THE BEGINNING AND END OF RAPE

THE BEGINNING
AND END OF RAPE

❖

Confronting Sexual Violence
in Native America

SARAH DEER

University of Minnesota Press
Minneapolis
London

Poetry by Connie Fife reprinted in chapter 9 was originally published as "Dear Webster" in *Reinventing the Enemy's Language: Contemporary Native Women's Writings of North America*, ed. Joy Harjo and Gloria Bird (New York: W. W. Norton, 1997).

Published by the University of Minnesota Press
111 Third Avenue South, Suite 290
Minneapolis, MN 55401–2520
http://www.upress.umn.edu

LIBRARY OF CONGRESS CATALOGING-IN-PUBLICATION DATA
Deer, Sarah, author.
The beginning and end of rape : confronting sexual violence in Native America / Sarah Deer.
Includes bibliographical references and index.
ISBN 978-0-8166-9631-4 (hc) — ISBN 978-0-8166-9633-8 (pb)
1. Rape—Law and legislation—United States. 2. Indian women—Crimes against—United States. 3. Indian women—Legal status, laws, etc.—United States. I. Title.
KIE3560.D44 2015
345.73'02532—dc23   2015017702
Printed in the United States of America on acid-free paper

The University of Minnesota is an equal-opportunity educator and employer.

21 20 19 18 17 16 15   10 9 8 7 6 5 4 3 2 1

For Lynnea

Contents

Introduction: Sovereignty of the Soul
ix

1. Knowing through Numbers?
The Benefits and Drawbacks of Data
1

2. *What She Say It Be Law*:
Tribal Rape Law and Indigenous Feminisms
16

3. At the Mercy of the State: Linking Rape to Federal Indian Law
31

4. All Apologies: The Continuing Federal Complicity
in the Rape of Native Women
44

5. Relocation Revisited: The Sex Trafficking of Native Women
59

6. Punishing the Victim: Dana's Story
80

7. The Enigma of Federal Reform: The Tribal Law and Order Act
and the Violence Against Women Act
92

8. Toward an Indigenous Jurisprudence of Rape
107

9. The Trouble with Peacemaking: False Dichotomies
and the Politics of Restorative Justice
123

10. "Righting" Tribal Rape Law: Proposals for Reform
137

Conclusion: The End of Rape in Native America
158

Epilogue
164

ACKNOWLEDGMENTS
167

NOTES
171

PUBLICATION HISTORY
205

INDEX
207

Sovereignty of the Soul

LET'S TALK ABOUT EPIDEMICS.

Accounts from the *New York Times*, *Washington Post*, National Public Radio, and other sources have used the adjective "epidemic" to describe the extremely high rates of violence perpetrated against Native women.[1] To make sense of the statistical data that consistently show that Native women experience the highest per capita rate of rape in the nation, journalists and activists have adopted a word we are accustomed to seeing within the context of disease outbreaks such as HIV or Ebola.

I think we've been using the wrong word. It's understandable: the word *epidemic* is used to attract attention to a particular problem that affects a growing number of people the longer it remains ignored or untreated. But this word doesn't quite fit. *Merriam-Webster* defines "epidemic" as a "sudden quickly spreading occurrence of something harmful or unwanted." It is an attention-grabbing word (and one I admit I have used in some contexts), but on reflection it can be misleading. The connotations of the word allow society to absolve itself of blame. The word suggests that the problem is biological, that the problem originated independent of long-standing oppression, that it has infected our society, twisting human relations. A biological epidemic is not a crisis of human origin; it is the result of the unchecked spread of microscopic viruses and bacteria. The word *epidemic* also suggests a short-term, isolated problem. We reflect on last year's flu epidemic, for example, and work toward ending the Ebola epidemic. Using the word *epidemic* deflects responsibility because it fails to acknowledge the agency of perpetrators and those who allow the problem to continue. The word also utterly fails to account for the crisis's roots in history and law. Using the word *epidemic* to talk about violence in Indian country is to depoliticize rape. It is a fundamental misstatement of the problem. If this book does nothing else, I hope to demonstrate why rape in the lives of Native women is not an epidemic of recent, mysterious origin. Instead, rape is a fundamental result of colonialism, a history of violence reaching back centuries. An epidemic is a contagious disease; rape is a crime against humanity.

Over the past twenty years, I have spoken to hundreds of Native women who have survived rape or domestic violence (usually both) throughout Indian country, from remote Alaska villages to Indian communities in dense urban areas. Most of my scholarship and activism has been directed toward the needs and rights of those survivors. I first began working with Native survivors of rape when I was an undergraduate at the University of Kansas in the early 1990s. I started volunteering at the local rape crisis center, called at that time the Douglas County Rape Victim Survivor Service (RVSS). I was twenty and eventually became a part-time employee. As a volunteer, I was trained to provide direct advocacy for victims who called us for assistance. Advocacy in this sense refers to a wide range of supportive services, which are offered at the request of a survivor, including accompanying survivors to the hospital, police station, or courthouse. We also offered private, confidential counseling over the telephone, and facilitated support groups for women who had experienced rape. In all things, we sought to provide compassionate emotional support. The women I met with and talked to during my first six years as an advocate served as the foundation for my life's passion. I answered desperate calls in the middle of the night from women besieged by nightmares and insomnia. I met women in the local emergency room and stood nearby as they made the agonizing decision of whether to report their husband/boyfriend/girlfriend/cousin/friend to the police for sexual assault. I sat in the waiting room reserved for witnesses at the local courthouse for hours, sometimes days. I walked in Take Back the Night marches and rallies and facilitated support groups for women. I talked to mothers, sisters, friends, lovers who had to watch amazing, beautiful women in their lives fall into very dark places as a result of the unspeakable trauma they were burdened with. If these women were fortunate, sometimes they called me months or years later to tell me, "Today I laughed for the first time since it happened." In all these memories, I remember most clearly the resilience of the women I met. Their stories and voices are today my most supportive and critical teachers. They taught me that, above all things, people who are violently assaulted should be the central focus of our criminal justice system.

The faces and voices of the women from Haskell Indian Nations University are what I remember most. Haskell is a federally funded university in Lawrence, Kansas, that is home to about eight hundred Native students from around the nation. Throughout both undergraduate and law school, I was privileged to work with Haskell students who called RVSS under a variety of circumstances (although I was never affiliated with Haskell in any formal way). For example, some students (both women and men) who had been assaulted as children called the crisis line when they arrived at Haskell because there was no crisis line back home on the reservation. They had suffered in silence for years. Just talking to someone who believed them was helpful. In other cases, I went to the emergency room or police station (usually in the middle of the night) after a victim was assaulted and requested an advocate. Some women were assaulted on campus; others off-campus, but almost always the assault triggered memories long suppressed about childhood sexual abuse. I listened to women as they realized they represented the fifth generation of women in their family to be victims of sexual assault—a realization that slowly emerged in a woman's eyes, casting a shadow across her face. *This happened to my gramma when she was my age. No one helped her. She was always sad and she never talked about it. Now I know the source of her sadness.* The eyes of these women then looked into the future, emptying out into a hollow vacancy as they considered the next generation, still girls or babies. *My niece. My baby sister. My daughter.* Native women experience the trauma of rape as an enduring violence that spans generations.[2]

I continued to work at the crisis center when I entered law school in 1996. I initially intended to become a prosecutor—in my work with RVSS I had attended at least a dozen jury trials, and I saw myself as joining the legal field in the courtroom. However, while in law school, I became attracted to Indian law as I thought about how achieving social justice for oppressed people was a question much larger than a single rape trial. Although I am a tribal citizen, I was not raised on or near reservation land, so I had the good fortune and privilege to be ignorant about the myriad legal obstacles and resulting day-to-day tragedies experienced by reservation residents as a result of the *law*. My naïveté and privilege led me to assume that most Indian law was confined to issues of contemporary civil law—for example, oil and gas law, tax law, gaming, and natural resources. Because I was focused almost exclusively on criminal law, I didn't think Indian law would provide me with skills I needed. I credit Robert Odawi Porter, a Seneca scholar and my Indian law professor, with challenging my assumptions and opening my eyes not only to the state of criminal law in Indian country but also the rich, textured universe of tribal jurisprudence. As a result of Porter's guidance, I began to see linkages between my interest in justice for victims of crime and my interest in enhancing tribal self-determination. I also began to think more about what it would mean to become a Mvskoke lawyer and my obligations to the Native women who had inspired my journey.

After law school, I worked for the federal government as a grant specialist, managing funds distributed as a result of the Violence Against Women Act (VAWA). As I traveled to various tribal nations and learned more about the high rates of violence committed against Native women, I began to confirm that the legal system, as far as Native women were concerned, was broken. Jurisdiction rules that I had critiqued in a law school classroom were suddenly more than just theories. I talked with tribal police officers who explained how rapists walked free on a regular basis—even taunting their victims and tribal officials because of legal loopholes. Some Native women told me that they tell their daughters never to report rape. *It only makes things worse*, they explained. I learned that, in some locations, federal and state officials who had obligations to respond to crime in tribal communities simply ignored calls for help or put in little effort to follow through with investigations. One location where I encountered numerous examples of such indifference was Alaska, the state with the highest rate of violence against Native women.

The response to crime in Alaska tribal communities is certainly complicated by the state's sheer vastness and the isolation of tribal villages—many are accessible only by air. In villages with populations ranging from one hundred to three hundred, nearly everyone is related by way of extended family relations. In one village in Alaska, it took state troopers three days to respond to a domestic homicide because the weather conditions were too poor to fly, and there is no other way to reach the village. The small community of two hundred residents and no law enforcement officials had to leave a woman's body in the home where she was killed so as not to disturb the crime scene. Meanwhile, her perpetrator freely roamed the village, terrorizing and traumatizing the whole community. In this vacuum of justice, sometimes women committed suicide after being ignored by officials for months after reporting a rape.

Despite the tremendous trauma I witnessed during my tenure with the federal government (1999–2002), I was also deeply moved and inspired by the activism and advocacy seeking to change a seemingly hopeless reality. In 1999, I first met Tillie Black Bear (Sicangu Lakota) and Lenora Hootch (Yup'ik), two Native women who started shelter programs for Native women in their communities in the mid-1970s. Tillie Black Bear, often affectionately referred to as a "grandmother of the domestic violence movement," established the White Buffalo Calf Woman Society (WBCWS) program on the Rosebud Reservation in southern South Dakota in 1977. The organization provides confidential advocacy services for women who are victims of domestic violence and sexual assault, including a twenty-four-hour crisis shelter, court accompaniment, and liaison with law enforcement. When WBCWS was established, it was the first formal contemporary organization on an Indian reservation that focused on gendered violence. Since that time, WBCWS has served as one of the most respected indigenous gender violence programs in the world. After her passing in the summer of 2014, Tillie Black Bear was memorialized by numerous organizations, including the National Network to End Domestic Violence, which released a statement reminding us that "Tillie taught us all to employ every option to advance women's safety."[3] Her broad-ranging approach to gender violence, informed by her own expertise as a survivor of battering, challenged and inspired many Native women to begin parallel programs in their own communities.

Lenora Hootch's understated revolutionary actions in Emmonak Village (Alaska) included the establishment of the first (and to this date, only) shelter for victims of domestic violence in an Alaska Native village. Ms. Hootch and her team of local women in Emmonak have sustained the shelter program even in times of financial uncertainty. Along with other Alaska Native organizations, the Emmonak Shelter program and its sister organization, the Yup'ik Women's Coalition, have taken their unique Alaska story to national and international audiences, always pressing for social change in Alaska that will include restoration of village sovereignty. Tillie, Lenora, and hundreds of other Native women have established a truth in their organizing; namely, that Native women who experience rape need and deserve a tribal-centric response to their experiences. By "tribal-centric" I do not mean a pan-Indian, romanticized response to trauma, but rather a response that centers a contemporary Native woman in her unique place and time, empowering her to access the collective strength and insight that have helped her people survive. What these and other women have taught me is that the origin of this human rights crisis can be tied to the very foundation of the United States as a legal and political structure. Indeed, the crisis of rape in tribal communities is inextricably linked to the way in which the United States developed and sustained a legal system that has usurped the sovereign authority of tribal nations. This colonial legal system has failed Native women by supplanting women-centered societies with patriarchal, oppressive structures that condone and thrive on violence as a way to control and oppress members of marginalized communities. These oppressive structures are predicated on hundreds of policies, regulations, and philosophies that underpin American justice.

Federal Indian law is the quintessential example of an oppressive America legal structure. Analyzing sexual violence against Native women requires a full exploration of the federal legal system as it applies to tribal nations. Indigenous people across the world share a common experience—namely, intrusion on their lands and culture by an exterior, hostile outsider. Rape victims experience the same dynamic, but it is played out on their bodies and souls rather than on the land. My intent in this book is to explore the interconnectedness of surviving colonization and surviving rape.

Sovereignty, Both Political and Personal

As indicated in my discussion of uses and misuses of the word *epidemic,* I am interested in the words we choose, what they mean, and the effects they have on the way we conceive of patriarchal power and control. In this book, I use the term *sovereignty* in two senses, referring to both political sovereignty and personal sovereignty. I conceive of sovereignty as a description of self-determination. However, it is a critically important word in today's political arena and even more so, I think, for the anti-violence movement. Self-governance or self-determination necessarily implies the development of concrete solutions to problems. Understanding the nature of the problem and developing solutions are straightforward manifestations of sovereignty. I attempt here to determine how tribal nations dealt with rape prior to colonization, to see if there are some creative ways that contemporary tribal nations can address sexual violence even within the limitations of the precarious position of Indian communities. The most important sources for the process of recuperation are oral traditions, stories, and traditional belief systems, as well as statutes and contemporary tribal appellate case law that sometimes encompass the traditional belief system.[4] History and anthropology can be helpful in a limited sense, but these disciplines have often failed to describe tribal justice systems accurately, so I refer to those kinds of materials with caution.

Rape is only one of a multitude of social and legal issues faced by tribal governments today, but it is deserving of the highest priority. Over the past five hundred years American Indians have experienced war, conquest, rape, and genocide, and all of these depredations have disconnected them from both their land and their own bodies.[18] Alienation from one's homeland provides a strong foundation upon which sexual victimization can take place. Indigenous scholar Jack D. Forbes explains the connection by asserting that colonial forces found it easy to shift "from the raping of a woman to the raping of a country to the raping of the world."[5] Perhaps Athabascan scholar Dian Million says it most succinctly: "Gender violence . . . marks the evisceration of Indigenous nations."[6] In this book, I take the position that rape should be the number one priority for tribal nations. All other challenges faced by tribal nations are linked to the history and trauma of rape.

Self-determination for individual survivors and self-determination for tribal nations are closely connected.[7] It is impossible to have a truly self-determining nation when its members have been denied self-determination over their own bodies. One of my mentors, Ho-Chunk anti-rape activist Bonnie Clairmont, writes, "Women's sovereignty is central to Indian sovereignty because nations cannot be free if their Indian women are not free."[8] Other social problems cannot be resolved unless psychological trauma is addressed in a systemic way.[9] Because rape played such a significant role in past attempts to destroy indigenous nations, it is critical that tribal nations develop and strengthen their responses to rape as part of broader political work toward achieving sovereignty. Without a system in place to respond to violence, it can only proliferate. I argue that for tribal nations, defining and adjudicating gendered crimes is the purest form of sovereignty. But reclaiming this authority must be more than an aspiration. As Congress restores inherent jurisdiction (never relinquished) to Native communities, tribal nations must prepare to use that restored jurisdiction in a way that does not replicate the worst flaws of the American legal system.

A Legal Framework of the Soul

In later chapters, I explore a legal framework for addressing rape from a Native survivor's perspective—the "sovereignty of the soul." The English word *soul* has spiritual connotations, but I do not mean to prescribe a static set of spiritual beliefs to all Native people. I use *soul* almost agnostically to refer to deep, fundamental aspects of identity, aspects that will be described differently depending on cultural beliefs. In some languages, the more appropriate word might translate to *heart* or *spirit*. Worldwide, victims of rape often describe their deep, psychic wounds as harming the very foundation of their identity.[10] This harm is almost always described as more profound and long lasting than physical or even emotional injuries. If our sexuality is part of that which defines who and what each of us is, then it is at the very core of our self-identity. I think this is because the very nature of sexuality represents the best of humanity—the creation of new life, or the sharing of deep mutual affection and attraction. When this manifestation of our humanity is violated, it has life-changing ramifications for one's feelings about self, others,

justice, and trust. In consequence, rape damages something critical to our being and personhood. Sexual assault often leads to feelings of great shame, humiliation, and guilt for victims. In Indian
country, violence is not always experienced as an individual; some
forms of violence manifest as systemic yet invisible structures that
accomplish the trauma of violence on a large scale. This is, not coin-
cidentally, a great description of colonization in the United States.
In fact, rape can be employed as a metaphor for the entire concept
of colonialism.[19] The damage to self and spirit that rapists cause
has some of the same features that colonial governments perpetrate
against entire nations.

People who have not experienced rape may not understand how
this works, but rape is different from other types of violent assault.
Hollywood often portrays rape as a one-time, relatively short-term,
violent event. In reality, sexual abuse can last for days, months, or
sometimes years. Perpetrators are sometimes woven into a kinship
circle such that they have access to dozens of young relatives and
carry out their crimes for decades. Men purporting to be spiritual
leaders use power and privilege to facilitate and justify their behavior. Victims may behave in unexpected ways; sometimes in ways
that make it hard to believe they are in pain. Some survivors, for
example, may appear to be madly in love with their perpetrators.
This is a survival technique—*if we're in love, this terrible thing couldn't
have happened.*

Distinguishing Rape from Domestic Violence

The phrases "domestic violence" and "rape" are often conflated
in the national discourse on gendered crime, leading to confusion
about how the legal system responds to violence against Native
women. Sexual assault and domestic violence are often overlapping
crimes, but they are not entirely interchangeable. I distinguish the
two categories of crime in this book for several reasons but certainly
not to suggest that the movements to end violence against women
be separated into different categories or that the movement to end
violence be bifurcated. I make this distinction for several specific
reasons.

First, domestic violence and sexual assault have different jurisdictional legal rules in Indian country. I discuss this in more detail

in chapter 7, but because domestic violence and rape are often used interchangeably, there has been some confusion about the full extent of the reform in the Violence Against Women Reauthorization Act of 2013. The 2013 reauthorization restored tribal criminal jurisdiction over non-Indians, a population that has been exempt from tribal criminal authority since 1978. The 2013 jurisdiction reform is explicitly limited, however, to violence committed by spouses, former spouses, or dating partners. Consequently, women who are raped by persons within other relationships (e.g., acquaintances, relatives, or strangers) are not covered by the recent legislative change, and authority over such crimes will require Congress to enact additional reforms to federal law.

The distinction between domestic violence and rape has to do with the relationship between the perpetrator and the victim. Domestic violence typically refers to violence and abuse perpetrated in the context of an "intimate partner" relationship. The perpetrator may be a spouse, a partner, a co-parent, boyfriend, or husband, among others. Any relationship marked by domestic violence is almost guaranteed to involve sexual coercion. Rape, however, often happens outside the context of an intimate partner relationship. Most rapists attack women they know well, certainly those who are in spousal or dating relationships, but the circle casts much wider than domestic violence. Native women are sexually assaulted by friends, neighbors, relatives, friends of friends, and strangers. The needs of survivors of domestic violence and survivors of rape may be quite different. We cannot assume that the legal remedies for survivors of domestic violence will always be appropriate or applicable to survivors of sexual assault.[11] A woman who is raped by a person who is not an intimate partner may experience many of the same emotions and challenges as a woman who is a survivor of domestic violence, but there are also some significant differences that warrant separate examination. For example, a survivor of domestic violence may need representation to file for legal separation, divorce, or child custody. A sexual assault survivor may have other kinds of civil legal needs, including housing (if she was assaulted in her home), employment, or education.

Rape as a Political Construct

I have made a conscious choice to use the word *rape* in this book, even though the word is falling out of favor in the legal field in favor of more clinical terms such as *sexual assault, sexual abuse, sexual violence,* and even *nonconsensual sex.* The word rape in the legal sense is admittedly reductive; it collapses a wide range of events into a single descriptor. By rape I mean to encompass a constellation of crimes that involves the abuse of sexual power, including child sexual abuse and adult rape, one-time incidents and ongoing abuse, even when not overtly physically violent. All forms of rape can cause tremendous trauma to victims. I object to a burden of proof that requires physical violence for there to be psychic harm. There are some legitimate reasons, from a government's perspective, to make legal distinctions between types of rape. But my intent here is to approach rape as a phenomenon with profound psychological and spiritual ramifications. Some legal scholars advocate for a legal distinction between violent rape and nonconsensual sex because the offenders in nonconsensual sex presumably do not truly intend to harm their victims. This has not been my experience as an advocate. Predation sometimes takes place over weeks and months; it is intentional and sadistic but may appear from the outside to be nonviolent. Psychologist David Lisak has provided a helpful critique of the myth of the "nice guy" who accidentally has nonconsensual sex. In his research, he has discovered that most men who rape have multiple victims. Lack of physical violence does not make these criminals any less dangerous.[12] Acquaintance rape, for example, is often facilitated by alcohol or drugs, and offenders are known to engage in planning and preparation in anticipation of the victim's intoxication.

There is no such thing as nonviolent rape. As I will explore later in the book, all rape is a form of intimate violation of the highest order. We must eliminate a legal distinction between the rapist who hits his victim and the rapist who waits, paying sinister attention, for his victim to pass out. In the latter case, a victim may not actively resist with her body, but she resists with her mind or her spirit.

There are many parallels between this experience and the larger efforts of colonization. Colonizers and colonizing institutions use tactics that are no different from those of sexual perpetrators, including deceit, manipulation, humiliation, and physical force. Because I hope to position rape in a sociopolitical context, I choose to use the word rape to describe all forms of sexual predation as experienced by Native people.

THE CHAPTERS IN THIS BOOK reflect a decade's worth of writing and thinking, from roughly 2004 to 2014. This was a decade that will go down in history as one of the most important eras for contemporary federal Indian law—not just for Native women but for tribal sovereignty more generally. Documenting this time period will help us assess what aspects of reform have been most successful from the vantage point of victims and advocates. My observations fall into two categories that form the basic framework for this book: chapters 1 through 6 explore how rape has harmed Native women and tribal governments, and chapters 7 through 10 focus on reform efforts, both tribal and nontribal.

Chapter 1 defines and describes the problem of rape in the lives of Native women. The oft-repeated statistics reflect a grim reality that rape has become the "norm" in tribal communities. Yet skepticism about the accuracy and reliability of hard numbers has at times threatened to eclipse the larger concern about the harm rape does to tribal societies. I argue that too much emphasis has been placed on "proving" a human rights crisis that Native women have been documenting and explaining for generations.

Chapter 2 explores precolonial responses to gender and rape, and in doing so responds to feminist theory's lack of a clear consideration of colonialism. This lacuna means that contemporary American feminist theory fails to fully address the problem of rape because it is the intersection of the two that allows and sustains gendered violence.

Chapter 3 describes the complicated matrix of criminal jurisdiction in Indian country. From a perspective that privileges tribal sovereignty, I explain how mechanical intrusions into the realm of tribal authority and the resulting jurisdictional complexity has created real, practical gaps in the formal systems of justice, gaps that have allowed perpetrators to assault Native women with impunity. In chapter 4, I move a step further, building on these mechanical and legalistic intrusions to view rape as encouraged and cultivated by colonialism. I examine the continued culpability of the federal government vis-à-vis specific federal officials who themselves commit individual acts of rape while serving in positions of trust and authority in tribal nations.

Chapter 5 explains how sex trafficking and prostitution in the lives of contemporary Native women are almost indistinguishable from the colonial tactics of enslavement, exploitation, exportation, and relocation. The chapter elucidates how some contemporary efforts to stop sex trafficking in the United States are disingenuous because they fail to account for the widespread sexual slavery of Native women throughout the past five hundred years. Recent reports of "man camps" at fracking sites make this issue even more salient today, as these camps repeat earlier histories of the rape of Native women during the Gold Rush and other moments in American economic booms.

Chapter 6 is a recent addition to my portfolio. It tells the story of a woman named Dana Deegan, whose life story as a survivor of rape and her subsequent prosecution and imprisonment demonstrates how colonial criminalization leads to tremendous revictimization for Native women today. Most incarcerated women are survivors of violence, and I end this first group of chapters with an account of how the American legal system punishes the people it purports to protect.

Starting with chapter 7 I shift to a discussion of contemporary policy and potential reform. In chapter 7 I provide detailed information about recent federal reform in the Tribal Law and Order Act of 2010 and the reauthorization in 2013 of the Violence Against Women Act. These reforms, largely spearheaded by grassroots Native women activists, present a new era in federal–tribal relations and provide a starting point for full reform. I have been fortunate to play a role in the federal reform efforts through my work with Amnesty International, congressional testimony, and direct communication with lawmakers. While many tribal-sovereignty activists may reject engagement with the federal systems that created the problems they seek to address, I make the case for working with the federal government to reform a system that has been deeply damaged by the failure to include tribal perspectives. Chapter 8 brings reform from the federal level back to the scale of individual tribal nations. I explore indigenous philosophical foundations for responding to rape. As contemporary tribal nations continue to strengthen their own response to rape, I suggest specific philosophical frameworks for tribal nations to consider in an effort to avoid some of the flaws of the Anglo-American criminal justice system. After examining the potential foundation for indigenous theories of rape, I critique some purported "indigenous" responses to rape in chapter 9, noting that an oversimplistic and potentially dangerous response to rape can emerge from a male-dominated approach to peacemaking and other restorative practices.

Chapter 10 is purposely forward-looking. In it I lay out a series of potential tribal legal remedies that can put the control over effectively responding to rape back in the hands of tribal nations. I describe these proposed remedies in detail and provide ideas for how such systems can be crafted to meet the unique needs of Native women.

THE JOURNEY OF A RAPE SURVIVOR to regain a sense of self-worth and self-determination often presents as a microcosm of the journey of a tribal nation to revitalize its own self-worth and self-determination. Each survivor has a different path in this journey, much like individual tribal nations. Survivors and tribal nations may experience dysfunction, despair, and obstacles. I hope to establish that the mission of tribal sovereignty advocates and anti-rape advocates are closely aligned—in both theory and practice.

I believe this mission can be successful only if it links conversations from the past to the present and into the future. We know that Native women have the knowledge and wisdom to reframe the way in which the dominant system responds to rape, and therefore our tribal nations need to turn to the wisdom of these women in an effort to end this human rights crisis.

For tribal governments, defining and adjudicating crimes such as sexual assault can be the purest exercise of sovereignty. What crime, other than murder, strikes at the hearts of its citizens more deeply than rape? Sexual violence impinges on our spiritual selves, creating emotional wounds that fester and infect larger wells of community trauma. For sovereign tribal nations, the question is not just about protecting and responding to individual women who are raped but also about addressing the foundational wellness of the community where it occurs.

THERE ARE MORE THAN 560 federally recognized tribal governments in the United States, each with a separate and distinct judicial system. My intent is not to provide a definitive plan of action for every tribal nation but to raise ideas, questions, and concerns about the contemporary legal response to rape. Certainly other powerful ceremonial and spiritual entities bear in this struggle—a struggle that focuses on social change. This book is not intended to provide all the answers or even the definitive review of the work done thus far but rather endeavors to add thoughts about tribal legal reform to the movement. National policy changes that will benefit all tribal nations are hard to come by because individual tribal nations may have conflicting strategies. The same can be said of rape survivors. Some rape survivors seek justice through the legal system, but that is not and should not be the only option available for solace and healing. Justice takes many forms and trauma does not resolve in the same way for everyone. Unfortunately, American culture emphasizes merely two modes of survival: legal and psychological. In the legal framework, victims in the American system are often told that they should report the crime to authorities if they truly want to end sexual violence—a terrible burden to place on a woman who has experienced a life-altering crisis. Simultaneously victims are often diagnosed with mental health problems for behaviors that are natural outgrowths of the trauma they have experienced. In this book, I explore how lessons from the survival of colonization and lessons from survival of rape can inform and reinforce one another, with the aim of directing this synergy to strengthen the international movement to end rape.

The Beginning and End of Rape focuses almost exclusively on indigenous women in the American context—an admittedly arbitrary and colonial distinction, largely as a result of my legal training in American law. I often consult literature describing the First Nation experience in Canada because of the parallel sociolegal history with the American experience. My legal training and focus have been on the

American legal system and tribal legal systems in the United States. I have concentrated here on law and legal remedies, understanding that such intervention is only part of the puzzle. This book is intended to offer one Native woman lawyer's perspectives on tribal rape law. In no way do I mean to speak for all Native women or all Native women lawyers.

The Relevance of This Book to Global Anti-Rape Activism

If we are to make true progress toward safe societies, the core experiences and realities of Native women must be central to the global movement to end rape. Rape is a political issue with settler colonial foundations, and an honest analysis of rape in America requires telling some difficult truths, including the fact that the U.S. government has cultivated the "epidemic" it now seeks to remedy. Any honest anti-rape movement must wrestle with the dark truths of colonial violence, because the movement will remain stagnant unless we can centralize the context in which Native women experience rape. We must enlarge the mainstream dialogue about rape to include the issues of tribal sovereignty and self-determination, not only because of the high rate of rape perpetrated against Native women but also because the very system on which the United States bases its claim to this land is shrouded in the trauma of rape. Avoiding that truth is what will keep us from true reform. Thus we must explore both the "beginning" of rape as well as the "end" of rape as experienced by Native women.

The efforts to address the humanitarian crisis in the lives of Native women are now at a critical stage; there is national momentum, largely fueled by the passion and advocacy of Native antiviolence advocates. I hope this book will be one of many tools that activists and tribal leaders will consult as the work continues. While I have advocated for most of the changes during this time period, I am cautious in concluding that all the changes will guarantee an improvement in the lives of Native women without sustained efforts and additional reform. What is most important is the conversations that have developed along the way and the continued dialogue centered by and for Native women.

ONE

Knowing through Numbers?

The Benefits and Drawbacks of Data

THE HEADLINES BEGAN TO APPEAR IN 1999. *American Indian and Alaska Native Women Experience the Highest Rates of Interpersonal Violent Crime in the United States.* During the past fifteen years, I have followed these headlines and their accompanying stories with great interest. It is irrefutable that, based on the available data, violent crime is experienced by Native women at per capita higher rates than almost all other groups in the United States. I have yet to see data that suggest otherwise. The most commonly quoted statistic is probably "1 in 3 Native women will be raped in her lifetime"—a figure originally derived from a 1998 report examining data from the National Violence Against Women Survey. This single statistic has garnered more attention than any other, inspiring investigative reporting, federal policy reform, a damning international human rights report, and an award-winning novel by renowned Ojibwe novelist Louise Erdrich, *The Round House.*

The data sets and corresponding reports that have been circulated throughout the nation have accomplished many things in the past fifteen years. Legislators made the issue a priority. Government agencies funded pilot projects. Journalists representing mainstream newspapers such as the *New York Times* and the *Washington Post* visited reservations to interview Native women. National Public Radio and PBS have broadcast extensive multipart reports about the problem. On July 29, 2010, President Barack Obama noted that the "one in three" reality "is an assault on our national conscience;

it is an affront to our shared humanity; it is something that we cannot allow to continue."[1]

Numbers are powerful players in American politics; the statistics about violence against Native women are almost always referenced in federal reports about rates of crime in Indian country and have served as valuable sound bites during the past ten years of reform. Without the publication and circulation of somber statistics, the federal law reform of the past few years would likely not have happened. In that sense, the data are invaluable, but numbers in and of themselves offer nothing in the way of long-term solutions to the crisis. Because of that, it is critical to develop a tribal-centric analysis of the knowledge we have about Native women and rape. This chapter explores the origin, nature, and application of statistical data related to violence against Native women and is followed by a discussion of the intangible harm rape does to the psyches of Native women and the survival of tribal nations. In the end, I consider the value and utility of our "knowledge" and encourage the continued development of research initiated by and for Native women.

How Do We Know What We Know? The Challenges of Collecting Data in Indian Country

It is notoriously difficult to gather data about Native people—on any topic. The dearth of data on Native people is not simply the result of indifferent researchers. In practical terms, Native people make up such a small percentage of the American population that a valid random sample is difficult to come by. In national studies, if data do not constitute a "statistically significant sample," then they are simply pooled with data from other groups of people who do not constitute a statistically significant sample and categorized as "other." This is commonly seen in criminology studies that classify Americans as "White, Black, and Other."[2] In more recent decades, criminologists and other social scientists have determined that the "other" should be more delineated so as to reveal additional nuances about the variety of American experiences with crime. Native people, however, have been largely overlooked in criminology. This changed in 1999, when the Bureau of Justice Statistics, a subdivision of the U.S. Department of Justice, issued a report titled *American Indians and Crime*.[3] The report combined a variety of different sources of federal data and noted a highly dis-proportionate level of victimization in the lives of Native people—specifically, the rate was two and a half to three times higher than for the nation generally. Since 1999 a variety of reports and studies have come to the same conclusion—namely, that Native women in particular suffer the highest rate of per capita rape in the United States.[4] Amnesty International investigated the high rates of rape, and media attention to the problem intensified after the release of its report *Maze of Injustice* in 2007.[5]

Where do the victimization data come from? Most of the data are collected by the federal government through surveys.[6] Prior to the development of victimization surveys, the government "counted" crimes by calculating the number of police reports that had been filed. However, because more than half of violent crimes in the United States are never reported to police, relying on law enforcement report data does not yield accurate results about the true extent of violent crime. Surveys such as the National Crime Victimization Survey (NCVS) and National Violence Against Women Survey (NVAWS) were designed to provide a more accu-rate picture of crime in the United States. The "victimization sur-vey" method is produced by contacting a random sample of house-holds in the United States and inquiring about their experience with crime.[7] If a survey respondent indicates that she has been a victim of crime, she is then asked a series of questions about the type of crime, the race of the perpetrator, the location of the crime, and other details.

The sample sizes for Native people in recent national surveys have become large enough that American Indian/Alaska Native (AI/AN) data have become "statistically significant" and some ten-tative conclusions can be drawn. Starting in 1999, the prevalence data have been consistent in concluding that there is a very high rate of crimes experienced by Native people generally, and Native women more specifically. I am not aware of a single study (federal, state, or tribal) containing a statistically significant group of AI/AN in which the data do not suggest that Native people suffer the high-est rates of victimization in the United States. However, the data we have still leave part of the story unwritten. Below, I consider what the data have led investigators to conclude, and the significance and relevance of those findings.

Data Dump: What Do We Know?

Despite the strength of the data in affecting legal reform, we still know surprisingly little about the nature of sexual assault in the lives of Native women. Here's what we *do* know: the national data tell us that Native women experience the highest per capita rate of rape in the nation.[8] National Crime Victimization Survey data consistently reveal a very high rate of rape against Native women, an average annual rate of 7.2 per 1,000 persons, compared to 1.9 per 1,000 persons for all races. The "one in three" statistic was originally published in a 2000 report on the National Violence Against Women Survey, which concluded that 34.1 percent of Native women will be raped during their lifetime (meaning that the more accurate statement is *more* than one in three Native women).[9] In 2010 the Centers for Disease Control and Prevention issued a report on the results of the National Intimate Partner and Sexual Violence Survey, which found that 49 percent of Native women report a history of sexual violence.[10]

Dr. Ronet Bachman, a statistician at the University of Delaware, is the national expert on interpreting NCVS data as it relates to violence against Native women. She has published additional findings from the data that serve as an important supplement to the federal reports.[11] Using an aggregated data set covering the years 1992–2005, Bachman and her coauthors uncovered some important trends about the qualitative nature of the sexual assault Native women experience.[12]

For example, the level of physical violence Native women experience during rape is significantly elevated when compared to that experienced by other races. For example, when asked whether aggressors physically hit them during the assault, over 90 percent of Native women responded affirmatively, compared to 71 percent of white victims.[13] In a related question, 25 percent of Native women victims report that their perpetrator(s) used a weapon, compared to 9 percent of white women.[14] Thus, there appears to be a particularly brutal physicality in assaults on Native women—a significant elevation that warrants further attention.

Unfortunately, based on my experience, none of these numbers are shocking. Nor do many Native women find these numbers shocking. Rape, in particular, is experienced at such high rates in some tribal communities that it becomes "normalized." Native women know that there is a high likelihood of experiencing rape at some point in their lives, and preparing for this inevitable violence resembles a full-time job. It is part of the daily lives of Native women, "normalized" but never acceptable. Charon Asetoyer (Comanche) and other women from reservations have explained the severity of rape this way: Native women "talk to their daughters about what to do when they are sexually assaulted, not if they are sexually assaulted, but *when*."[15]

In terms of the prevalence rates themselves, most experts I have spoken to (and by experts I mean the grassroots advocates and activists from tribal communities) almost universally assert that the federal statistics represent at best a very low estimate. Actual rates of sexual assault against Native American women are actually much higher. Through my work in Native communities, I heard more than once, *I don't know any woman in my community who has not been raped.*

Lingering Questions: What We Do Not Know

Despite the fact that fifteen years have passed since the initial release of *American Indians and Crime*, we still have remarkably little information about Native women and rape. Some generalized conclusions can be drawn from the available information but it must be remembered that the gatherers and publishers of these numbers are researchers from academia and the federal government. Australian criminologists Chris Cunneen and Simone Rowe refer to this kind of data as "legal-bureaucratic knowledge," and they maintain that it often does not consider the "implications of Indigenous approaches . . . to the production, analysis and presentation of quantitative, statistical Indigenous data."[16] It is as though Native women must repeatedly cite Western data for there to be a legitimate critique of the status quo.

Although the victimization survey method is a dramatic improvement over the older methodology of counting police reports, obvious shortcomings remain. The National Crime Victimization Survey has not typically included homeless people (or people living in shelters) as part of its population sample—and Native people are overrepresented in the homeless population. Moreover, while victimization surveys certainly uncover more crime than do police reports, many victims likely will not disclose—even to a stranger—that they have been victims.

Using these data to describe the scope of the problem in individual tribal nations is problematic because each community is different. Tribal governments have struggled for over a century with the "one size fits all" federal approach to problem solving in tribal communities. Our tribal communities are often lumped into a single category (e.g., "Indian country" or "Native people"), which does not account for the wide disparity in specific problems faced by individual sovereign nations. Most of the time, we do not have specific data about individual tribal communities, and of course the crime rates vary widely among various tribal nations.

The Controversy over Interracial Rape Statistics

Much of the national conversation about statistics on violence against Native women has centered on the rates of "interracial" rape statistics, which become critically important when discussing legislative reform. As a baseline, the vast majority of rapes in the United States are intraracial, meaning that victims are usually attacked by persons of their own race. The only exception to this general rule is AI/AN women, who report that the majority of assailants are non-Native. The original 1999 Bureau of Justice Statistics report concluded that about nine in ten American Indian victims of rape or sexual assault had white or black assailants.[17] Another report indicated that over 70 percent of the assailants were white.[18] The numbers have fluctuated over the last decade, but the majority of Native women interviewed in these national studies consistently report that the majority of their perpetrators are non-Native.[19] This is an anomaly in American criminology; violent crime in America is almost always intraracial.[20]

Interracial statistics have significant policy implications for tribal criminal jurisdiction and all reform efforts related to tribal jurisdiction. As I discuss in-depth in chapter 3, tribal governments were stripped of power to prosecute and punish non-Indians for crimes committed in Indian country in 1978, when the Supreme Court issued a notorious decision in *Oliphant v. Suquamish Indian Tribe*.[21] In *Oliphant*, the court relied on a curious doctrine known as "implicit divestiture" to conclude that tribal courts had lost certain attributes of sovereignty—in particular, the criminal authority over nonmembers—owing to historical presumptions of federal lawmakers. From a survivor's perspective, the *Oliphant* decision means that non-Native men who rape Native women on tribal lands completely escape tribal criminal sanctions. (One hole in *Oliphant*, by the way, was addressed in 2013 legislation for domestic violence victims, but not for rape victims. The 2013 legislation is the focus in chapter 7.) Many have asked whether *Oliphant* is the reason most Native women experience such a high rate of interracial crime. It is a compelling question, but I am not sure we have the precise answer, because we do not have pre-*Oliphant* data about the rate of interracial rape experienced by Native women.

There is a noteworthy amount of skepticism, cynicism, and confusion about the accuracy and utility of interracial statistics.[22] Some commentators simply claim that the data are wrong—that somehow a glitch in the data-gathering system is to blame. Some of that skepticism might be based on the fact that most violent crime in the United States *is* intraracial. Why would the experience of Native women be different? I have noticed that some skeptical politicians will try to claim the statistics are being manipulated to further tribal sovereignty interests, but these same politicians usually do not provide alternative data. Perhaps they are too uncomfortable with the fact that white men are still raping Native women with impunity.

Another important conversation in light of these statistics is the culpability of Native men as perpetrators of rape. A small number of tribal nations are so remote or closed that non-Native people are largely absent from the community. So when the data suggest most perpetrators are white, those tribal members may be understandably skeptical of the data's accuracy. If the data do not reflect the reality in a particular community, then that community's members view the data with skepticism. When we focus too heavily on interracial statistics, we may lose sight of the fact that there remain a significant number of Native men involved in these crimes. The colonial connection necessarily frames rape as a crime committed by colonizers against the colonized. But the reality is that Native men and boys have also become perpetrators of sexual violence. We cannot absolve Native men from responsibility—even if they represent the minority of perpetrators. We also cannot forget that Native men and boys are also victims of rape—at a much higher rate than their counterparts in other races.

The other wrinkle is that the national interracial data often do not distinguish between on-reservation crime and off-reservation crime.[23] Knowing where these crimes occur is critical because, due to a complicated legal history, the jurisdiction of tribal governments is much more limited than the jurisdiction of the state and federal systems. Tribal governments currently have jurisdiction only over crimes committed in Indian country.[24] Some skeptical policy makers have challenged the accuracy of the non-Indian perpetrator statistics as reflecting the "urban" reality but not the reservation reality. Most Native people do not live on land subject to tribal jurisdiction. Those who are skeptical of federal reform will sometimes contend that since tribal nations do not have jurisdiction over crimes occurring off-reservation, the urban-based interracial statistics should not influence policy making. The argument is that if these numbers do not reflect what is happening on reservations, they pertain to what is happening off the reservation, so tribal jurisdiction is irrelevant and restoration of tribal authority is thereby not justified.

For me, it boils down to simple justice: even if one non-Native man rapes one Native woman on one reservation, the tribe should be able to assert criminal jurisdiction over that case. I do not see the need to "prove" that most perpetrators on reservations are non-Native. However, studies showing that most perpetrators of violence against Native women are non-Native are certainly a compelling reason to address the 1978 *Oliphant* decision directly. Ultimately we really cannot say for certain whether most Native women who experience crime on tribal lands are more likely the victims of Native people or of non-Native people. However, whether the rate is 20 percent non-Native or 80 percent non-Native, tribal nations should have full authority to respond to crimes committed by all persons. Future studies in this area should include this critical point so that we can address skepticism about the data.

Even when someone dismisses the data by suggesting that the numbers reflect the urban experience but not reservation settings, we are still left with a problematic situation. If the data are more accurate in the urban settings, shouldn't we be concerned that most Native women in urban settings are reporting this high rate of interracial crime? Again, remember that most crime in the United States is intraracial. Since we know that Native women are reporting a high rate of interracial crime (this fact alone is difficult to rebut), this suggests there is a significant American problem regardless of tribal jurisdiction. At the very least, these numbers should justify further inquiry by social scientists and activist groups into the lives and experiences of urban Native women.

For example, what factors make it more likely than not that a Native victim in an urban setting will be attacked by a non-Native? If Native women are being targeted by rapists, there may very well be racially motivated components to some of these crimes. There is a sense that a "rapeability" factor stems from the United States' long history of anti-Indian and anti-woman policies, which have become part of the fabric of our society.[25] As Deborah Miranda notes, "Indian bodies are inferior bodies. Indian women's bodies are rape-able bodies. Indian bodies do not belong to Indians, but to those who can lay claim to them by violence."[26] Predators may target Native women and girls precisely because they are perceived as marginalized and outside the protection of the American legal system.

In short, the data we currently have do little more than "prove" that Native women experience extremely high rates of rape. But do we need more data in order to move forward? Bachman's report concludes: "We contend that new resources directed at counting 'how many' American Indian and Alaska Native women are victims are misguided. . . . The limited resources that are available would be better invested in developing intervention and prevention programs."[27] I agree with this sentiment because even if contradictory data came out next week suggesting that "only" one in four Native women will be raped in her lifetime and "only" 20 percent of the offenders were non-Native, we would still be faced with a serious harm to tribal nations that needs and deserves critical attention. A continued emphasis on the aggregate data about the rate of rape committed against Native women may serve to eclipse long-term victim-centered solutions.

The Ripple Effects of Trauma

I want to move now to a more important question: "What harm is rape doing to tribal nations?" Answering this question requires a more difficult inquiry than number crunching because each dehumanizing number in a data set represents a woman's life. Each woman's life is connected to many other women's lives—daughters, sisters, mothers, cousins, and friends.[28] Trying to conceive of the community harm that is done by extremely high rates of rape can be overwhelming. Louise Erdrich's novel *The Round House* tells the story of the rape of one Native woman from the perspective of the woman's thirteen-year-old son, a perspective that underscores the ripple effect. In the novel, both son and father suffer greatly in processing the experience that their mother and wife has suffered. Their lives are forever changed, which in turn, changes the other people in their worlds.

I approach this topic with some degree of trepidation because this kind of exploration has not always benefited Native people. Native communities are too often portrayed as traumatized, broken, and dysfunctional—all stereotypes of inferiority that neglect to honor the resilience and survival of the people by focusing on the bad rather than the good. Nonetheless, many of the challenges experienced by Native people today can be connected to the experience of rape, and the failure to confront these issues will be to the detriment of all Native people. There has been a growing trend among Native women's organizations to share painful information in ways that also celebrate and honor the strength in Native cultures. A prime example is the Barrette Project of the Minnesota Indian Women's Sexual Assault Coalition. MIWSAC, a grassroots coalition of tribal anti-rape organizations, created the project as a public awareness exhibit. The "living memorial" exhibit (and its companion book) is made up of beaded and quilled barrettes, each accompanied by the testimony of a Native woman or girl affected by rape. The exhibit thus contains elements and images of honor, beauty, and strength while simultaneously offering up difficult truths. MIWSAC's description of the project is particularly instructive in this regard:

We utilize beaded barrettes because they represent so much to us as Native women; pride and beauty—a piece of our dance regalia—the love we feel when clipping a barrette in our daughters hair—or fear and helplessness, knowing that the same barrette may have been jerked from her hair as she was being assaulted. It is because we feel that beaded barrettes carry with them this strong symbolism that we wanted to use them as a physical representation of our stories, that we share on our traveling memorial—red, velvet covered boards with the stories and barrettes displayed.[29]

MIWSAC and related organizations have provided a platform for Native women to tell their stories on their own terms, and these perspectives, I believe, carry more significant information than any statistical report. LeAnn Littlewolf (Leech Lake Band of Ojibwe) describes the experience of widespread rape in the lives of Native women:

The issue of sexual violence is too familiar. I can reach out around me and see so many faces of women I know who have lived through this incomprehensible experience. I can feel its deep reach into the lives of women and see the way it unfurls its effects into our families and to our communities. This is the Native way, as we find ourselves inextricably connected. And yet, being raped disconnects everything. The violation cannot be explained and this makes it impossible to reconcile. It changes the very reality of life.[30]

It is, of course, impossible for statistics themselves to convey the incredible amount of pain and trauma experienced by survivors of rape. The devastating long-term impact of rape has been well established in a variety of fields, including psychology, medicine, sociology, ethnography, and anthropology. Feminist philosopher Claudia Card writes that rape "breaks the spirit, humiliates, tames, [and] produces a docile, deferential, obedient soul."[31] The harm is simultaneously physical and spiritual, and is perhaps best captured by phrases like "soul murder"[32] and "spiritual murder."[33] Unresolved trauma can often be the source of substance abuse and addiction—frequently described as "self-medicating" in the world of anti-rape activism. Mainstream studies of the aftermath of rape have concluded that survivors are at a high risk for developing mental and physical problems as a result of the assault.[34] For Native women, the widespread nature of rape infiltrates every aspect of life. Renowned psychiatrist Judith Lewis Herman, who has dedicated her career to studying the experience of sexual assault survivors, has described the impact of rape as having lifelong implications: "resolution of the trauma is never final; recovery is never complete."[35]

Context is always critical. Imagine living in a world in which almost every woman you know has been raped. Now imagine living in a world in which four generations of women and their ancestors have been raped. Now imagine that not a single rapist has ever been prosecuted for these crimes. That dynamic is a reality for many Native women—and thus for some survivors, it can be difficult to separate the more immediate experience of their assault from the larger experience that their people have endured through a history of forced removal, displacement, and destruction. All these events are attacks on the human soul; the destruction of indigenous culture and the rape of a woman connote a kind of spiritual death that is difficult to describe to those who have not experienced it. It is not only Native women who have been raped but Native nations as a whole.

Survivors not only struggle to cope with their own feelings but also bear the burden of society's judgment. There is no one "right" way to respond to being raped. Myriad reactions are justifiable and "logical" in the aftermath of an assault, and most of the counterintuitive behavior people observe is shrouded in the shame and confusion experienced by survivors. Victim blaming is not just external—feelings of self-blame and guilt can be even more overwhelming than the trauma itself. Survivor and professor Susan Brison explains this dynamic aptly when she writes, "It can be less painful to believe that you did something blameworthy than it is to think that you live in a world where you can be attacked at any time, in any place, simply because you are a woman."[36]

Several studies have found self-blame to be a significant factor in the recovery and general well-being of survivors.[37] If she was assaulted outside her home, a survivor may fear leaving her home, or if she was assaulted in her home, she may never want to return home. If someone she trusted raped her, she may doubt her own intelligence, decision-making ability, and sanity. Rape victims often struggle with "triggers" or memories of the assault associated with sight, smell, and sound. If the rapist was a doctor or nurse, a survivor may avoid necessary medical care. If the rapist was a police officer, she may never call for help again (and may teach her daughters not to call, either—no matter how bad things may seem).

In short, rape affects more than the individual victims; it has an impact on the entire community. Women play significant roles in tribal communities, culturally, spiritually, and politically, and have been referred to as the "backbone" of tribal sovereignty.[38] Sovereignty thus suffers when the women suffer. The fact that over one-third of Native women have been traumatized by rape inhibits their ability to contribute productively to the community. The insidious and cyclical nature of sexual violence compounds the trauma, particularly in communities where there has been no effective intervention for centuries.

This is not to say that women who experience sexual assault are doomed to a life of despair and pain. On the contrary, Native women survivors who have shared their stories of survival with me have impressed upon me their strength of will and resolve in the face of brutality and oppression. Native women can indeed survive and heal after rape, but the immediate and lingering aftereffects of the crime can result in significant (if temporary) impairments in their lives. I seek to acknowledge and document the devastation left in the wake of rape, and to address how tribal legal systems might play a role in responding to this devastation.

What We Need to Know

The most important research being done on rape in the lives of Native women takes place under the auspices of locally initiated and implemented projects. The surveys, roundtable reports, and safety audits that are done in local communities are much richer in terms of information because of the depth that can be achieved with methodology that reflects the unique experiences of particular tribal communities.[39] These kinds of studies do not often appear in academic journals because the Native women who conduct and publish them are not particularly concerned with how the outside world understands their trauma. (Or, as one elder chided me, "It's nobody else's business.") These localized research projects are designed to craft customized, tribal-specific interventions. However, the distribution of such reports (when appropriate) can serve as examples or models for other tribal communities. For example, in 2013 the White Buffalo Calf Woman Society (an organization dedicated to ending violence against women in the Sicangu Lakota nation) released two important reports that focused inward on the real experiences of Lakota women.[40] Tribal members developed the survey instruments with the assistance of social scientists. These kinds of reports typically contain much richer information about the unique needs of survivors in that community than any outside survey could ever capture. The WBCWS studies provide insight into what the community members are truly experiencing without revealing any private information. Consider the value of the following data points:

> The majority of those polled felt domestic violence (92.8%), sexual assault (92.8%), and teen dating violence (91.2%) were all problems on the Rosebud Reservation. A lower percent (82.0%) thought that stalking is a problem. . . . More than three-quarters (77.5%) of all female respondents who had experienced both domestic/dating violence and sexual abuse or rape had considered or tried hurting themselves.[41]

This information is far more valuable to the tribal leaders than aggregate national data available from the federal government. When Native women design studies that reflect their own concerns, then the research will truly advance change.

Conclusion: Categories of Knowledge

There are different categories of knowledge. There is the kind of knowledge we gain from years of careful study, consulting as many experts as possible and analyzing the empirical data. Then there is the kind of knowledge we gain from experiencing something; a visceral knowledge that can invoke the physical senses and the genius of memory. I find Athabascan scholar Dian Million's description of this dynamic as "felt theory" particularly worthwhile because it honors and values the real, lived experiences of Native women as legitimate sources of knowledge.[42] Both categories of knowledge are critical for addressing rape.

I hesitate to call one form of knowledge more "Western" and one more "Native." Such binary distinctions tend to oversimplify the worldview and reinforce the stereotype that Native people somehow do not value quantitative scientific study. In my experience, Native people are no less interested in empirical data than other people.[43] Western science, however, has largely operated from a place of patriarchal oppression that both steals data and disrespects fundamental tenets of basic kinship protocol. If Native people distrust scientific data, it is because it has largely been used to critique Native society and reinforce dehumanizing stereotypes. As Linda Tuhiwai Smith explains, " 'Research' is probably one of the dirtiest words in the indigenous world's vocabulary."[44] The scientific process and the use of the data can seem dehumanizing, exploitative, and pointless.

So while gathering empirical, scientific data has been critical in convincing the outside world to take notice of the crisis, we must not forget local realities. National numbers are flat; they lack dimension and stifle future exploration. For Native women, surviving rape is a journey with texture and dimensions that are shaped by history, language, and ceremony.

TWO

What She Say It Be Law

Tribal Rape Law and Indigenous Feminisms

THE PEOPLE OF MY NATION, the Mvskoke, have always governed themselves pursuant to laws. Like most tribal nations, the Mvskoke people relied for millennia on sacred oral traditions and ceremonies both to establish and enforce legal standards. These laws were not written down. In fact, for many Native people, reducing laws to writing weakened their power by limiting accessibility to a few and losing the value of rhythm and intonation. Europeans utterly failed to understand this kind of system. Seeing no judges, courtrooms, or attorneys, settlers assumed that Native people were without law. This assumption made it morally palatable to impose foreign laws upon Native people, and also facilitated the application of racial epithets such as "uncivilized" and "savage." Starting in the early nineteenth century, federal Indian agents encouraged, cajoled, manipulated, and bribed Native people into reducing their laws to writing, while simultaneously mandating the development of an American-like system to replace tribal legal traditions. The earliest written laws of tribal nations thus provide fascinating case studies on how the clash of culture and ideas played out in everyday legal relationships.

Mvskoke leaders started writing down laws much earlier than most other tribes. By the early nineteenth century, Mvskoke people were largely intermarried and intermingled with Scottish immigrants. Federal officials encouraged and expected assimilation, and writing down laws (in English) was a central component of these efforts. Some of the earliest known Mvskoke written criminal laws date to 1825, when Chilly McIntosh, the son of a well-known Mvskoke chief, handwrote fifty-six criminal laws in English to satisfy the local Indian agent that the Mvskoke people were law-abiding. The thirty-fifth law clearly addresses gendered violence. While the crimes were not labeled with any particular title, it is safe to say that this is the first written Mvskoke rape law:

> And be it farther enacted if any person or persons should undertake to force a woman and did it by force, it shall be left to woman what punishment she should satisfied with to whip or pay what she say it be law.[1]

Several interesting concepts emerge from this forty-three-word sentence, although the syntax is confusing and the word rape itself is never used. The word "force" (used twice) is an important clue that this passage describes a physical attack and the law clearly refers to women as victims (although it does not indicate the gender of perpetrators). There is a clear reference to corporal punishment ("whip or pay")—which is consistent with observed Mvskoke law in practice in the early nineteenth century. Perhaps most remarkable component of this law is the last six words: "what she say it be law." This phrase, suggesting a rape victim had legal standing to participate in sentencing decisions, is fundamentally inconsistent with Anglo-American rape law in the same time period.[2]

For most of American legal history, rape was framed as a *property* crime perpetrated against men.[3] In fact, the phrase "marital rape" was an oxymoron in American law until the early 1990s (married women had no legal right to deny sex to their husbands). In 1825, most state laws often required two eyewitnesses to convict a man for rape—a woman's word alone could never be sufficient. In addition, settler women were not allowed to be attorneys, judges, or jurors, meaning there could literally be no female voice to "say the law." Yet the 1825 Mvskoke law—in the same era—ends with the phrase "what she say it be law." Somehow, despite the persistent effort and pressure to develop an American-style government and legal system, the Mvskoke law suggests a legal tradition that acknowledged the decision-making capacity of women. This does not mean the Mvskoke people were feminists in the modern sense of the word, but it does tell us the precolonial legal system likely operated with a fundamentally different worldview.

The pressure to assimilate laws and governments continued (and continues today), and less than fifty years later, the Mvskoke rape law read as follows: "Be it enacted, That should any person be convicted of rape, he shall for the first offense receive fifty lashes, for the second offense he shall suffer death."[4] Several fundamental changes are expressed in less than fifty years. Note that the gender-neutral 1867 law does not mention a victim at all. The voice of Mvskoke women appears to have been lost or at least eclipsed through the forced Americanization of the Mvskoke people.

With Mvskoke law as a starting point, this chapter considers the relevance of precolonial responses to sexual violence in tribal nations by exploring general foundational structures and belief systems about gender that existed prior to the imposition of foreign legal structures. This chapter will also consider the limitations of mainstream American feminism in developing solutions to violence against Native women and how Native women's perspectives can be muted by the dominant discourse about patriarchy. This chapter closes by exploring the role of contemporary tribal jurists in documenting and enforcing tribal-specific gendered justice.

Gender Equity in Traditional Law

Patriarchy is largely a European import. Native women had spiritual, political, and economic power that European women did not enjoy. That power was based on a simple principle: women and children are not the property of men. I am guarded about pan-Indian essentialisms suggesting tribal nations were all "matriarchal" and therefore rape free—Plains Cree Métis scholar Emma LaRocque cautions that "it should not be assumed that matriarchies necessarily prevented men from exhibiting oppressive behavior toward women."[5] I often provide forty-five- to fifty-minute lectures on Native women and rape, and I have sometimes been guilty of overgeneralizing and overromanticizing precolonial gender roles—if for no other reason than time constraints. Still, there are some common themes in tribal histories and epistemologies that serve as counterpoints to patriarchy. Women exercised power in ways that weren't always readily recognized by a non-Native observer because they did not always perform tasks associated with European leadership.

Power should not be confused with pure equality. Tribal societies were generally not gender neutral. In fact, gender was often explicitly prescribed in the division of duties, based on a dualistic scheme with a significant emphasis on balance. Often, this duality is presented in a reductive way (e.g., "The women farmed while the men hunted"). In reality, it would be more accurate to say "most women farmed" and "most men hunted"—there were always exceptions based on personal abilities, ceremonial expectations, or the need to balance responsibilities.

Exploring a particular tribal epistemology can illuminate some specific ways in which this gendered balance was achieved. In Mvskoke culture, "The balance of male and female principles permeates all Creek thinking. The balances, therefore, involve the division of various powers, functions, and privileges."[6] This framework for gender can also be described as *nonbinary complementary dualism,* wherein binary gender lines are fluid without fixed boundaries. This is evidenced by the role that Two-Spirit or gender nonconforming people played. Sometimes a man would perform a woman's role, and vice versa.

In a gendered epistemology, all persons have valued roles and duties, which balance one another; "dualism embraces difference in principle, not as division but rather as complementarity."[7] It is a versatile description that continues "to offer exceptional sanctuary to an attitude about gender that cherishes a wide arena of personal autonomy and freedom."[8] Women and men often had separate duties, but the separation took the form of horizontal distinctions rather than a vertical hierarchy of authority. The gender lines, as part of a creation story or cosmology, are set up to complement each other, to provide "equilibrium."[9] In some cosmologies, gendered identity is transcended by those with particular spiritual gifts.[10]

Even the fundamental foundation for Native identity was women centered; many tribal kinship systems are organized around a matrilineal clan system whereby a child's primary identity is based on the mother. In matrilineal societies, women are often vested with the power to name the leaders of the clan who then execute the chosen laws of the people. Property was conveyed through women, and they often chose the leaders of their tribal councils. In some political structures, like that of the Haudenosaunne, women held "veto" power over decisions to go to war based on their willingness to provide food for warriors.

Many traditional tribal gender laws have been lost or damaged through assimilation (particularly Christian assimilation). It is difficult to re-create or reimagine how precolonial systems adjudicated rape, but there are clues in historical records that affirm the presence of significant anti-rape sentiment in most tribal cultures. One of the most significant clues comes from tribal constructs of sexual autonomy and bodily integrity. In the Lakota culture, for example, Mark St. Pierre and Tilda Long Soldier write, "the woman owned her body and all the rights that went with it."[11] European settlers were fascinated and sometimes horrified by the sexual autonomy of Native women. Their journals and observations, especially those from the eighteenth and nineteenth centuries, provide important (though often flawed) information about women's sexuality in Native communities. In Europe and early America the legal system was used to limit, penalize, and punish sexual choices of women. Not so in tribal nations. In 1722 Diron D'Artaguiette, a French settler, wrote that young Native girls "are the mistresses of their own bodies" as though this were somehow a noteworthy observation.[12] Many European settlers judged cultural values about women's sexuality as savage and primitive if not altogether inhuman. French Jesuits, who were the primary European contact for many tribal nations, were "baffled and sometimes horrified" by the sexual and political autonomy exhibited by indigenous women.[13] Christian missionaries and federal agents used Native women's autonomy as justification for conversion and assimilation. Native women who expressed and celebrated their sexuality had no place in mainstream America and were often shamed and marginalized. Many Europeans were alarmed by the powerful role played by Native women within their nations, and efforts were made to reduce the status of Native women through numerous means.[14] Missionary records from throughout the continent indicate that many religious groups formally imposed severe consequences on Native women who dared exercise independence and sexual autonomy.[15]

Likewise, Europeans were often fascinated by the anti-rape cultures they encountered, particularly when they discovered that Native men did not rape women war prisoners.[16] For example,

Laurel Thatcher Ulrich (the Harvard historian who coined the phrase "well-behaved women seldom make history") writes that the Puritans were "amazed at the sexual restraint of Indian men, who never raped their captives."[17] Even Europeans who wrote disparagingly about Native people noted that Native people abhorred sexual violence. Brigadier General James Clinton of the Continental Army told his troops in 1779, "Bad as the savages are, they never violate the chastity of any women, their prisoners."[18] Another account comes from George Croghan, who testified about Indians in the Middle Atlantic colonies in the late eighteenth century: "I have known more than onest thire Councils, order men to be putt to Death for Committing Rapes, wh[ich] is a Crime they Despise."[19] Despite the proliferation of "captivity narratives" in the nineteenth century, which were framed with the intent to dehumanize the brutish behavior of Indians, there is very little historical documentation of Native men perpetrating rape against white women.

Precolonial Responses to Rape

There is, of course, no database of stories or laws that we can consult to understand how tribal nations articulated and enforced rape laws. We do have anecdotal evidence that tribal nations took rape seriously enough that punishments in some regions included corporal punishment, banishment, and even the death penalty.[20] Native women's activists have documented the traditional response of tribal communities to violence against women.[21] Ojibwe scholar Lisa Poupart explains:

> According to the oral traditions within our tribal communities, it is understood that prior to mass Euro-American invasion and influence, violence was virtually nonexistent in traditional Indian families and communities. The traditional spiritual world views that organized daily tribal life prohibited harm by individuals against other beings. To harm another being was akin to committing the same violation against the spirit world.[22]

While my research is generally consistent with Poupart's conclusion, I hesitate to claim that all tribal cultures were entirely 100 percent "rape free." But the frequency of the crime was low, in part because of the immediate and severe consequences for disrupting balance in society. Evidence lies in both the experience of Native women prior to contact as well as the behavior of Native men, as recorded by European explorers, settlers, and traders.

Historically, tribal nations, as sovereigns, exercised full jurisdiction over crimes against women. Crimes such as rape, domestic violence, and child abuse may have been extremely rare, but when they did occur, tribal systems provided a powerful system of social checks and balances that held offenders accountable for their behavior.[23] Unlike the American legal system, wherein victims of violent crime have historically had no voice in the criminal justice process,[24] most indigenous legal systems were victim centered. Tribal governments strived to provide a sense of spiritual and emotional recovery from violent crime, by providing both material goods and spiritual sustenance designed to restore the victim to her previous place in life. Although no system is perfect, indigenous philosophies of justice generally provide more protection and healing to victims than the American system.[25] Moreover, many "responses" to rape were incorporated naturally as part of the way in which people lived. There were political consequences as well. In Iroquois culture, a man could not achieve a leadership position if he had ever raped a woman.[26] As Dakota scholar Elizabeth Cook-Lynn explains, "Men who caused stress in the community or risk to the survival of the tribe by dishonoring women were held accountable by the people. They could not carry the sacred pipe, nor could they hold positions of status."[27] Many of these principles need to be revitalized and enforced.

As tribes began to develop written laws in response to pressure from the U.S. government, it is possible that some of the values that had been transmitted orally found their way into the early written laws. The Mvskoke law described at the beginning of this chapter is one such example. When compared to the European and early American laws on rape, which often punished women for the actions of rapists, the tribal response to sexual assault was comparatively victim-centric and respectful of survivors.[28]

American Rape Law

Nineteenth-century American rape laws, based in large part on the common law of England, treated women as subordinate, at best, or as chattel at worst.[29] They were not intended to protect women as much as they were intended to control them, preserve chastity, and curtail their sexual independence. And as part of the colonial project, Europeans imposed their own expectations and standards for appropriate female sexuality on tribal people. In Spanish law, women were considered to be the legal subjects of their fathers, brothers, or closest male relative.[30] Through the process of assimilation and acculturation, many of these European constructs of gender and sexuality have become incorporated into some contemporary indigenous communities. Reclaiming an indigenous jurisprudence of rape, therefore, requires a reexamination of tribal conceptions of sexuality, independence, and autonomy. This is a topic that I discuss more thoroughly in chapter 8.

The origins of sexual assault law in the American system developed as an offshoot of property law.[31] The traditional American legal paradigm of rape (a stranger attacking a virgin) did not address the experience of most women, as rape law placed women in the same category as inanimate property. Legal scholar Michelle Anderson has carefully studied these early paradigms, and has a described a culture which is fundamentally at odds with sexual autonomy:

> Historically, [Anglo-American] rape law raised unique procedural hurdles for rape victims that victims of other crimes did not have to surmount. Derived from English common law and applicable in most jurisdictions until the mid to late 1970s, these formal rules embodied clear presumptions against women who complained of having been raped. These rules included absolute exemptions from criminal liability for men who raped their wives. They included requirements that the victim establish that she resisted her attacker to the utmost, freshly complained of having been raped and corroborated her testimony with other evidence. They included biased suppositions about victims who had previously engaged in sexual intercourse outside of marriage. Finally, they included special cautionary instructions read to the jury to warn them of the fallibility of the testimony of those who allege they have been raped.[32]

Until the mid-twentieth century, most state systems only criminalized rape when the victim was a white woman and left indigenous women and other women of color with no recourse.

At the same time, the colonial mind-set could not conceive of a legal wrong in raping a Native woman. As a result, Native women were devalued and debased, and their abuse was seen as being outside the law.[33] In a 1909 congressional debate regarding punishments for perpetrators of sexual assault against Native women, U.S. Representative George W. Norris of Nebraska stated on the floor of the House of Representatives, "the morals of Indian women are not always as high as those of a white woman and consequently the punishment should be lighter against her."[34] Accordingly, in 1968, the Ninth Circuit Court of Appeals (ruling on an Arizona case) upheld a law that imposed a harsher penalty for the rape of a non-Indian woman than for that of an Indian woman,[35] presumably because Congress viewed Native women as immoral and therefore unworthy of protection.[36] While this particular legal distinction is no longer on the books, the legacy of official disparate treatment is apparent from the statistics we see today.

Advancing Native Feminisms

Starting in the mid- to late twentieth century, Native women activists sometimes clashed with liberal feminists on the issue of "equality." Tribal cultural values often do not strive for the utopian ideals of pure equality in the form of a gender-neutral society. This contemporary tension between Native and non-Native feminists can be traced back to the "clash" between Europeans and Indians during colonial expansion over the two groups' fundamentally different epistemological views on the nature of gender and the appropriate roles of women in society.[37] Today's mainstream feminist theories about rape are often responding to a culture grounded in a patriarchy of European origin. When tribal governments respond to gendered violence, though, they are responding to a phenomenon fully entrenched in abusive colonial power. Thus, the many solutions proposed by mainstream feminists, who focus on patriarchy as the cause of gendered violence, are often a poor match for the responses of tribal societies.

Skeptics may contend that whatever matrilineal/matrilocal aspects of Native society existed have largely been abandoned or lost as a result of hegemony and assimilation, and it is merely hopeful idealism to suggest we could rekindle concepts of precolonial gender balance. In response to that concern, this chapter concludes by highlighting a few published tribal court decisions that offer evidence that women-centered values and practices still exist, in some form, in some of today's tribal legal systems. Such cases demonstrate that the effort to sustain and revitalize precolonial gender norms is not merely an academic exercise. Reviewing these cases can illuminate tribal courts as one avenue of confirming or reestablishing respect for women in contemporary tribal communities. Many tribal judges have, at least from outward appearances, based their legal analysis on standards established by American common law. What I have highlighted are cases in which tribal jurists have resisted this patriarchal tradition and tapped into unique tribal conceptions of gender to resolve disputes.

Contemporary tribal court cases addressing gender issues demonstrate a unique tribal perspective or way of thinking about legal cases dealing with gender that is based on tribal customs and traditions. The cases in this section focus on matrilineal clans, family law, criminal law, and property. Cases dealing with child custody, divorce, and sexual assault exemplify these principles of gender equity. These cases are not presented as tribal feminism in action but rather as acknowledgment of gendered law that could be explored further in the efforts to intervene in entrenched gendered violence.

Kinship Circles: Women at the Center

Matrilineal descent may be one of the salient gender characteristics that has survived over the centuries in some communities. Many Native people may not know much about their language or precolonial government structures, but still retain a strong connection to their clan and matrilineal ancestry. The following tribal court cases demonstrate that clan identity is still relevant enough to appear as a central focal point in some tribal judiciaries. If one is using a strictly Western lens, some of these custody/kinship cases may look like a preference for women, but only if one characterizes gendered analysis as centered on rights as opposed to responsibilities.

Hepler v. Perkins is a 1986 child custody decision from the Sitka Community Association Tribal Court in Alaska.[38] The case ultimately turns on a Tlingit matrilineal society and values based on the mother's clan responsibilities. In *Hepler*, a Tlingit mother from Sitka attempted to regain custody of her child from the non-Indian father and grandparents. Both mother and child were Sitka tribal members. The descriptions of familial and clan relationships are distinctly those of the Sitka Tribe and are based on the role of mothers within the Sitka community. The mother and child were living away from the tribal community when the paternal grandparents went to the state of Washington to gain custody of the child. The mother asked the Tribal Court of the Sitka Community Association to rule on whether under customary tribal law the tribe continued to assume responsibility for her child even when she and her child were away from Sitka. The Tribal Court of Sitka referred the case to the Court of Elders to rule on this important issue of clan jurisdiction over children of female members.

The Court of Elders found that

> children of female members of a clan are children of the clan regardless of where or under what circumstances they may be found. Clan membership does not wash off, nor can such membership be removed by any force, or any distance, or over time. Even in death clan membership continues, and in re-birth is it renewed.[39]

Based on the tribal custom of female clan membership and their responsibility to care for children, the Tribal Court decided that it had inherent authority to protect the clan relationship, even when a child was not currently living within the tribal territory.

The Sitka case demonstrates the continued relevance of matrilineal descent, which is intertwined with the power Sitka women have in the tribal community. In a matrilineal society, clan membership is determined through the mother. As described by the elders, clan membership does not "wash off" and is not diluted by distance. The court ruled in favor of the Indian mother, based not on an assumption that the mother was a more nurturing or effective parent but based rather on Sitka values about clan membership and clan responsibility for children.

In the Matter of JJS is a 1983 adoption case from the Navajo Nation with a similar acknowledgment of clan identity.[40] The District Court of Window Rock in the Navajo Nation located in northern Arizona made a decision to grant custody of a neglected child to the mother's extended family. After considering Navajo customary law, the court awarded custody of the neglected child to the maternal relatives, based on the principle that "the Navajo view of the relationship of children to parents is not one of a simple parent and child relationship, but an entire pattern of expectation and desirable action surrounding children."[41] There is a distinct relationship between Navajo children and their parents based on reciprocal expectations and relations. Children are highly valued in Navajo society as "an integral part of a functioning self-reinforcing and protecting group."[42] This group consists of a large extended family based on matrilineal society. A child can be adopted by the extended family for an indeterminate amount of time in order to retain the family and clan ties. The entire extended family is expected to care for the child as a natural part of community and clan obligations.[43]

Instead of using federal law to decide the case, the court relied on Navajo tradition that dictates the importance of the extended family in raising a child. The bonds between children and grandparents are extremely important, and the court reflected these values by allowing the child to stay with his or her extended family.

The Navajo Nation Supreme Court has also infused contemporary divorce law with traditional gender norms. One example is the 1997 case of Naize v. Naize in which the court ordered that the husband pay alimony and attorney's fees to the wife based on Navajo custom and tradition, which dictates that you "do not throw your family away."[44] In exploring these obligations, the court noted that in traditional Navajo marriage, the husband moves into the wife's home upon marriage, and the joint efforts of the man and woman work to benefit the family. Moreover, the court concluded:

If the marriage does not survive, customary law directs the man to leave with his personal possessions (including his horse and riding gear, clothes, and religious items) and the rest of the marital property

> stays with the wife and children at their residence for their support
> and maintenance. Whatever gains the marital property generate[s]
> goes to support the wife and children and to a lesser extent the wife's
> close relatives.[45]

With these words, the court upheld the wife's request for spousal maintenance. The court decided to grant spousal support to the female divorcée based on Navajo customary law that indicates that the marital home, all possessions within, and the children belong to the women. The ex-wife's request for attorney fees was also upheld.

However, the Navajo Supreme Court reversed one aspect of the maintenance decision of the lower court, which ordered the ex-husband to provide wood and coal to his ex-wife for the remainder of her life. The Supreme Court referenced another Navajo custom in reversing this decree, noting that divorce should have "finality," and a lifetime obligation was inconsistent with this tradition. Customary law dictated that to restore balance and harmony after the divorce, each party should return to his or her own home and leave the other person alone. In this case, the Navajo court relied entirely on Navajo customary law and traditions regarding the position of women within Navajo society.

In 1993 the Tribal Court of Appeals for the Sicangu Lakota (Rosebud Sioux) Tribe in South Dakota carefully considered the role of gender imbalance in a child custody case captioned *Spotted Tail v. Spotted Tail*.[46] The court reviewed a custody decree in a domestic violence case and concluded that the trial court correctly awarded custody to the mother in a divorce case. The mother in this case was apparently accused of abandoning her children and thus of being unfit for custody. However, the court based its decision on the welfare of the children, which it ruled should never be subservient to the interests of the parents. In this case, the mother had to flee from the abuse of her children's father. She tried to make contact with her children, but her husband denied her access and demonstrated a pattern of dominion and vengeance over both the children and the mother.

The tribal court put the interests of the children first, instead of focusing on alleged shortcomings of the parents. Despite the fact that the mother had not been able to parent for several years, the court considered how domestic violence affected her access to the children. Domestic violence cases are especially challenging for mothers who have suffered abuse at the hands of their partners, because judges often unfairly consider the mothers to be a threat to their children. But in *Spotted Tail*, the court noted that the evidence "reveals a father who was domineering, abusive, and revengeful, who seemed bent on keeping the children away from their natural mother."[47] This case alludes to the special place children and women hold within most tribal communities. Children's interests are of primary concern to the tribe, because they represent future generations and the continuation of the tribal community.

Contemporary Accountability: Rape in Tribal Court

Tribal courts have also considered gender norms in the context of rape cases. In *Winnebago Tribe of Neb. v. Hugh Bigfire* (1998), the Winnebago Supreme Court was asked to use the American concept of "equal protection" in a sexual assault case in which the tribal code differentiated between men and women. The male defendants argued that men and women should be treated equally under the law. The court rejected this argument, explaining that

> under traditional Winnebago customary law, gender differences commonly were drawn for the punishment of offenses related to sexual misconduct because of the natural biological differences in this area between the sexes, the different consequences of misconduct for men and women, and different roles ascribed by the tribal tradition to men and women (without creating any hierarchy or cross-gender disrespect). . . . Ho-Chunk tradition recognizes and respects different roles for males and females in the Winnebago Tribe, and particularly, tolerates and encourages different responses to sexual misconduct for men and women.[48]

After considering research into the tribal gender values through consultation with tribal members, elders, and research on Ho-Chunk customary law, the Winnebago Supreme Court concluded that gender differences constitute a natural part of Ho-Chunk life, and that men and women have different roles to provide for each other in relationships. The equal protection claims failed because the charges against the males made them more accountable, which coincided with traditional male roles of respecting women within the community.[49]

Fort Peck v. Martell (2000) is another tribal court case that involves interpreting tribal rape law.[50] The defendant, Martell, coerced a young girl to leave the reservation with him by promising her drugs and alcohol, and then he raped her outside tribal territorial jurisdiction. The defendant argued that the crime took place off-reservation (in Havre, Montana), thus falling outside the jurisdiction of the tribal court. The Fort Peck Court of Appeals ruled that key elements of the crime took place on the reservation, namely, the "coercive methodology" used by the defendant. This is an innovative analysis of the crime, framing rape as a series of actions for which the perpetrator should be held accountable, a ruling that reflects an understanding of rape that is typically absent from American law.

Conclusion: Reclaiming Indigenous Feminisms

The tribal cases in this chapter suggest that some contemporary tribal courts are seeking to address gender issues in a distinctly indigenous way. By reclaiming their own tribal perspectives on gender, they are engaging in a unique ethic of decolonization—an ethic that balances traditional views on morality with contemporary needs and problems. Of course, tribal courts are not the only tribal entities that continue to consider how precolonial conceptions of gender can inform contemporary issues. Tribal courts are, however, the living manifestation of tribal law, and the fact that women's roles are respected and valued is indicative of a larger movement to stop violence.

Analyzing the 1825 Mvskoke law is a useful exercise because it illuminates uniquely Mvskoke values that can help shape contemporary tribal rape law. While the actual substance of the law has little applicability today, it is through these traditions that tribal nations have the opportunity to revisit traditional gender roles and determine how the values of protecting women and holding perpetrators accountable have relevance for today's tribal laws.

THREE

At the Mercy of the State

Linking Rape to Federal Indian Law

IN NOVEMBER 2013, the Indian Law and Order Commission, a national bipartisan independent investigatory body created by language in the Tribal Law and Order Act of 2010, released a report titled *A Roadmap for Making Native America Safer.* Among its many conclusions was the assertion that "more lives and property can and will be saved once Tribes have greater freedom to build and maintain their own criminal justice systems." The report's recommendations are part of a larger contemporary movement to disentangle federal law from tribal law. Tribal governments have struggled to respond to rape because federal Indian law has placed both legal and practical barriers in the exercise of criminal jurisdiction.

Today's tribal legal systems operate under bizarre constraints imposed under even more bizarre conditions, creating a patchwork of various federal and tribal laws that work in tandem to utterly obfuscate justice. Nowhere does this patchwork affect the day-to-day lives of Native people more directly than in the area of criminal law. Native people are both overvictimized and overincarcerated at significant rates, and nearly everyone who has worked in Indian country can tell you that the criminal justice framework is to blame.

Tribal sovereignty is a critical component to addressing gendered violence in tribal communities today, because a sovereign political entity has duties to protect citizens from abusive power. Seneca legal scholar Robert Odawi Porter writes that political sovereignty for tribal nations is expressed through three core components: belief, ability, and recognition.[1] Using this structure in the context of rape, political sovereignty might be best articulated as, "Our tribal nation *believes* it has the legal and moral authority to respond to rape. Our tribal nation has a *strong system* in place to hold offenders accountable. Neighboring nations *recognize* our authority and respect our decisions about responding to rape."

All three aspects of Porter's construction of sovereignty have been damaged by colonialism. The federal government has systemically stripped power from tribal nations, leaving tribal nations without effective legal remedies that are grounded in tribal law. Understanding how this process has diminished the power of tribal governments is a critical step in the process of strengthening today's tribal criminal justice systems. I will explore the complicated calculus of contemporary criminal jurisdiction in Indian country and demonstrate how the dysfunction of federal Indian law has created barriers that continue to make Native women particularly vulnerable to rape. For the purposes of this chapter, I will limit the discussion to the most significant federal actions that have an impact on the tribal response to rape.

A Brief History of Federal Indian Law, from Columbus to Today's Reforms

Understanding the historical context in which federal Indian law developed is critical to any proposal for reform. In the context of rape in tribal communities, then, it is also necessary to examine the history of rape committed by European men against Native women. In raping Native women, European men were certainly breaking tribal law. This fact mattered little to the colonists and rapists, who completely misunderstood, ignored, and otherwise disrespected existing tribal legal systems.

We can begin our historical investigation with the arrival of Christopher Columbus in North American in 1492. An iconic symbol of colonization, Columbus's arrival represents not only the beginning of the destruction of indigenous cultures but also the moment when European men introduced rape as a major tool of that destruction. A passage from the diary of one of Columbus's aristocratic friends who accompanied him on the second voyage describes one such encounter:

> When I was in the boat, I captured a very beautiful Carib woman. . . .
> Having brought her into my cabin, and she being naked as is their
> custom, I conceived desire to take my pleasure. I wanted to put my
> desire to execution, but she was unwilling for me to do so, and treated
> me with her nails in such wise that I would have preferred never to
> have begun. But seeing this . . . I took a rope-end and thrashed her
> well, following which she produced such screaming and wailing as
> would cause you not to believe your ears. Finally we reached an
> agreement such that, I can tell you, she seemed to have been raised
> in a veritable school of harlots.[2]

The symbolism of this boastful passage and its arrogant entitle-
ment is extremely important, for it exemplifies the logic of colonists
who would continue to deploy rape as a tool of conquest. Historian
Albert L. Hurtado notes of the nineteenth-century California gold
rush, "Part of the invading population was imbued with a conquest
mentality, fear and hatred of Indians that in their minds justified the
rape of Indian women."[3] The same men who brought the trauma of
rape with their physical presence also represented the powers that
would ultimately put a stranglehold on the type of tribal authority
they would recognize.

Indian "Uprisings" as a Response to Sexual Exploitation

Throughout the nineteenth century, tribal leaders often protested
and resisted when women and children were mistreated. Indeed,
many tribally initiated conflicts and "uprisings" were responses
to kidnapping and sexual mistreatment of women. One example
comes from the 1862 U.S.–Dakota War in Minnesota, popularly
referred to as the "Sioux Uprising." While many historians describe
the precursor to this war as hunger and anger about delays in distribution of treaty-promised annuities and supplies, a closer review
of the record also reveals Dakota concerns that the Office of Indian
Affairs had "failed to investigate charges of . . . mistreatment of
Indian women by white men."[4] Jerome Big Eagle, one of the Dakota
warriors condemned to die by the military after the war, received a
reprieve from President Abraham Lincoln and was exiled to a prison
camp in Iowa, where he was ultimately pardoned by President

Lincoln in 1864. He spoke to an author in 1894 and told him that just prior to the uprising, "some of the white men abused the Indian women in a certain way and disgraced them, and surely there was no excuse for that." Attacks on Native women and children aggravated the already tense relationships between frontier communities and Indian tribes. Violent "uprisings" often came after nonviolent attempts had failed and all legal procedures available to Native tribes were exhausted. Indians did kill whites, though clearly acts of violence were measures of last resort.[5]

The Problem of Jurisdiction

In law, jurisdiction is a term of art referring to government power, usually centering particularly on the power of the courts. There are three main categories of jurisdiction in the American legal system: territorial, personal, and subject matter. As sovereign nations, tribes exercised full jurisdiction in all three contexts. Tribal governments exercised inherent authority over territory, people, and relevant subject matters as developed through cultural practices and legal norms.

In the United States, tribal jurisdiction (at least that recognized by the federal government) has suffered greatly in the past 150 years at the hands of unilateral federal laws passed with no input or vote from tribal leaders. In a variety of contexts (including legislative and judicial), the federal and state governments have drastically diminished recognized tribal power. As a result of this complicated federal legal scheme, tribal governments have been denied jurisdiction over the vast majority of sexual violence that happens to Native women. This chapter focuses on four of the most significant laws in the lives of Native rape survivors today: the Major Crimes Act, a federal law passed in 1885;[6] Public Law 280 (PL 280), a federal law passed in 1953);[7] the Indian Civil Rights Act (ICRA), a federal law passed in 1968;[8] and the 1978 U.S. Supreme Court decision in *Oliphant v. Suquamish*.[9] This combination of federal laws and policies has created one of the most complicated jurisdictional frameworks in the American law.[10] Professor B. J. Jones, who has served as a judge for a variety of tribal courts in North Dakota, South Dakota, and Minnesota, notes that in the midst of jurisdictional uncertainty, the "security of women is compromised and the legal system is diminished in the eyes of both victims and offenders."[11] The limitations I describe here are not unique to the crime of rape but rather apply to all criminal cases. However, I explore the ways in which Native rape survivors experience the criminal justice system, in order to highlight the ways in which the system can aggravate trauma for individual victims.

Federal Intrusion: Major Crimes Act

In 1885 Congress passed the Major Crimes Act (MCA), which forcibly imposed the federal criminal justice system on tribal communities and still has significant relevance for Native rape survivors today. The MCA provides the federal government with criminal authority on many contemporary reservations, meaning that a rape survivor will navigate a federal criminal justice system if she reports the rape to law enforcement.

The impetus for the MCA was non-Native outrage over a controversial 1883 U.S. Supreme Court case, *Ex Parte Crow Dog*.[12] *Crow Dog* did not involve rape on its surface, but the statutory response to the case changed the framework under which rape would be addressed by tribal nations. *Crow Dog* began as a Lakota homicide case in the Dakota Territory (now parts of Montana and western North and South Dakota), when Crow Dog, a Brulé leader, killed Spotted Tail, a rival Brulé leader. The Lakota people exercised their inherent authority over intratribal crime and adjudicated Crow Dog in a traditional setting, imposing traditional penalties. Unsatisfied with the perceived leniency of the tribal sanctions, federal officials subsequently arrested and prosecuted Crow Dog in the federal territorial court, a process that concluded with a death sentence. Crow Dog petitioned the Supreme Court, arguing that he was not subject to U.S. authority as a citizen of a foreign government accused of violating foreign law on foreign soil.

When I lecture about this case, at this point I usually ask the audience whether they think Crow Dog won or lost his case in front of the Supreme Court. Most people guess that Crow Dog surely must have lost the case given the hostile relationships between tribal and federal officials at that point in history. Most people are surprised when I tell them that Crow Dog actually won in front of the Supreme Court and was subsequently released from federal custody. In freeing Crow Dog, the Supreme Court reviewed federal law (as it existed in 1883) and somewhat reluctantly concluded that tribal nations continued to operate as independent sovereigns. Ultimately, the court found that the only government with authority to respond to that particular homicide was that of the Lakota people. The non-Indian population was outraged and demanded that Congress intervene to change the laws governing tribal–federal relationships to ensure that Native defendants would be prosecuted in the Anglo legal system.[13] Responding to this public outcry, Congress passed the MCA, which unilaterally imposed the federal prosecutorial framework on the territories of tribal nations. The MCA provided the federal government with the authority it had requested in *Crow Dog*. The practical effect was that federal officials could now prosecute defendants like Crow Dog in federal court— because Congress said they could. A great article written by Judge B. J. Jones and attorney Chris Ironroad explains that laws like the MCA endorse a federal "tautological rationale" (we have jurisdiction because we say so).[14]

Although it is unlikely that Congress (or the outraged public for which it purported to speak) was particularly concerned with the plight of Native women who had been raped, the MCA included rape in its original list of offenses that could trigger federal prosecution (along with other "major crimes" like murder and kidnapping). The list of crimes over which the federal government can assert authority has been expanded over the years, but child sexual abuse was not added until 1986.[15]

Since the efforts of the government were designed to extinguish the very existence of tribal nations, it is more likely that Congress intended to infiltrate and control the indigenous populations through increased legal authority.[16] However, tribal nations have successfully sustained authority over rape (and other major crimes) by arguing that the doctrine of inherent sovereignty requires Congress to divest tribes of concurrent jurisdiction in clear language. The MCA never explicitly divested tribal nations of authority over the enumerated crimes.[17] Tribes therefore technically retain authority over *all crimes* (including those listed in the MCA), subject to the limitations noted later in this chapter. A tribal nation and the federal government thus share "concurrent" jurisdiction over the crimes, and in theory can operate independent of one another.

Although some have argued that the MCA was meant to supplant tribal authority, tribal nations prosecuted crimes such as rape and homicide in the twentieth century, and federal courts have recognized that tribes retain inherent jurisdiction over crimes enumerated in the Major Crimes Act.[18]

The federal government has largely controlled the development of contemporary tribal legal systems, and tribal governments have not consistently exercised concurrent jurisdiction over violent crimes. Many tribes do not pursue cases against rapists, or will wait until a declination from a federal or state prosecutor before proceeding with an official tribal response. Thus, the practical impact of the Major Crimes Act is that few tribes have pursued prosecution of crimes such as murder and rape for more than one hundred years. Instead of a rape case being handled within a community that applies the laws, beliefs, and traditions of its people, rape cases became the domain of the federal government. Until recently, there was no acknowledgment of this critical obligation of the federal criminal justice system, and the vast majority of rape cases in tribal communities were rarely adjudicated in federal criminal court. A simple summary of the MCA from the perspective of Native rape victims is as follows: on reservations where the MCA applies, federal law enforcement agencies (FBI and BIA) work in conjunction with prosecutors from the U.S. Attorney's Office to respond to rape. This means a rape survivor who reports the crime will necessarily interact with federal representatives carrying the official badges of colonization.

State Intrusion: Public Law 280

Approximately seventy years after Congress passed the MCA, federal jurisdiction over criminal matters (as established by the MCA) was transferred in 1953 to some state governments through a federal law known as Public Law 280 (PL 280).[19] PL 280 was part of a larger mid-twentieth-century federal effort to ultimately "terminate" recognition of tribal nations—an official government policy that has since been abandoned. The termination policy was designed to eliminate federal recognition of Indian nations and force Native people to assimilate into the mainstream U.S. population. PL 280 relinquished federal control over Indian territories in certain states

(Alaska, Oregon, California, Nebraska, Minnesota, and Wisconsin), turning the law enforcement authority over to the state governments. In communities affected by PL 280 and similar laws, the federal government's authority to respond to rape has been replaced by the authority of the state government.

Neither the states nor the tribes, however, consented to this arrangement, and states were not provided with any additional resources with which to enforce crimes in Indian country. As a result, PL 280 has led to widespread criminal justice dysfunction in those states.[20] This dysfunction was exacerbated when the federal government decided not to fund the development of tribal courts in these states. Many reservations thus operated without any consistent criminal justice system.

Moreover, a history of hostile relations between states and tribes has limited the possibility of cooperative law enforcement ventures. Today, states and tribes are often engaged in protracted litigation about issues related to natural resources, taxation, gaming, and, increasingly, child welfare. Although the obligation to provide criminal justice services to tribal governments is not often questioned, it is understandable that victims of crime might see the state government as a political body that challenges the rights of Native people on a regular basis.

Though the termination policy of the 1950s has largely been abandoned, the legacy of PL 280 remains for many tribal governments. For tribal nations located within the boundaries of states affected by PL 280, criminal activity and violence fall under the authority of the state. However, many of the states have not responded with effective law enforcement, leaving tribal communities at the mercy of criminals who prey on the vulnerable. For all practical purposes, tribal governments in PL 280 states have historically been at a distinct disadvantage when it comes to crime control.

Like the MCA, PL 280 did not specifically divest tribal governments of concurrent jurisdiction over crime.[21] However, the practical impact of PL 280 has included a weakening of tribal justice systems and a lack of response to criminal behavior, leaving many victims of crime without recourse in either the state or the tribal system. Native rape victims affected by PL 280 are beholden to a state criminal justice system that may have expressed outright hostility to tribal rights such as treaty hunting and fishing rights.

Capping Tribal Sentences:
Indian Civil Rights Act of 1968

A third federal law that has limited tribal governments' ability to address rape is the Indian Civil Rights Act of 1968, which places a cap on tribal sentencing authority. Congress passed ICRA in an era generally known for progressive legislation. Unfortunately, the Indian "Civil Rights" Act is largely a misnomer, for it actually restricts tribal court authority in several significant ways. ICRA serves as another example of federal statutory imposition of assimilated tribal justice systems because it requires that tribal governments enforce American legal norms as enshrined in the language of the Bill of Rights. The story of this federally imposed sentencing restriction is particularly noteworthy because of the context in which Congress passed the law.

Native people aligned with other social justice movements in the late 1960s to raise concerns about police brutality and disparate treatment in the American legal system. But the effort to address the inequities that Native people faced took a curious turn. Instead of concentrating on the racial discrimination and political disenfranchisement suffered by Native people in the state and federal systems, Congress focused on overstated abuses by tribal court systems—a legitimate problem, to be sure, but abusive tribal governments were no more or less common than abusive state governments. Federal lawmakers were motivated to pass ICRA when they learned that tribal governments are not bound by the U.S. Constitution (a principle confirmed by the U.S. Supreme Court in 1896).[22] Of course, tribal governments have never been hostile to civil rights; principles of individual autonomy and systemic checks on government are hardly the exclusive brainchild of the Western world. In truth, ICRA is a Eurocentric response to challenges that developed in tribal courts due to forced assimilation and hegemony.

ICRA mandates that tribal governments enforce certain individual rights in tribal court—and those rights are defined using selected language from the First, Fourth, Fifth, Sixth, and Eighth Amendments to the U.S. Constitution. Tribal courts are the primary enforcers of ICRA, but there is a mechanism for federal review in limited circumstances (thereby perpetuating colonial control over tribal courts). One practical outcome of ICRA is that defendants actually have more protection in tribal court—because both ICRA and any tribal constitutional or statutory civil rights laws will apply.

In addition to the civil rights provisions, ICRA imposes a limit on the punishment a tribal court can impose. When the law first passed in 1968, incarceration was limited to six months and fines were limited to five hundred dollars.[23] Thus, from the American legal perspective, tribes were limited to misdemeanor (minor crimes) jurisdiction. Later, as part of drug control legislation, ICRA was amended to allow tribes to sentence offenders to one year of incarceration, a five-thousand-dollar fine, or both—which still amounts to a misdemeanor under American law.[24]

ICRA is almost always discussed in the context of a criminal defendant. I raise the issue from the perspective of a rape victim. Consider that almost all sex crimes in American law are categorized as felonies. Even though the MCA had not divested tribes of felony jurisdiction, the ICRA sentencing restriction reflected a common belief that tribal governments could not (and would not) exercise authority over serious, felony-level crimes (such as rape). While tribal governments did not typically rely on incarceration as a response to violence, American law responds to violent crimes with long periods of imprisonment; ICRA has furthered the myth that tribal governments have no power to respond to felony-level crimes. Assimilated tribal justice systems will often resist prosecuting extremely violent crimes, having internalized the Anglo-American belief that incarceration or monetary sanctions are the only possible response to violence. As with the Major Crimes Act and PL 280, however, there was no explicit divestiture of jurisdiction. Therefore, tribes can prosecute rape—but have not been able to imprison the defendant for more than one year per offense. This restriction was "lifted" again in 2010 (chapter 7 explores the Tribal Law and Order Act, which authorized tribal courts to impose sentences up to nine years in certain situations).

ICRA does not affect a tribal government's ability to impose alternate or traditional sentences, such as banishment, community service, probation, counseling, or public apologies. Nonetheless, the limitation on the ability to incarcerate has had a disparate impact on victims of rape and other violent crime. Native women who are victimized often discover that their tribal nation lacks strong contemporary laws or prosecutorial policies on felony-level criminal behavior. If the federal or state systems choose not to prosecute, the victim is left at the mercy of the perpetrator.

Rehnquist on (non)Sovereignty:
Oliphant v. Suquamish

A fourth jurisdictional barrier is the 1978 Supreme Court decision in *Oliphant v. Suquamish,* which divested tribal courts of criminal jurisdiction over non-Indians.[25] This decision has created a practical vacuum of justice for victims who have the misfortune of being attacked by a non-Indian. Since the *Oliphant* decision, tribal nations have lacked the power or authority to prosecute crimes committed by non-Indians—at least as far as the federal government is concerned. As a result, any tribal government that prosecutes a non-Indian for a crime risks a federal review and reversal of the conviction (basically, the federal courts will see such a conviction as void *ab initio*).

This decision has created a crisis situation in some tribal communities, because non-Indian sexual predators, drug manufacturers, pimps, and other violent people are attracted to Indian country as they perceive it as a location in which crimes can be committed with impunity.[26] Pedophiles and sexual predators also commit crimes within Indian country because of the vulnerability of the citizens and the jurisdictional gaps. If a non-Indian rapes a Native woman, the tribe has absolutely no criminal jurisdiction to punish the offender. Tribal police may be able to arrest a suspect if they are cross-deputized with a local or state government, but the tribal government cannot criminally prosecute that offender.

Tribal leaders and others have vocalized their concern about the federal government's low rates of prosecution of rape and other violent crimes.[27] Certainly there have been prosecutions of non-Indian rapists in federal and state courts since 1978, particularly in some areas where the federal or state government has developed strong relationships with the tribal governments.[28] But when comparing the numbers of Native women who are experiencing rape with the number of prosecutions, we find a significant disparity. In some cases, it is difficult even to gain access to prosecution statistics that specify Native victims, because American Indians and Alaska Natives are often classified in the "other" racial category. In the case of the federal government, different bureaucracies located in various departments have completely separate ways of counting and classifying sexual violence against adults. The Tribal Law and Order Act and Violence Against Women Act were designed to enhance the federal government's approach (see chapter 7). The *Oliphant* decision does not limit the ability of a tribal government to impose civil sanctions on a non-Indian.[29] Civil sanctions are a weak substitute, however, for the important punitive power imposed by a criminal justice system for a crime such as rape.

Poverty and Sovereignty: How the Lack of Resources Undermines Legal Effectiveness

In addition to the multitude of legal barriers restricting tribal governments from responding to rape, there is an insidious practical limitation to stopping rape—tribal nations are notoriously underresourced. More than one Native woman has said to me, *even if jurisdiction is restored, my tribal government doesn't have the money to implement a comprehensive anti-rape strategy.* In the past fifteen years, multiple federal government reports have concluded that high tribal crime rates are due in part to the impoverished condition of tribal criminal justice systems. In particular, the United States Civil Rights Commission issued a report in February 2003 that strongly critiques the lack of resources allocated to tribal governments.[30] The report, however, covers many different kinds of resource limitations, including law enforcement and tribal justice systems. Despite the prevalence of crime, law enforcement in Native communities remains inadequate, with understaffed police departments and overcrowded correctional facilities. There are fewer law enforcement officers in Indian Country than in other rural areas and significantly fewer per capita than nationwide. In addition, per capita spending on law enforcement in Native American communities is roughly 60 percent of the national average.[31] These resource limitations have resulted in inferior systems of justice at the tribal level. Even a reported rape may not result in a comprehensive investigation, because staffing shortages and low morale at the tribal level can interfere with their respective counterparts at the federal or state level. Despite these limitations, a few tribal governments have successfully prosecuted rape, such as the Standing Rock Sioux Tribe and the Navajo Nation.[32] Overall, tribal governments face numerous barriers in adopting strong anti-rape laws and procedures. The barriers are both legal and practical, and the solutions will require additional widespread reform of federal law to restore tribal authority over violent crime.

Aside from the problem of relying on the federal government to prosecute rapists who prey on Native women, there are numerous practical problems, including geographical distances and language and cultural barriers. The length of time between an assault and the sentencing, assuming a conviction is achieved, can be significant. Federal prosecutors are often very selective about the cases they pursue, leaving many victims without recourse. Federal prosecutorial decision making is "largely hidden from public scrutiny," and many victims feel abandoned.[33] Indeed, most rapes in the United States are never reported to law enforcement. Professor Michelle Anderson, who has studied the legal response to rape in America, writes that "women have little to no faith in the formal structures of police power to remedy violence motivated by gender animus."[34] Several General Accounting Office reports released during the past ten years also bear out this reality. In 2012 the GAO reported that U.S. Attorneys declined to prosecute 67 percent of sex crimes.[35]

It is clear that federal laws and policies are insufficient to address the fundamental needs of Native women living in tribal communities, who have not been able to trust the federal or state systems to respond to their experience. That is why deliberate restoration of tribal authority is crucial for long-term change. Decision-making authority and control over violent crime should be restored to indigenous nations to provide full accountability and justice to the victims. Even as systemic federal agency reform is taking place, there will always be the foundation of wide gaps created by a system originally designed to destroy, not heal. Tribal jurisdiction (both civil and criminal) must be completely restored without restriction. Nothing less will do.

FOUR

All Apologies

The Continuing Federal Complicity
in the Rape of Native Women

They trespass her body like they trespass this land.
—Ryan Red Corn, *To the Indigenous Woman*

SUPPOSE A RAPIST has offered to apologize to his victim for the violence he committed and his victim has agreed to listen to his words in a public forum. In delivering the apology, though, the perpetrator admits only to psychologically and physically hurting the victim. He refuses to acknowledge that he actually raped her.[1] Most people would object that such an apology only minimizes and erases the extent of the violence he committed. Many would conclude that the victim would be in danger of even more trauma as a result of such a spectacle.

What does it mean to apologize without apologizing?

In this chapter, I seek to align the federal government's culpability with the high occurrence of rape of Native women. As Australian criminologists Chris Cunneen and Simone Rowe explain, "Change can occur only when colonisation is brought 'front and centre and named as the root cause' of Indigenous overrepresentation, both as victims and offenders."[2]

Chapter 3 discussed the legal framework that has allowed the continued harm of Native women. This chapter focuses on the reality of this continuing harm. The United States has been complicit in this ongoing harm, and I argue that part of its complicity is lodged in the ways the U.S. government has sidestepped its culpability in the continuing rape of Native women. I use two national apologies as entry points for examining the culpability of the federal government for perpetuating a system that allows continued widespread rates of rape of Native women. The apologies help establish what the federal government has acknowledged in terms of harm. Next, the chapter provides specific examples of a continued federal assault on tribal communities, which I hope will demonstrate just how hollow those apologies can ring.

For Native survivors of sexual assault, relying on the federal or state systems to respond comes with a painful dose of irony. If the tribal legal system is not able to provide safety and accountability to victims, some choose to forgo justice altogether. Prominent Pawnee lawyer Larry EchoHawk writes, "Many Indians distrust the legal and social authorities that could be most helpful to them because of past experiences of unjust treatment."[3]

Trauma truly threatens the future of tribal nations. And without an adequate system for intervention, trauma and victimization create a cyclical sense of despair and desperation, indeed, a very continuation of the colonization process. But the culpability of the federal government must be named. Bonnie Burstow is a feminist psychologist who has critiqued her own discipline's approach to trauma. Her explanation of state culpability is particularly helpful in this discussion. She notes that it is a "common but serious mistake to downplay the traumatic impact of the various institutions of the state" as if the "state has no role."[4]

Symbolic Sorrow

Many people don't know that the U.S. government has issued three general apologies to Native people, including one that was offered to Native Hawaiian people in 1993. These apologies are largely symbolic efforts to acknowledge past wrongs and have significance for many (but not all) Native people. The significance, of course, can *only* be symbolic. Indeed, there are few expectations for such national apologies other than raising awareness.[5] Notably, most political apologies admit to past wrongs but rarely acknowledge the continuing legacy of such harms. Law professor Brent White explains that government apologies "are often phrased passively and carefully crafted by lawyers as statements of regret rather than real apologies that accept responsibility and acknowledge the extent of the harm caused."[6] The two apologies I explore in this chapter are in line with White's assessment. In 2000, before a room of tribal leaders, Kevin Gover apologized for the historical actions of the Bureau of Indian Affairs. In 2009 Congress ostensibly apologized to Native people through a buried resolution signed by President Barack Obama as part of Department of Defense appropriations.

Skeptics and critics of these apologies are certainly warranted. Often the critique focuses on the fact that without structural or substantive reform, an apology is useless as anything other than a political spectacle. Whether the apologies should even be formally "accepted" is itself a volatile political issue—many Native people are justifiably incensed that the United States would be arrogant enough to offer an apology in the midst of the current state of Native nations.

At best, these apologies signal that potential change for the better may be forthcoming. Apologies presumably provide, at the very least, an acknowledgment of harm. But honestly addressing centuries of violence, maltreatment, and neglect requires major changes and adjustments to the current structure of federal laws, policies, and regulations affecting tribal nations—these things cannot be accomplished in a short speech or document.

Given that apologies in the context of rape can be fraught, I approach the national apologies with the same skepticism. The federal government has never formally acknowledged sexual violence as a harm that has been inflicted as a result of colonization. By documenting the specific federal actions that have contributed to the high rates of rape in Indian country, this chapter will conclude that federal contrition must be an ongoing process rather than a single event.

Other common techniques used by an admitted sex offender include excusing or justifying the behavior, usually by framing the victim's behavior as culpable. This is known as "victim blaming" and can appear at both societal and individual levels. Perpetrators will claim that they didn't "mean" to hurt the victim, or sometimes feign ignorance ("I didn't know what I was doing was wrong"). Others deflect responsibility by pointing to intoxication or mental illness as the cause of their actions. In this sense, I argue that an apology that falls short of accepting true accountability provides the foundation for the assaults to continue.

The 2000 Gover Apology

On September 8, 2000, the 175th anniversary of the establishment of the Bureau of Indian Affairs (BIA), then Assistant Secretary of the Interior for Indian Affairs Kevin Gover (Pawnee) delivered a broadly worded and emotional apology to Native people on behalf of the BIA. In the apology, Gover acknowledged the failures of Indian policy and many of the atrocities committed by U.S. government officials against Native peoples. The apology was delivered near the end of the Clinton administration in front of many tribal leaders, although the White House did not endorse the apology. Christopher Buck describes the apology as suffering "a death by silence."[7] The text of the speech was initially posted on the BIA website but disappeared when President Bush took office in 2001. Only a handful of media outlets covered the event.

While Gover encouraged those in attendance to share his message of sorrow and contrition with others in their communities, it is unlikely that the message reached more than a few people. There was, at the time, no good vehicle for transmitting the information to a wide audience of Native people. A video of the speech is now posted on YouTube but has still not received wide circulation (less than 2,500 views as of April 13, 2015).

Kevin Gover's apology, like any government apology, provoked strong feelings among the small number of Native people who have actually heard its message, and for the most part the apology has been met with skepticism by many Native people.[8] These skeptics lodge two primary objections. First, that as a Pawnee Indian, Kevin Gover was not an appropriate person to deliver an apology to other Indians. With indignation and frustration, critics of Gover's apology ask if it would be acceptable for, say, a Jewish person to apologize on behalf of the German government for the Holocaust, or for an African American to issue an apology on behalf of the United States for the horrors of slavery. Second, the apology failed to propose any new policies or specific philosophical directives from the Bureau of Indian Affairs that might persuade Native communities that the apology was the first step on a path toward real reform and redress. Gover's apology was not endorsed by the Clinton administration, and Gover himself indicated that he was guided by "moral sensibilities" in drafting and delivering the apology.[9] An apology can never be all things to all people, especially one delivered by a state to a population that it has, for centuries, systematically worked to exterminate and traumatize. Yet, Gover's apology in 2000 failed to resonate with even a minority of Indians.

I personally find Gover's apology lacking because it did not directly acknowledge sexual assault. I cannot say I am terribly surprised by this omission, whether it was intentional or not. Ignoring sexual violence may sidestep painful realities, but silence is also one of the most insidious weapons invoked by rapists. Survivors experience tremendous shame and guilt, which is compounded by the secrets they must keep to survive.

Where the Gover apology was explicit was in its acknowledgment of the wrongs committed or facilitated by the federal government in the area of federal Indian policy. The apology included hard-hitting words like "cowardly" and "annihilate" to describe the implementation of federal policy in the nineteenth century. Gover acknowledged that these actions have created "shame, fear, and anger" for Native people. He even included the phrase "ethnic cleansing" in the apology (which may have been one reason the White House did not comment on the event).

The closest the apology came to acknowledging rape was a description of the treatment of Native children in boarding schools. Gover acknowledged that the BIA had brutalized children "emotionally, psychologically, physically and spiritually." While some of these words could describe rape, the omission of the word remains significant. At less than twelve minutes long, the speech could hardly have included every atrocity in American history (for America's rap sheet is very long indeed), but it is noteworthy that "sexual violence" or "rape" was not listed among the crimes committed against children. In most legal systems, rape is the second most serious crime, surpassed only by murder. So to neglect rape is to fall short of truly acknowledging the extent of harm done by colonization. Silence about sexual atrocities is the norm, and shame is routinely placed on the victims of rape rather than on the perpetrators.[10]

The 2009 Congressional Apology

On December 19, 2009, President Obama signed legislation titled "Native American Apology Resolution" without any public fanfare. That day, the White House press secretary issued a one-sentence release that only mentioned the Department of Defense Appropriations Act of 2010, to which the apology resolution was attached as a rider. Authored by Republican senators who were likely seeking to stimulate some additional votes from their districts, the apology language had been circulating in Congress for several years. One key difference between Gover's 2000 apology and Obama's 2009 resolution was regarding culpability. Instead of apologizing for actions of the U.S. government, the resolution instead apologized for the actions of U.S. *citizens* as opposed to the actions of the *government.* As with the Gover apology, there was no mention of rape or sexual assault. Specific acknowledgement of the governments actions included *violence, maltreatment, and neglect*—but, as with most national apologies, the text clearly limited the application of the apology to symbolism.

As a Native woman, I have mixed feelings about the nature and format of these apologies, but I understand why federal officials might feel compelled to offer them. Both the 2000 and the 2009 apologies, though clumsy, seemed to express sadness—and did offer some acknowledgment that Native people continue to suffer social maladies today as a result of historical actions. But that is all they really did. If a rapist apologizes to his victim, does he acknowledge her sadness? Does he recognize that there is continued harm as a result of his actions? What action should follow?

The Explicit Truth about Rape

Rape has been used—is still used—as a weapon to control and colonize Native peoples. Tribal nations were not mere passive recipients of this violence, however. Many so-called Native rebellions, outbreaks, or uprisings have been linked to the rape of Native women,[11] thus linking resistance of rape to the exercise of tribal sovereignty. Native men in many nations retaliated against the colonial rapists. Historian Virginia M. Bouvier has documented the links between rape of Indian women and Indian "revolts" against Spanish missions in the eighteenth century.[12] Letters from priests in the San Diego region, for example, indicate that the rapes of indigenous girls and women in four nearby *rancherías* by Spanish soldiers were cause for great concern.[13]

Consider this passage from historian James A. Sandos that describes how the confluence of religion and law terrorized entire communities:

> Priests taught Indians patriarchy and, in the process, lowered the status of Indian women within Indian culture. Such devaluation was further compounded by the shameful rape of Indian women by Spanish and Mexican soldiers and settlers. Angry Indian men were killed for their opposition to the rape of tribal women. Partly to protect them from soldiers, priests in the missions had unmarried Indian women above the age of seven locked together at night in a room known as the *monjería* (nunnery) to preserve their chastity. Female separation from the extended family must have been emotionally painful. Confining them in a group, moreover, spread infectious disease, making them more vulnerable to microbes than men. All of these changes created tension and required personal adjustment, profoundly difficult for some, less so for others.[14]

Widespread rape also threatened the balanced gender roles in tribal societies. Tribal social and economic structures were disrupted as a result of rape by outsiders.[15] For example, in the Paiute culture, women served as the primary food gatherers and were unable to continue this practice because it left them without protection from the predatory acts of the settlers.[16] Even seemingly consensual sexual relationships and marriage between Native women and European men were not immune from a context of power and control. Historian Albert Hurtado writes that Native women often married or had sexual relationships with European men as a "survival strategy."[17] Indeed, descriptions of historical accounts of sexual relationships between European fur traders and Native women sound remarkably similar to descriptions of modern-day sex trafficking, a dynamic I explore more fully in chapter 5. The United States endorsed and facilitated forced removal and relocation by means of the Trail of Tears[18] and the Long Walk.[19] The American legal system rarely, if ever, responded to rapes.[20] Rape during these forced marches only amplified the deep psychic harm that came with removal. Psychologist Leslie E. Korn notes, "The invasion of development disconnects people from their land and its plentitude of resources just as rape leaves an individual disconnected from her and others and in somatic, psychic and spiritual pain."[21]

Justification for colonial violence and justification for rape have similar goals and share a common history and language of dehumanization, power, dominance, and conquest. Although women of all races experience rape, the high rate and elevated violence experienced by Native women (and other indigenous women) indicate that the history of conquest and seizure has a disparate impact on the indigenous populations. The continents of the Western Hemisphere are themselves the namesake of Italian cartographer Amerigo Vespucci, who took note of Native women during his journey to present-day South America:

> The women as I have said go about naked and are very libidinous; yet they have bodies which are tolerably beautiful and cleanly. Nor are they so unsightly as one perchance might imagine; for, inasmuch as they are plump, their ugliness is the less apparent, which indeed is for the most part concealed by the excellence of their bodily structure. . . . When they had the opportunity of copulating with Christians, urged by excessive lust, they defiled and prostituted themselves.[22]

As noted in chapter 3, Native women who are raped in the United States today face a legacy of laws that historically have protected perpetrators, allowing them to commit rape with impunity. Rape is more than a metaphor for colonization, however; it is integral to colonization. Laguna scholar Paula Gunn Allen notes that "the oppression and abuse of women is indistinguishable from fundamental Western concepts of social order."[23] Rape embodies the worst traits of colonization in its attack on the body, disrespect for physical boundaries, and disregard for humanity, and thus a survivor of rape may experience many of the same "symptoms"—shame, fear, self-hatred, depression—that survivors of colonization experience. Key federal mantras, such as Manifest Destiny and the Doctrine of Discovery, are played out on the bodies of the women it displaced. The U.S. government, as a perpetrator of colonization, has attempted to assert long-lasting control over land and people—usurping governments, spirituality, and identity.

Federal Officials Who Rape:
Colonial Impunity Continues

As discussed in chapter 3, federal laws have supplanted effective tribal legal systems with dysfunctional foreign legal systems.[24] The laws and practices of the United States thus continue to be implicated in the high rates of rape of Native women, because they continue to restrict the strength and form of tribal justice systems.[25] However, the federal systems that have replaced the tribal systems continue to perpetuate the problem by failing to provide accountability on a number of levels. First, the federal system has typically failed to adequately investigate and prosecute crime when it does occur.[26] Native people are an extremely vulnerable population and are often invisible and forgotten in public discourse regarding social and community issues.[27] Even when the federal system prosecutes rape, the adjudication often occurs in a distant place, outside the construct and control of the local community. Moreover, some federal employees who would be in a position to respond to the rape of Native women have themselves been offenders.

The abuse of power to facilitate rape has a particularly sinister flavor. The dynamic becomes even more sinister when a federal employee rapes a Native woman. Even one case—in a small community suffering aspects of historical trauma—can quickly break down any federal–tribal trust that has been cobbled together despite circumstances. Federal officials working with tribal communities are probably no more or less inclined to abuse their power than federal officials working in other capacities, but these incidents should be acknowledged for what they represent. It is a hard truth that some federal agencies entrusted with providing safety and support to Native people have tolerated, concealed, or excused the behavior of employees who rape during or prior to their employment with the agency. While these incidents may not be the norm, rape committed by federal officials is the purist manifestation of continuing colonial violence. Beth Richie's analysis of sexual aggression in the lives of black women has parallel application in the Native context: "There is a profound impact when women are sexually assaulted and exploited by state institutions that are theoretically designed to protect or support them—or at least not harm them."[28] The following list gives a few examples of criminal conduct committed by people entrusted with the most personal and sensitive aspects of Native people's lives; all the events occurred within a single generation. I will preface this list by acknowledging that the vast majority of federal employees would never conceive of committing acts of violence and abuse. But when you consider how small and isolated most tribal communities are, crimes like these have long staying power in the context of categorical distrust.

- In 1990 a Senate Special Committee on Investigations issued a report detailing widespread sexual abuse committed against Native children by non-Indian Bureau of Indian Affairs (BIA) teachers.[29]
- In 1991 Thomas W. Michaelis, an obstetrician-gynecologist, was convicted of attempting to sexually assault four teenage girls. He was then hired by an Indian Health Service hospital in Arizona, where he worked for eight years before being fired in 2001.[30]
- In 1996 Phillip G. Daugherty was hired as a nurse by the Oklahoma City Indian Health Service, despite his conviction in 1982 for a sex crime in the Marine Corps. After he was accused of fondling a female patient in 1998, Daugherty's criminal record was discovered and he was removed from federal service in 1999.[31]
- In 1997 an Oklahoma state court convicted Dr. Richard Clay Hudson, a doctor at Creek Nation Community Hospital, of the rape and sodomy of one of his patients. Dr. Hudson had previously worked for the U.S. Air Force, where he was also accused of assaulting patients.[32]
- In 1998 a former family practice physician at the Navajo Area Indian Health Service Agency pleaded guilty to seven counts of shipping child pornography.[33]
- In 2000 a jury found a Bureau of Indian Affairs employee guilty of aggravated sexual abuse.[34]
- In late 2003 a sixteen-year-old girl died of alcohol poisoning at Chemawa Boarding School (a federal institution) after apparently being abandoned in a holding cell.[35]
- In 2004 an IHS doctor from Gallup was charged with assaulting his girlfriend and groping a flight attendant.[36]
- In 2004 the chief investigator at the FBI Internal Affairs Office pleaded guilty to child molestation. A former FBI whistleblower noted that he had not aggressively investigated child sexual abuse in Indian country during his twenty-year career.[37]
- In September 2010 (less than two months after the Tribal Law and Order Act became law), an Arizona journalist wrote a scathing

report about how the BIA and tribal police bungled a serial rape investigation of the White Mountain Apache Tribe in Arizona, arresting innocent people and failing to follow through on victim reports.[38]

- A BIA jailer in North Dakota pleaded guilty to having sex with an inmate in August 2009.[39]
- In 2010 a BIA police officer was charged with stabbing his wife in the chest.[40] The charges were dropped when his victim recanted.
- In 2012 a registered nurse employed by the Indian Health Service pleaded guilty to possession of child pornography. He had used his government-issued laptop to download images of children engaged in sexual acts.[41]
- In 2013 the BIA detention facility on the Pine Ridge Indian Reservation had the highest per capita rate of staff sexual misconduct in the United States.[42]
- In 2015 a federal computer security expert who once worked at the Indian Health Service was sentenced to twenty-five years for distribution of child pornography.[43]

The demoralizing impact of these numerous accounts cannot be underestimated (and, of course, these are just the tip of the iceberg. Most perpetrators are never caught). Native people, already vulnerable to criminal victimization, may choose to go without necessary health care rather than risk being victimized by a federal employee. Furthermore, there is no guarantee that federal officials who perpetrate crimes against indigenous people (or those who fail to conduct appropriate background checks) will be held accountable for their behaviors.

Even though these cases can be characterized as anomalies in the sense that they do not represent the behavior of most federal officials, these incidents have fundamental colonial attributes and should be acknowledged as such. Many of the perpetrators wearing federal badges are Native themselves, but this does not mitigate the harm they cause; in some ways, a Native perpetrator with a federal badge is the saddest outcome of colonization. Existing federal laws fail to provide justice to victims of these federal perpetrators. For example, even today, IHS regulations allow federal officials "discretion" in placing a person with a criminal history in a federal position that "does not involve regular contact with or control over Indian children, if a determination has been made that such placement would not put Indian children at risk."[44] While we do not know how many persons with criminal history currently work for IHS, it is hard to imagine a local tribal health care job in which the employee could truly avoid regular contact with children. This also presents a problem in terms of the assumption that someone with a criminal record against children would not also have proclivities for adults. In small, isolated communities, it could be the parent of a hurt child who is receiving services from the person who harmed a child in that community.

When these tragedies occur, it would behoove the federal agency involved to acknowledge (if not apologize) for the harm the act has caused the community. Such measures are no doubt avoided for liability or public relations reasons, but individualized apologies along with a planned remedy for deterrence could be more useful to tribal governments than larger symbolic apologies on the national stage. The Obama administration, starting in 2009, has devoted extensive time and energy to improving the relationship between the federal government and tribes in the context of criminal law. But for some reason we still do not hear them acknowledge the specific truth about this history.

Holding Federal Officials Accountable: An Uphill Battle

If a federal employee rapes a Native woman, and the federal government fails to intercede, then where can the victim find justice? Suing a federal employee or a federal agency is difficult and usually requires attorneys with a special expertise in litigating civil rights claims. In addition, litigation can be drawn out over several years, requiring a survivor to wait long periods of time with no guarantee of victory. Moreover, plaintiffs in civil suits are almost always a matter of public record. So for Native survivors to succeed in lawsuits against the federal government, they must disclose, find a qualified and interested attorney, come forward publically, and potentially wait for years for a resolution. This is not a particularly tenable option for someone suffering the aftereffects of trauma.

Sovereign immunity protects the federal government from tort claims in federal and tribal courts, with a few exceptions encapsulated in the Federal Tort Claims Act (FTCA).[45] In the past twenty years, numerous federal lawsuits have been filed on behalf of Native people, alleging negligence by the federal government in hiring and supervising particular employees. Some federal courts, however, have barred suits by victims against the federal government when the primary charge is assault and/or battery, citing a narrow provision of FTCA. As Jack W. Massey noted, "The courts have willfully blinded themselves to the harm their obeisance causes victims and the law . . . and people are shut out from being made whole by a perverse system."[46]

A 2009 court victory for a Native rape survivor presents a promising approach by returning to the foundational documents governing the relationship between tribal nations and the United States. In *Lavetta Elk v. United States*, a young Lakota woman successfully sued the federal government for the actions of a military (army) recruiter.[47] Ms. Elk's perpetrator, Joseph Kopf, assaulted her on the Pine Ridge Reservation in 2002 after lying to her about being accepted into the army and driving her to a remote part of the reservation.[48] As a result of this assault and the perpetrator's abusive behavior (she had to file a restraining order against him), Ms. Elk suffered from flashbacks, insomnia, and depression. She sought compensation from the federal government for her injuries and filed a lawsuit in the Federal Court of Claims. For most Native plaintiffs in similar situations, the case stops here—dismissed for lack of jurisdiction or federal sovereign immunity.

Her attorneys, however, presented a novel treaty argument to overcome two important legal obstacles to sustaining such a lawsuit.[49] Through a careful review of treaty language, the Court of Claims ruled that Ms. Elk's lawsuit could bypass years of administrative appeals and that federal sovereign immunity was waived under a strict reading of the treaty language itself. The key phrase is referred to as the "bad men" clause and reads as follows:

> If bad men among the whites, or among other people subject to the authority of the United States, shall commit any wrong upon the person or property of the Indians, the United States will, upon proof made to the agent and forwarded to the Commissioner of Indian Affairs at Washington City, proceed at once to cause the offender to be arrested and punished according to the laws of the United States, and also reimburse the injured person for the loss sustained.[50]

The court reviewed the historical context of the "bad man" treaty clause (which appears in a total of nine treaties with thirteen tribes signed between 1867 and 1868).[51] After concluding that a "bad man among the whites" had indeed committed a wrong upon the person of Elk by raping her, the court then considered what obligations come with the word "reimburse" in the final clause of the treaty section. The federal government argued that any reimbursement should be limited to out-of-pocket expenses only and not extend to pain and suffering. However, the court considered the meaning of the word "reimburse" in the late nineteenth century and determined that the treaty language should be interpreted to cover all costs, particular since the next clause talks about a "sustained" loss, which necessarily exceeds that of out-of-pocket expenditures. The court concluded that a contemporary application of the treaty language "requires that Ms. Elk receives here the types of damages that, in the modern view, would make her whole, that is, those that indemnify her loss."[52] In calculating the various harms Ms. Elk experienced because of the rape, the judge ordered the federal government to reimburse her nearly $600,000.

Although Ms. Elk's litigation strategy had a positive outcome, the trial judge's opinion exposes how the federal government spent significant time and money to fight her lawsuit by trying to prove she was a liar. In defending the United States, attorneys from the Department of Justice attacked Ms. Elk's credibility by hiring a forensic psychiatrist who evaluated her and "opined that Ms. Elk was exaggerating both the severity of the attack and her resultant symptoms." From the ruling judge's perspective, much of the expert witness's testimony could be characterized as victim blaming, especially since the rapist who committed the acts had been adjudicated by a military court and found responsible for sexual assault as well as lying to federal officials. The judge noted that "in short, while Dr. Mills [the forensic psychiatrist] repeatedly accused Ms. Elk of being 'unreliable' and 'manipulative,' it was he that best fit that description."[53]

Thus we see two federal responses to this event that give pause. The federal prosecutor declined to take the case to provide criminal justice relief; and the Department of Justice responded to Ms. Elk's civil complaint by suggesting that the victim overstated her pain and suffering. These two actions (especially when considered as a pair) present a troubling picture of a federal government that has made a commitment to improving the status quo.

Lavetta Elk's victory over the federal government is important, but it will likely not be replicated widely. Only a handful of tribes have the "bad men" language in their treaties, and without a specific legal "hook" to federal culpability, it is nearly impossible to sustain a lawsuit for damages against the federal government. Moreover, it is not always the case that a survivor seeks compensatory damages for a rape—a harm that is difficult to quantify. The use of treaty arguments to provide justice to victims has certainly piqued the interest of some Native lawyers, however. Creative legal minds will continue to develop novel approaches to holding the federal government accountable.

Tribal judge and Apache scholar Carey Vicenti writes, "We must insist that repose, finality, and closure each are laden with moral consequence given the manifest injustice of the predominant society's attitude toward Native America."[54] In the case of rape, the United States must acknowledge the harm that has been done, and tribal nations must reclaim their rightful role as protectors and responders. Tribal governments have fundamental cultural values and beliefs that will contribute to a comprehensive response to violent crime—if only provided with the necessary resources. A sincere and comprehensive apology will provide the reforms and resources necessary to put indigenous nations at the center of the response to rape.

FIVE

Relocation Revisited

The Sex Trafficking of Native Women

IN JULY 2009, after years of effort, local community members renamed a hiking trail in coastal Yachats, Oregon, in remembrance of a brutal journey experienced by a Coos woman known only as "Amanda."[1] Amanda's Trail sits on property owned by Yachats resident Joanne Kittel, who told reporters, "This property is so precious, so that I didn't really feel like an owner, I felt like a steward."[2] The story of the trail's namesake, Amanda, is a grisly and brutal account of a young, blind Coos woman who was kidnapped by U.S. Cavalry in 1864 and forced to walk eighty miles along the jagged rocks of the Oregon coast to the so-called Great Reservation.[3] According to tribal council member Wendy Williford (Confederated Tribes of Coos, Lower Umpqua, and Siuslaw), the cuts on Amanda's feet left a "trail of blood in her wake."[4] Little else is known about Amanda or her eleven-year-old daughter, Julia, whom Amanda was forced to leave behind because she had a white father. U.S. soldiers accompanied Amanda, forcing her to walk the eighty miles to ensure that not a single Coos person was left to roam free within the borders of the state of Oregon.[5] Oregon, which had achieved statehood only a few years earlier, in 1859, had criminalized assault and abduction. But Amanda would not have been considered worthy of equal treatment under the law. Even the murder of Indians was, for all intents and purposes, legal at that point in time in Oregon.[6] There are no doubt dozens of tribal communities scattered across the United States who have their own "Amanda" stories, still circulating as common knowledge in the community, cautionary tales and lessons that carry with them fear and terror in their retelling.

In this chapter I consider the many forced walks by Native women like Amanda, walks both literal and metaphorical. Most urgently today, these "forced walks" take the form of the scourge of sex trafficking of Native women. Sex trafficking is really a contemporary phrase for sexual slavery. I first started thinking seriously about sexual slavery in the lives of Native women after attending a local event focused on human rights violations in the Minneapolis/ St. Paul area in 2008. A local study had discovered that nearly 30 percent of women arrested for prostitution in arrests in a particular Minneapolis neighborhood were Native women. Native people make up only 2–3 percent of the Twin Cities' population. As I thought more about the historical documentation of coerced "sexual favors" on reservations, I wondered if things had changed much over the past hundred years. I wondered if the Native women in Minneapolis were experiencing the same kind of traumatic walk as that of Amanda.

In 2000 Congress passed the Trafficking Victims Protection Act (TVPA)[7] and funded a comprehensive public relations campaign to bring attention to this form of "modern day slavery." As a result an unprecedented amount of attention has been given to sex trafficking in the United States during the past fifteen years. Congressional appropriations have funded dozens of task forces to develop collaborative relationships among law enforcement, prosecutors, and victim advocates to combat sex trafficking in several metropolitan areas. The United States has also undertaken an extensive research agenda to better understand the nature of human trafficking, funding more than twenty-five studies and reports on human trafficking since 2000.[8]

Many of these reports proclaim the United States as a world leader in the international efforts to address this crime.[9] The federal government has often framed human trafficking as an "import problem"—in that the victims are being smuggled into the United States from foreign countries.[10] In truth, America is not only a destination for the commercial trade in human beings but also a point of origin.[11] In fact, the primary trafficking problem in the United States is domestic trafficking, wherein women and girls are sold within the United States for use in the commercial sex industry (primarily pornography, stripping, and prostitution). Domestic trafficking within the United States is as much a problem as, if not a bigger problem than, international trafficking into the United States. The full extent of modern sex trafficking is extraordinarily difficult to document because the sex industry involves both legal and illegal activities. Moreover, the victims of this crime are often reluctant to come forward for fear of the legal system or their captors.

Failure to acknowledge the truth about domestic trafficking makes the U.S. government's efforts seem disingenuous, if not dishonest, in the eyes of victim advocates around the world. The government's pronouncements on sex trafficking reflect an inconsistent double standard that absolves the United States and its allies of blame.[12] Vine Deloria Jr. aptly summed up this dynamic in 1969 in his book *Custer Died for Your Sins:* "There has not been a time since the founding of the republic when the motives of this country were innocent. Is it any wonder that other nations are extremely skeptical about its real motives in the world today?"[13] Focusing on foreign governments as the source of the problem erases the brutality Native women have experienced as a result of actions within the United States. The contemporary definition in this country of human trafficking is, in many ways, a perfect descriptor of the experience of many Native women throughout the history of American imperialism.

I seek to set the record straight. Although women from all segments of society are victims of sex trafficking, I focus on the history of the trafficking of Native women. I use the United States' definitions and descriptions of sex trafficking to help frame the analysis. The aim of this chapter is not merely to lay blame but to understand how historical events and policies continue to shape the lives of Native women and girls today. Amanda's journey is not an isolated, historical event. Native women today continue to take their own, arduous marches whenever they are sold, bought, and objectified.

The Colonial Roots of Prostitution

The tactics of contemporary traffickers are consistent with many of the tactics used by colonial and American governments to subjugate Native women and girls. The commoditization and exploitation of the bodies of Native women and girls, although theoretically criminalized through contemporary prostitution laws, have not been the subject of rigorous investigation and intervention. In fact, this ubiquitous form of predation was not only legal throughout most of history but encouraged by dominant culture. Today, the eroticized image of Native women is so commonplace in our society that it is unremarkable—the image of a hypersexual Indian woman continues to be pervasive in American culture. For example, a popular Halloween costume is a racist rendition of "Poca-hottie," and an entire fetish porn industry has developed around the image of the "rez girl"—an erotic woman who is perpetually sexually available.

Dispossession and relocation of indigenous peoples on this continent both necessitated and precipitated a highly gendered and sexualized dynamic in which Native women's bodies became commodities—bought and sold for the purposes of sexual gratification (or profit), invariably transporting them far away from their homes. As European and American law gradually supplanted indigenous law, Native women's bodies became increasingly commercialized. Removing Native women from their lands, homes, and families was an essential factor in depriving them of their personal liberty. The result was that the transport and sale of sex slaves throughout the Americas became so widespread because criminal laws—if they existed—were rarely enforced. Often, this exploitation was de jure legal (in that it was sanctioned by the government). Even in those instances where sex slavery was explicitly illegal, it continued to flourish as a result of official indifference and in large part institutionalized racism and prejudice. Racism and Indian sex slavery were, therefore, de facto legal.

Trafficking in North America long predates the U.S. government; the tactics used by sex traffickers today were used against Native peoples from the first moment of contact. These tactics were pioneered by the Spanish, Portuguese, French, English, Dutch, and Russians. Colonial legal systems historically protected (and rewarded) the exploiters of Native women and girls and therefore encouraged the institutionalization of sexual subjugation. This dynamic continues today, albeit in a different guise.

Indian Enslavement and Exploitation

In describing trafficking in the TVPA, Congress explicitly states that "traffickers often make representations to their victims that physical harm may occur to them or others should the victim escape or attempt to escape" and further acknowledges that "such representations can have the same coercive effects on victims as direct threats to inflict harm." This description is really a sanitized description of slavery enforced by violence, and Native people experienced these realities in multiple ways. The federal law goes on to acknowledge that trafficking is "often aided by official corruption in countries of origin, transit, and destination."

The European governments that purported to "settle" North America also instituted widespread slavery of Native bodies. Most early European settlements were largely financed through the slave industry, and once the institution became the foundation of local and regional economies, it took centuries to eradicate. Europeans usually employed legal mechanisms (in addition to physical force) to stake their claim in the land and the people. Settlers kidnapped Native people to facilitate western expansion, often forcing them to work as interpreters or informants. While no European government officially condoned the institution of slavery, settlers and soldiers of Spanish, Portuguese, French, and English origins engaged in the behavior with little or no interference from their respective continental monarchies. Far from being criminalized, much of this behavior was encouraged or incorporated into the transplanted colonial legal systems.

Enslavement of Indians continued to be widely practiced in many regions of the United States after the 1700s. Although human enslavement was technically abolished throughout the United States upon the ratification in 1865 of the Thirteenth Amendment, slavery-like conditions persisted for many years. In California, for example, the "Law for the Protection of the Indian," (passed in 1850) allowed Indians convicted of certain crimes (including vagrancy) to be bonded out to "the best bidder."[14] The Indian would then be compelled to work for said "best bidder" until such time as the fine was paid in full.[15] Sexual slavery is part and parcel of chattel slavery. Most forms of human slavery throughout history can be characterized as de facto sex trafficking; historically, enslavement of Indian people in the Americas facilitated widespread sexual abuse.

Legal definitions of slavery almost always include language referencing ownership by the enslaver, which strips the enslaved of legally recognized personal autonomy.[16] Sexual exploitation is a logical result of enslavement, and trafficking flows naturally from the combination of slavery and sexual violence.[17] First, the slave, by virtue of her captivity, is contained and unable to freely travel or migrate without the permission of her captor or captors. Second, under most forms of legal slavery, she has no legal right to refuse sexual contact with her captors.[18]

The ironic undercurrent to documented accounts of mistreating Native women is that state actors and settlers often prided themselves on "rescuing" Native women from sexual subservience.[19] Because American perspectives on sexuality (especially in the late nineteenth-century Victorian era) contrasted sharply with indigenous perspectives on healthy sexuality, many European and American policies penalized Native women for engaging in consensual sexual activity. Even seemingly sympathetic reformers, such as the "Friends of the Indians," minimized the harm caused by sexual exploitation by pointing to the failure of Native women to adhere to Western standards of femininity.[20] This perception of Indian women as demure, helpless, or sexually exploited facilitated significant paternal and patriarchal constraints on their behavior.

The nineteenth century is replete with examples of brutality against Native people. Jesuit scholar Francis Paul Prucha notes that "the frequency of offenses committed against Indians by the frontier whites—among which outright murder was commonplace—was shocking."[21] Rape of Native women, like the rape of other nonwhite women, was not truly considered rape and received little (if any) response from the legal system. Lawrence Friedman has noted that

the law really protected only "respectable" white women (and their menfolk). Women who were not "respectable," or who were black, or Native American, were effectively outside the circle of protection. Of course, the words of the statutes never said as much, but that was the practical result; it was rare for poor or black women to seek or get justice after rape.[22]

The failure to enforce laws or apply them to Native people resulted in the de facto legalization of sexual servitude. Collusion, indifference, and corruption all played roles.[23] Consider that Native women who were exploited by frontier settlers had little recourse, even when suffering extreme forms of physical violence. In my research, I discovered the advice of a "Rocky Mountain hunter" who purchased a Native girl in 1868: "The girl, when sold to a white man, is generally skeary for a while and will take the first chance to run away. . . . Should you take her again, and whip her well, and perhaps clip a little slice out of her ear, then she will stay."[24]

Once Native people were confined to reservations, they were often completely dependent on the military and local traders for food, clothing, and shelter. Indian agents throughout the West documented how soldiers exploited this dynamic to secure sexual "favors" from women. In 1885, W. L. Lincoln, an agent in Montana, wrote:

> There is but little said in their favor regarding their moral standing, and for this there is no doubt but that the Government is largely to blame. . . . [When I first came here] the soldier had also come to stay. The Indian maiden's favor had a money value, and what wonder is it that, half clad and half starved, they bartered their honor . . . for something to cover their limbs and for food for themselves and their kin."[25]

Prostitution was (and is) often the last resort in order to avoid starvation and death. In this historical framework, "prostitution did reflect the destruction of the Indian social order."[171] William B. Hennessey, a Minnesota historian, explained that after the 1862 U.S.–Dakota war, Dakota women were forced to prostitute themselves "in a large measure [owing to] their indigence. They would resort to anything to the end that they might procure wherewith to eat."[26] These practices were well known and widespread, but I have never located any evidence of a soldier being prosecuted for the mistreatment of a Native woman.

Commoditizing Native Women through Marriage

Among the myriad ways Native women have been subjugated throughout history, one method is seldom discussed: the commoditization of Native women through marriage. At isolated times in American history (largely related to the discovery of oil or other valuable natural resources on tribal lands), a white man could profit handsomely from marrying an Indian woman and thereby gaining access to her wealth.

In the early nineteenth century, a complicated intermarriage dynamic developed in the southeastern United States when non-Indians sought valuable farmland held by tribes. At that time, most tribal legal systems did not readily make these lands alienable to nonmembers. Some non-Indians devised a plan to become legal owners of tribal land by marrying into the tribe. When the Cherokee Nation was engaged in ongoing legal disputes with the state of Georgia regarding land holdings, "marrying Indian wives was the only way for non-Cherokee men to gain control over land and citizenship rights within the Nation."[27] After allotment, when federal law required a dissection and dispersal of tribal lands to individual Indians, white men married Indian women as an attempt to gain ownership of valuable land. Thomas Priestly, who was the federal Indian agent for the Yakama Agency in Washington State in the 1880s, noted that the white men who married Indian women for such purposes were "not of the better class."[28]

In the early twentieth century, a few tribes benefited from cash windfalls after the discovery of oil or other natural resources. In these cases, a non-Indian man could gain access to the riches if he married into the tribe. This made Indian women and girls particularly attractive to outsiders. A 1910 Oklahoma City newspaper article titled "Dusky Maidens Are in Demand" reported that

> dusky maidens of the Yakima Indian reservation are receiving no end of attention from white suitors. Many a mixed blood marriage has been made lately because of the money that Indian maids bring their husbands. A Toppenish quarter-breed was recently married to a white man after a two weeks' courtship. She owns a well-placed allotment of Indian lands and her mother's real estate is figured at $50,000. [The] very pretty Indian belle, who is still heart whole and fancy free . . . has many admirers among the palefaces, as well as among the redskins.[29]

Once a white husband had access to the land and/or wealth, the Native women were often abandoned or mistreated.[183] The social dynamic, then, was one in which Native women were valued not as human beings but rather as commodities to leverage land and power. In Oklahoma a number of Osage women were murdered for their land rights in the early twentieth century—so many that the Federal Bureau of Investigation initiated one of its earliest serial murder investigations.[30]

Removal and Relocation

When you hear the term *sex trafficking,* what images come to mind? In contemporary American culture, the phrase often conjures up images of a woman who has been abducted or tricked into leaving her homeland (usually an Asian or Eastern European country) by organized criminals who then coerce her into sexual slavery once she arrives in a foreign country, a country where she has no friends or family, no language fluency, and an illegal alien status that will lead to deportation should she try to escape. Isolation and distance are key tools of the contemporary international sex trafficking trade—no different from the isolation and forced removal to distant, unfamiliar reservations to which Native people were subjected through forced migration, mandatory boarding school education, and urban relocation.

For many Native people, leaving ancestral homelands is traumatic in and of itself because of the spiritual connections to a particular place that are broken in the process. Forced removals of Native people are not just an infringement on liberty and autonomy; the removals harm entire nations.[31] When coupled with rape, the forced removals completely subjugated the victims. As noted earlier, the dynamics of the Gold Rush in California during the late 1840s quickly deteriorated into wholesale abduction and sale of Native peoples.[32] There are numerous accounts of kidnapping, rape, sex slavery, and murder associated with the influx of white settlers into California.[33] The original official Humboldt County history (published by the Historic Record Company in 1915) includes several accounts suggesting that kidnapping of Native women for sexual purposes was quite common in the 1800s. In one example, the description is that "bands of white men, consisting of three or four depraved wretches, would often catch a young squaw or two and detain them for several days or weeks at their cabins and then permit them to make their way home as best they could."[34]

One Lassik woman, T'tcetsa (also known as Lucy Young), "fell prey to men engaged in the widespread practice of kidnapping Indian children and selling them as servants to white settlers" during the 1860s.[35] After numerous escapes and recaptures, T'tcetsa was sold to a white trader, Arthur Rutledge, who "kept her chained at his place because she always ran away."[36] Rutledge's sexual abuse of T'tcesta resulted in so many pregnancies and miscarriages that she lost count.[37] T'tcestsa's story is a rare first-person account of this widespread treatment. In the early twentieth century, she was interviewed by several ethnologists who were able to record her poignant perspective:

> White people come find us. Want to take us all to Fort Seward. We all scared to dead. . . . I hear people tell 'bout what [Indian] do early days to white man. Nobody ever tell what white man do to [Indian]. That's reason I tell it. That's history. That's truth. I seen it myself.[38]

Forced Migrations and the Many Trails of Tears

The history of the United States is replete with examples of using military authority to force the relocation of Native people.[39] Nineteenth-century "Indian removal" was originally developed as a solution to the challenges posed by conflicts between white settlers and Indians in the southeastern United States and federal removal law was often explicit in its terms. The Indian Removal Act (1830), for example, provided legal authority and military funding to move Indians to an area west of the Mississippi.[40] The "Trail of Tears" of southeastern Indians (Cherokee, Mvskoke [Creek], Seminole, Chickasaw, and Choctaw Indians) in the 1830s is the best known of these forced marches, but there were numerous other forced migrations and "relocations," almost all of which were hardest on women and children, who were at the mercy of a colonial military that neither prevented nor punished rape. Forced migrations decimated Indian nations, with many dying from crippling fatigue, starvation, and disease.[41] Losing both the very young and the very old in large numbers during the journey meant that the wisdom and cultural knowledge of the elders, and the sense of hope for the continuance of the tribe, died with them.

It is impossible to count the number of rapes that occurred during these forced migrations, just as it is impossible to count the number of deaths. All we have are glimpses of the brutality offered through accounts that survive in the historical literature. Navajo scholar Laura Tohe writes that the Diné people call Fort Sumner (the place where they were marched), "Hwéeldi" (the Place of Extreme Hardship) because of their experiences of starvation and rape at the hands of the U.S. government.[42] Native people often arrived at their new "home" or place of captivity with little more than the clothes on their back; soldiers often took advantage of this state of affairs to coerce Native women into providing sexual services to receive food, clothing, and blankets.[43]

Firsthand oral narratives from this time are exceedingly rare—probably because, as scholar Tohe notes, "the response to such death and violence was to not speak of it in any casual way."[44] Most records of these experiences have been preserved, not on paper, but in the oral histories of tribal people. A typical passage in this rare oral history comes from a series of stories transcribed by a Creek woman, describing her grandmother's recollection of the Trail of Tears: "Sometimes, as weeks went by these soldiers would tear the clothing off young girls twelve years of age . . . or young mothers and molest them."[45] Women and girls in this scenario had no legal system to turn to for justice.

Assimilation and Gendered Slave Labor

The last official major military actions on Indian land occurred near the end of the nineteenth century. The experience of Native women did not improve, however, as the government's control over Native women's sexuality took on new, sinister forms. With the collective trauma of surviving war and relocation not yet fully addressed, new government policies launched a different kind of attack on tribal cultures: forced religious conversion and boarding schools. Unlike the earlier nineteenth-century migrations, which were the result of overt violence, boarding schools involved official coercion of a different kind. However, when viewed in the context of a century of rape, murder, and starvation perpetrated by soldiers and Indian agents, the boarding schools strategy is clearly a continuation of the legacy of oppression.

Targeting children is one of the most sinister methods of attacking a community, because it can destroy a society from the inside out. American Indian children were easy victims for this strategy, which reached its peak in the early twentieth century. In an effort to promote assimilation of tribal people, after war failed to exterminate all of us,[46] the government endorsed the widespread removal of children from their communities to be "educated" in government- and church-run boarding schools throughout the United States and Canada.[47] Under the authority of the U.S. government, Native children were forcibly removed from their homes and taken to boarding schools at a rate exceeding 70 percent in some communities. This era brought a new level of sexual violence to indigenous communities in the form of sexual abuse of children.[48] The extent to which children in boarding schools were raped may never be fully known, but the volume of anecdotal accounts from survivors would lead one to believe that some boarding schools were fraught with sexual abuse.[49] Certainly, there are documented efforts to control the sexuality of Native girls, which resulted in more secrecy and shame in tribal communities.[50] In many tribal communities, then, the imposition of foreign legal systems occurred simultaneously with widespread rape.

This involuntary movement of Native children was often directly or indirectly tied to sexual exploitation. The boarding school era is synonymous with sexual abuse and sexual exploitation on a mass scale. For example, forced attendance at boarding schools, where youth often were sexually, physically, emotionally, and verbally abused, was a traumatic event with the potential for being internalized and later manifesting as psychological symptoms:

> The resulting psychological symptoms may have been transmitted . . . onto family members (secondary traumatic stress) and passed onto subsequent generations (intergenerational transmission), in the absence of culturally appropriate ways for healing (unresolved grief).[51]

Children were sent hundreds, sometimes thousands, of miles from home on steamboats, trains and wagons.[52] If they refused to go, their families were threatened with starvation and incarceration.[53] Some Indian schools engaged directly in the abduction of Native children in order to "maintain student enrollment levels."[54] Government documents indicate that there were efforts to keep members of the same tribe apart, a tactic that was likely designed to facilitate assimilation, and the institutions themselves were "often harsh and repressive."[55]

As part of the overall effort to separate children from their homeland and culture, many schools did not allow children to return home during the summer months.[56] Although assimilation or indoctrination was the primary goal of the boarding schools, commercialization and profit were convenient by-products of these boarding school efforts; the local non-Native communities often benefited from cheap or free labor.[57] In Phoenix, for example, Native girls and young women in school were required to provide domestic services for white families—often with substandard (or no) pay.[58] Indian girls who worked in these settings were also expected to follow strict social codes of Victorian-era morality.[59] "In the minds of many [V]ictorians, Indian women by nature were prone to filth, 'animal gratification,' lewd, licentious, and promiscuous behavior."[60] The federal agenda was clear: "Train Indian girls in subservience and submission to authority."[61] In other words, indoctrinate the dominant paradigm of the patriarchy into Native women.

Corporal punishment was commonly deployed in boarding schools, combining identity destruction with physical punishment. Most tribal cultures did not use corporal punishment as a disciplinary tool, but school beatings were acceptable, expected, and, in fact, were the subject of some well-publicized controversies in the early twentieth century.[62] Moreover, boarding school facilities often included jail cells used to punish children who disobeyed orders.[63] At Chilocco Indian School in Oklahoma, "Punishment . . . was solitary confinement in the 'dark room,' where the only light entered through a four-inch square in the door."[64] In recent years, some survivors of the boarding schools have disclosed that sexual abuse was common in the schools.[65] In some, corruption and cover-ups allowed for the continuous sexual abuse of Native children for decades.[66] There was rarely any option for filing grievances in these situations—indeed, children were powerless to take any action to stop the abuse.[67]

Relocation Revisited: Urban Migration

Under the TVPA, Congress established that "traffickers lure women and girls into their networks through false promises of decent working conditions at relatively good pay as nannies, maids, dancers, factory workers, restaurant workers, sales clerks, or models. Traffickers also buy children from poor families and sell them into prostitution or into various types of forced or bonded labor."[68] Replace "traffickers" with "the United States government"—and the definition aptly describes the next phase of American Indian policy.

This section seeks to reframe the relatively sanitized word *relocation*, which has often been used to refer to the Indian urbanization policies of the 1950s. In practice, "relocation" is a continuation of the colonial determination to destroy the inherent protection offered by one's relatives in one's own homeland and apathy toward the conditions in which the relocated people find themselves. As with other strategies implemented by the United States and its European predecessors, this process created new avenues for predators to manipulate, coerce, and force Native women into the commercial sex industry.

In the 1950s, as tribal communities continued to make efforts to remobilize and establish roots in the prescribed space, the government again retooled its approach to tribal people—this time, moving them from their reservation communities to urban centers.[69] When viewed through the lens of contemporary human trafficking laws, these federally facilitated migrations left Native people vulnerable to victimization. Indeed, these relocations ensured that yet another generation of Native women would be exposed to sexual abuse and degradation and the genocide of Native peoples would be advanced.

The federal actions were swift and effective. In 1940 only 7.2 percent of Native people lived in urban areas.[70] In 1943 the BIA launched a pilot program to transition Indian people from the reservations to the cities, followed by a second, more comprehensive initiative in 1952. The goal of these projects was clear: no more tribal identities; no more reservations. Native people should assimilate completely into the American body politic. Within a few short years, the number of Native people living away from their tribal community had dramatically increased.[71] By 1960, 33,466 Indians had been

relocated and the number continued to rise. Today, nearly 60 percent of Native people reside in urban areas.[72]

The relocation project was often presented to young Native
people as a generous opportunity.[73] Living conditions on many
reservations had deteriorated to a level of abject poverty by the
mid-twentieth century.[74] Representatives of the BIA traveled to
reservations and recruited young Native people to move to the
city, where, it was promised, jobs and housing were plentiful. The
BIA presented some of the opportunities as competitive and highly
valuable by implementing an application, interview, and approval
process. A successful applicant would receive a small stipend to
cover travel expenses.[75] Usually, there was no stipend to support a
return home (even in cases of family illness or death).[76] Not surprisingly, there were no documented efforts to ensure that Native
women had access to any social services should they fall victim to
sexual exploitation in the cities, which is significant since Native
people often found themselves unemployed soon after arriving in
the city.[77] In 1965 one social scientist concluded that "more than 75
percent of the Indians who have relocated would choose to return
to their reservations as soon as possible."[78] By 1969 the average per
capita income for Native people was less than half of the national
poverty level, and the unemployment rate had skyrocketed to nearly
ten times the national average.[79] All these "urbanization" factors
created the perfect opportunity for pimps and predators to gain a
foothold in the lives of Native people.

Situating Native people within urban settings also provided more
convenient opportunities for social scientists to "study" Indian culture and adaptation styles. A review of this literature is illuminat-
ing, as it becomes clear that non-Indians blamed tribal culture as
the root cause of "deviant" behavior, rather than considering the
effects of forced acculturation, institutionalized racism, and poverty.[80] In one sociological report, the author explained that Indians
suffered poverty and other social ills in the urban locations because
they were incapable of comprehending the "basic instrumental values of modern urban industrial society."[81]

Although most of the studies of urban Indians focused on men
(who relocated at a higher rate than did women—at least initially),
some reports did devote attention to gender dynamics, and a few
focused exclusively on women. Social scientists often described

sexual exploitation by white men, but the exploitation was rarely characterized as predatory behavior—sometimes vulnerable Native women were described as engaging in experimentation as a result of alcohol use. Social scientists often concluded that Native women were simply behaving promiscuously with non-Native men—with no indication that some of the women might have been victims. Consider the following observation from 1963: "For the young [Native] females, drinking seems to help them overcome sexual inhibitions; this is crucial to their popularity with many of the young Whites."[82] Another social scientist in the same decade wrote:

> This rejection of native males, and the valuing of transient white males, results in a situation of *mutual* exploitation between the transients and the [Native] girls. The girls will go so far as to seek out Navy men, construction and barge workers (both single and married), gaining presents from them, most notably in the form of beer.[83]

This typical characterization of the relationships as "mutual exploitation" is directly followed by observations that reveal a more one-sided dynamic:

> Generally speaking, the [Native] girls do not profit in the long run from this mutual sexual exploitation. Many of them are burdened with illegitimate children and contract venereal diseases which are especially prevalent. Very few of the transients marry native girls.[84]

No empirical data are available to determine the extent to which sex traffickers in the mid- to late twentieth century may have targeted Native women. Anecdotal evidence, however, indicates that Native women who left the reservations for urban areas were vulnerable to such exploitation.[85] For instance, testimony provided to Congress by Amabel Bulin in 1944 indicates that the sex trafficking of Native girls was common in Minneapolis. Bulin, an advocate for Native women and girls in Minneapolis in the 1940s and 1950s, testified in 1944 in front of a U.S. House committee that Indian girls in Minneapolis were illegally being sold liquor and that this made them vulnerable to "exploitation" and "immorality."[86]

A 1970 article titled "Promiscuity and Prostitution in Urbanized Indian Communities" provides some insight into the approach mainstream (white male) experts had toward prostituted Native women.[87] In one of the only articles written about Native women in prostitution before 1990, the authors conclude that Native prostitutes are "habitual liars" and "chronic alcoholi[cs]."[88] The authors further claim that "random factors and forces" are responsible for Native women entering prostitution, ignoring the role of sexual predators (and history) in the criminal ecosystem of sexual slavery.[89]

Contemporary Sex Trafficking in the Lives of Native Women

Sex trafficking is formally criminalized in the United States, but the legacy of enslavement, exploitation, and exportation is reflected in the lives of Native women who are victimized by prostitution and sex trafficking. Of course, the U.S. government has, for the most part, ceased officially engaging in the reprehensible activities described throughout this chapter. The military no longer permanently occupies reservations or forces Native people at gunpoint to travel hundreds of miles on foot. Tribal members are no longer directly pressured by federal agents into leaving the reservation for the city. However, the legacy of relocation, chronic poverty, and historical trauma significantly reduces the opportunities available to Native women and makes them vulnerable to prostitution and sex trafficking.

Documenting the Invisible

As explained in chapter 1, providing "proof" of widespread crime is often a critical prerequisite to reform. But trafficking of any kind is notoriously difficult to research because of the invisibility of the victims.[90] We do know a few things, however. For example, statistics indicate that most women become prostitutes as juveniles.[91] We also have evidence that most women used in prostitution have experienced child sexual abuse and extreme poverty. These so-called risk factors are certainly elevated in a tribal community, suggesting that Native women are victimized by prostitution at a higher rate than other women. Recent studies bear this theory out. There is significantly more research on Native women in prostitution in Canada, which shares a boundary with the United States and also a similar history when it comes to the oppression of its indigenous population.[92] Canadian statistics have demonstrated that indigenous women and girls are prostituted at disproportionate rates.[93] "A study conducted in 2000 estimated that 70 percent of street prostitutes working in the most dangerous and lowest paying 'tracks' in the Downtown Eastside [Vancouver] were Aboriginal women under the age of twenty-six, and most are mothers."[94] In Winnipeg, one advocate reported that hundreds of teen and pre-teen girls, some as young as eight and averaging about thirteen, are working the streets.[95] Even more are abused behind closed doors, with about 80 percent of child prostitution taking place in gang houses and "trick pads."[96] An estimated 70 percent of these girls were indigenous.[97]

Native women as sex trafficking victims in the United States have only recently received attention in a few select regions. For example, in September 2009 the Minnesota Indian Women's Resource Center issued a report titled *Shattered Hearts,* which offered a graphic description of the lives of Native women and girls who have experienced prostitution and sex trafficking.[98] In 2011, I was invited to contribute to a report about contemporary sex trafficking titled *Garden of Truth: The Prostitution and Trafficking of Native Women in Minnesota.* Garden of Truth was the product of a partnership between the Minnesota Indian Women's Sexual Assault Coalition and Prostitution Research & Education. The study was designed by Native women (Nicole Matthews, Cristine Davidson, Guadalupe Lopez, Eileen Hudon, and Christine Stark) in collaboration with Dr. Melissa Farley, who has studied prostitution in more than seven countries.[99] *Garden of Truth* presents findings from a multiyear research project that involved interviews with more than one hundred Native women in Minnesota who self-identified as prostitutes or former prostitutes.[100] The findings include the following:

- About half of the women met a conservative legal definition of sex trafficking which involves third-party control over the prostituting person by pimps or traffickers. Yet most (86%) interviewees felt that no women really know what they're getting into when they begin prostituting, and that there is deception and trickery involved.

- 98% of the women were currently or previously homeless.
- 92% wanted to escape prostitution.
- 92% had been raped.[101]

The stories in *Garden of Truth* are heartbreaking. I struggled with the material myself, and I did not participate in the face-to-face interviews that MIWSAC and PRE conducted. Reports like *Garden of Truth* can help educate law enforcement, prosecutors, and judges about the invisible reality that has been ongoing for centuries.

In 2010 the Anchorage Police Department and the Federal Bureau of Investigation confirmed that they had identified a pattern wherein Alaska Native girls and women were coming to Anchorage "only to be lured into prostitution by pimps and the promise of security."[102] Apparently, Alaska Native women are particularly valuable because they can be marketed to fetish markets as Native, Asian, and Hawaiian.[103] Girls are trapped almost immediately— one in three Alaska Native runaway girls are targeted for prostitution within forty-eight hours of arrival.[104] In 2010 law enforcement agencies said that about one-third of women and girls arrested for prostitution were Native, even though less than 10 percent of the city's population is Native.[105]

Organized Crime, Fracking, and Man Camps

Native women are still "trafficked" today, both literally and figuratively. The methods of trafficking have changed, but organized crime and corporate greed are intersecting in yet another perfect storm. Perceived and actual limitations on tribal criminal authority attract criminals, including sex traffickers. Global trafficking research has suggested that "poverty or political instability" can create environments conducive to predatory criminal enterprises.[106] Gangs are a particular problem in impoverished communities throughout the nation, and the isolation of some Indian reservations makes them even more attractive to drug manufacturing rings. Generally, the sex industry is inseparable from organized crime rings. There is ample evidence that organized criminal behavior and gangs have infiltrated many tribal communities. The federal government itself has acknowledged this problem and in response funded programs to focus on the illegal drug traffic associated with some tribal communities.

In the past five years, a phenomenon that is all too familiar to Native women has begun making news again. The dynamic has to do with large numbers of non-Native men relocating to temporary living quarters near reservations. In North Dakota these shantytowns are commonly called "man camps." Descriptions of these camps are eerily similar to the frontier dynamic as chronicled in the history of the discovery of gold and oil. The following description comes from the Fort Berthold Reservation in western North Dakota, but presents perpetrators in a sympathetic light:

> These oil workers usually come from desperate conditions. These workers usually have a family they have left elsewhere so they are not looking to start new relations. These workers are paid an excessive amount of money. These workers are well aware their employment is only temporary. These workers know they are living in a remote environment where law enforcement is already stretched beyond its limits and the temptation for criminal behavior is very strong.[107]

There has been a significant increase in crime committed against Native people in North Dakota since 2008, likely attributable at least in part to the man camps associated with the oil boom.[108] Journalists and tribal leaders have described a higher-than-usual rate of prostitution, drug use, and crime in the man camps.[109] Law enforcement officers struggle to respond effectively to crime in these boomtowns. The crime that Native women are experiencing as a result of the exploding fracking business has parallels with the harm being done to the planet—the land and water are being poisoned as the hearts and spirits of Native women break. Thus another generation experiences displacement and abuse.

Conclusion

The U.S. State Department has found that prostitution and related activities "fuel the growth of modern-day slavery,"[110] yet the standard American law enforcement response to prostitution continues to be to arrest and prosecute women and girls who are prostituted.[111] Incarcerating and stigmatizing the women and children engaged in prostitution further alienates these victims from networks of assistance and safety. Native women are already overrepresented in the prison population, and some common reasons are related to the traumatic experience of many young Native women today.[112]

The time has come to ensure that all Native women are accorded full value and protection by the American legal system. Native women and girls deserve tailored interventions that recognize the historical legacy they live under. We can start by recognizing that transporting (or coercing) a Native girl or woman across sovereign lines (i.e., from a reservation to a city in the United States or Canada or from one reservation to another) for the purpose of slavery and/or sex work should be considered "international trafficking." Defining it in such a way will help ensure that more appropriate and stringent measures are taken by tribal, state, and federal governments to stop it.

The victimization of Native people is a story five hundred years in the making and we cannot remedy these problems overnight, but our best chance of breaking the cycle of victimization is the development of culturally appropriate interventions to help Native women and girls break the shackles of history and prejudice. The "Amandas" in the twenty-first century may not leave physical blood in their wakes, but the psychic and physical harm continues. Holding perpetrators accountable for trafficking Native women and girls should be compulsory.

SIX

Punishing the Victim
Dana's Story

DANA DEEGAN is a resilient and talented Native mother and grandmother from the Fort Berthold Reservation, nestled against the shores of Lake Sakakawea in western North Dakota. She designs and sews beautiful powwow regalia for her children and grandchildren, spending long hours thinking about their well-being and planning for their future. Dana is also a part-time student and keeper of a sweat lodge. In her spare time, she does beautiful beadwork and crochets toys and hats for her children and grandchildren. But Dana is also a federal prisoner, currently serving a ten-year sentence for a crime that was quite literally born of tragedy and despair. Dana's story epitomizes the ultimate tragic consequence of the historical trauma experienced by her people—the death of a child.

Her story came to my attention almost by accident. I discovered her case while researching the federal judiciary's response to violence against Native women. I had clicked on a criminal appellate case from the Eighth Circuit Court because it contained my search words "Native & women & violence." What I read took my breath away. Dana Deegan had received a ten-year sentence for her crime (described in more detail later in this chapter) and had appealed the length of the sentence to the federal appellate court. The Eighth Circuit did not rule in her favor—the court affirmed her ten-year sentence by a vote of two to one, but what captured my attention was a remarkable, impassioned dissent authored by Judge Myron Bright that contains an impeccable analysis of how the federal legal system has failed Native women. Judge Bright had served more

than forty years on the federal bench when he penned this important legal text, so it is telling that he opened his opinion with the
following statement: "The . . . imposition of a ten-year-plus prison
sentence on Ms. Deegan, a young American Indian woman, represents the most clear sentencing error that this dissenting judge
has ever seen."[1] That's not the type of sentence you typically find
in a federal case. I had to know more.

I eventually reached out to Dana by writing a simple letter to
her in prison, and as I learned more about her and her baby boy, I
came to understand that Dana's incarceration directly embodies the
warped outcome of a society where rapists are not held accountable for their behavior and victims are not treated with honor or
respect. Survivors of rape like Dana often pay the ultimate price for
the unresolved trauma, with lives marked by fear, shame, substance
abuse, and self-harm—often ending in incarceration. Dana's story
is a painful reminder of this reality, but her resilience is an inspira-
tion. Nonetheless, she is steadily working to prepare for her return
to her family with a renewed sense of health and hope.

Truly understanding Dana's story requires a careful consideration of how Native motherhood has been threatened and criminalized in the context of rape and domestic violence. Dana is a documented survivor of numerous rapes and instances of physical abuse,
and her multiple perpetrators were never held responsible for their
crimes. She bears the brunt of the criminal justice system and has
been separated from her family, separation being the only constant
in her life other than rape and abuse. Dana is not a generic woman
in a generic legal system. Her conviction and incarceration are a
direct result of trauma—as uniquely experienced by many Native
women. This chapter tells part of Dana's story.

I am grateful to Dana and her family for trusting me with her
story, and to my colleague Joanna Woolman, for encouraging me to
approach the issue of incarcerated Native women through a feminist lens.

How Moses Died

Baby Moses Deegan died in 1998. His mother, Dana, was twenty-five
years old and living on an isolated, remote part of the Fort Berthold
Reservation with three young daughters. Dana's living conditions

at the time Moses was born were utterly hopeless. Her children's father regularly beat her, and she had no money to pay for food or diapers because he monopolized the household expenditures for drugs and alcohol. She was suffering with emotionally paralyzing memories of severe childhood sexual abuse, and was completely overwhelmed and even out of touch with reality at times.

In October, Dana gave birth to Moses, unassisted and alone in her shower while her daughters played in the next room. She has few coherent memories of that day, but she remembers feeling suicidal and desperate. She also remembers having been in denial about her pregnancy, which she would keep secret from everyone in her family for years to come. Suffering from dissociation, terror, and panic, Dana did the unthinkable. She left the hours-old infant in her home and fled with her three daughters to a place of refuge with her mother where she tried to put the pieces together in her own mind, telling no one about the birth. Sadly, Dana's absence from her home extended for two weeks. Moses died alone. When Dana found Moses, her panicked behavior continued; she kept the birth and death secret and buried Moses in a makeshift grave near a tree that she could see from her home—suffering in silence, in part, because of her justified fear that disclosing Moses's death could result in losing her children.

During the next nine years, Dana's life substantially improved because of her personal strength, resolve, and resilience. She continued to raise her three daughters and contributed in meaningful ways to their lives and the lives of others in her community. She took college classes and secured a full-time job. Her resilience was cut short, however, when Moses's remains were discovered on her family's property in 1999. The local community expressed outrage over the death of the Baby Doe, but Dana stayed silent, hoping and dreaming that her desperate act would not separate her from her daughters. For a variety of reasons, Dana was not positively identified as Moses's mother until 2007, when DNA analysis matched mother and son. The case fell under federal jurisdiction pursuant to the Major Crimes Act and the U.S. Attorney charged Dana with first-degree murder, calling Moses's death a "slow motion murder."

After a federal grand jury indicted her on that charge, Dana confessed to causing her baby's death and entered into a plea agreement with the government for a reduced charge of second-degree murder. Despite numerous mitigating circumstances, Dana was sentenced to over ten years in federal prison in 2008.[2] At her sentencing hearing, the judge imposed 121 months after ruling that a downward departure from the federal sentencing guidelines was not justified despite numerous mitigating circumstances.[3] Dana is currently serving her ten-year sentence in federal prison with a release date of March 6, 2017.

How Moses *Really* Died:
Dana's Lifelong Struggle to Survive

Dana has admitted to causing the death of Moses. As she has painfully put the fragments of her memory back together, she now understands that her crime is very much connected to her past—she has survived horrific emotional, physical, and sexual abuse perpetrated by nearly every man in her life. Notably, none of the perpetrators have ever been held accountable for their actions in any criminal justice system. Dana's history of abuse is chronicled in the sentencing transcript and features information Dana shared with forensic psychiatrist Dr. Phillip Resnick. From an early age, Dana witnessed and experienced extreme domestic violence at the hands of her father, a violent alcoholic who ultimately died from complications of his addiction. She remembers seeing her father beat her mother severely about once a month, resulting in broken bones and blackened eyes. Dana's father also beat her on a daily basis for many years; she and her many siblings learned how to hide serious injuries from school officials and lie about absences. In childhood, Dana began to experience what she now understands were dissociations as a result of these beatings.

If physical violence weren't enough, Dana was also sexually abused by her father's friends starting when she was five. By the time she was nine years old, Dana had experienced repeated rapes and torture. At age eleven, she summoned the courage to report the abuse to her mother, who felt guilty for not protecting her. When her mother told her father, he beat one of the accused men so badly, the man almost died. As a result of this abuse, Dana and her numerous siblings were in and out of the foster-care system starting when

Dana was eleven. Sometimes her father would stop drinking and the children would return home—but ultimately he would resume drinking and the children would be removed again.

Dana met the man who would become the father of her children when she was fifteen. They began a romantic relationship, which quickly became abusive. When Dana was seventeen, he assaulted her for the first time and from there his violence and substance abuse became a regular experience for Dana. She had three daughters with her partner, and his violence toward her escalated in intensity over time. She had few options for safety. As a former foster child herself, Dana knew firsthand the pain of being removed from a family. She legitimately feared that disclosing the abuse would separate her from her children. Her partner's mother, who was a central stabilizing figure in her life, provided some stability and support between the beatings (her husband tended to avoid violence and drinking in front of his mother).[4]

At the time Moses was born, Dana was severely depressed and suicidal. Although she probably realized she was pregnant around the four-month mark, she could not come to terms with the reality of a fourth child and entered into deep denial about the pregnancy. She made no plans for the birth and did not receive any prenatal care.[5] By the time Moses was born, Dana reported feeling at the end of her rope.[6] She did not think she could care for another baby and knew she could not return to her parents' home because of her father's physical abuse and drinking.[7] At the time of Moses' birth, her partner was beating her on a regular basis and spent nearly all of their household income on alcohol and drugs, leaving Dana with few resources to feed her daughters.[8] One can imagine many scenarios in which Dana's family could have been quickly split apart if she were to admit that she was struggling. She was terrified of losing her three daughters at the time.[9]

The History of Child Removal

Many may ask why Dana didn't simply reach out for help when she found herself in the midst of such a crisis. Part of the answer lies in her mental and physical state at the time Moses was born. But Dana was also reluctant to contact child protection or a social services program because she feared a system that has destroyed

Native families for generations. In this section, I explore the history of child removal in tribal communities and its intersection with today's legacy of violence and exploitation. Native women like Dana have few options, especially when they are in constant danger of physical, sexual, and emotional abuse.

Child removal is a common feature of colonialism and has sent a variety of messages to tribal communities, particularly to mothers. The dominant society disapproved of the way Native people parented. As discussed in chapter 5, child removal has been a common feature in many tribal communities. Some boarding school systems "threatened and sometimes eliminated Native women's ability to supervise their daughters."[10] Ultimately, the imposition of Euro-American parenting standards was the foundation for the erosion of traditional parenting structures in many tribal communities. Isolation and shame replaced healthy parenting norms, which had included the support of extensive kinship networks and child-rearing responsibilities. Native families have been targets of social workers for more than a century—and, by extension, the child protection system—and the results have been devastating.

Today's Native pregnant women and mothers wrestle with a dark legacy of child removal when assessing their options for help in times of crisis. For good reason, there is a great deal of distrust of outside intervention.[11] In many tribal communities, disclosing domestic violence or child abuse is considered to be an inexcusable betrayal, because alerting authorities to any potential harm within the home can open the door to child removal.[12] Given the trauma of mass child removal in tribal communities, it has been safer for parents in crisis to try to resolve the problem internally rather than seek help from third parties. Outside agency intervention from state and federal agencies may not be overtly racist today, but there continue to be vestiges of superiority and disrespect for Native cultures. Even today, standard social work curriculum does not explain the historical context in which Native people parent.[13] Social workers continue to separate Native mothers from their children at rates far exceeding those of any other race, almost always under the guise of "neglect"—not violence.

Meanwhile, due to the breakdown of extended kinship networks and systems of care, the once-strong internal tribal structures themselves might not be able to take on these issues and protect children from harm.[14] Many tribal governments have actually replicated the child protection systems of state governments. Dakota scholar Elizabeth Cook-Lynn has observed that "the modern attack on the civil and tribal rights of Indian women of childbearing age on reservation homelands . . . has often resulted in staggering, violent, misogynistic practices previously unknown to the tribes."[15] In many tribal communities today, a Native mother suffering from addiction, poverty, abuse, or neglect may be effectively trapped. Disclosing the challenges to outside authorities risks child removal; therefore, from this perspective, it is better not to seek help. This strategy, however, effectively isolates Native women who fear for their well-being and that of their children. When a woman receives no intervention, support, or advice, the situation can deteriorate rapidly, resulting in devastating consequences for mothers and children, including death.[16]

A system that is supposed to protect and nurture children has thus been crudely warped by a patchwork of policies rooted in racism and oppression. It is no wonder a Native woman like Dana might avoid seeking help when she is suffering and scared—there are many rational disincentives to seeking help.[17] Mothers and pregnant women suffering from chronic psychological distress may have few options; in some tribal communities, the only mental health service is emergency psychiatric care.[18] Reaching out for help was the last thing Dana could do.

Making Dana Pay

The crime Dana committed is known in psychiatric literature as "neonaticide" (the killing of an infant within the first twenty-four hours of life). The American legal response to neonaticide differs from that of other countries. Women who commit infanticide are largely demonized by American society and have received life sentences for abandoning their newborns. In other countries (England, Australia, Canada, and Hong Kong, for example) the legal system has recognized that the conditions under which women commit neonaticide place the crime in a different category from most filicide cases.[19] In both England and Hong Kong, women charged and convicted under these acts often receive lenient sentences, consisting of probation with court-ordered psychiatric treatment.[20] The origins of these infanticide statutes are based on a two-pronged rationale. First, there is concern about the harsh treatment in the criminal justice system of young, single, and low-income women. The second consideration is the psychiatric issues that occur before, during, and after birth.[21]

These foreign laws clearly incorporate notions of feminist legal theory. That is, they recognize that immediately after the birth of a baby, in certain circumstances, hormones, postpartum depression and psychosis, and other gendered differences have real and significant impacts on the events leading up to a crime.[22] As such, when a mother kills or abandons a newborn immediately after birth, the laws of these countries explicitly recognize that gender matters. They then go on to provide different outcomes for women in these circumstances based on these biological differences.

There are no "infanticide specific" laws in American law, meaning that crimes like Dana's are treated no differently than other types of homicide. However, all fifty states have adopted "safe haven" laws whereby a parent can leave an unwanted newborn at a safe place in complete anonymity.[23] Unfortunately, the North Dakota safe haven law was passed long after Moses died. One of the many ironies in Dana's story is that the story of Moses was one of the cases that inspired the North Dakota Safe Haven law.[24] While Dana serves her sentence, other women in North Dakota can benefit from the law that offers an "out" for women in her situation.

Dana was ultimately sentenced for second-degree murder in a federal criminal justice system that was not equipped to provide justice and healing to Dana and her family. Was Dana truly culpable of coldhearted murder deserving of a lengthy prison sentence? Dana provided some information during her sentencing about her motivations at the time of the birth, but it is impossible to know what really happened because of the level of dissociation and trauma she experienced. We know that Dana was not in a position either before or immediately after the birth to seek or receive help. She was completely isolated and terrified of losing custody of her daughters. Dana herself had entered the foster care system at age eleven after reporting the sexual and physical abuse she experienced.[25] The trauma of being removed from her mother and siblings likely made Dana extremely wary of reaching out for help as a mother with children of her own. This memory of trauma in her childhood also represents a clear example of historical trauma affecting the choices and life of an individual Native woman. This is part of what makes Dana's story so compelling. We can see the implications of historical trauma played out in her life.

At the core of Dana's case is the story of a Native woman and mother living in constant fear and danger, in extreme poverty, and without access to support, legal or otherwise. She exists in the world as someone aware of the historical trauma of Native women through time, and this historical context is part of her individual story. Examining Dana's life story and crime through the lens of feminism may help us understand what could have been done to help Dana and her family.

Indigenous Feminism as a Tool
for Understanding Dana's Story

Indigenous feminisms, as explored in earlier chapters, have roots in precolonial conceptions of gender.[26] Like intersectional feminism, indigenous feminism considers gender and race—but also the role of colonization in the lives of Native women.[27] A legal analysis informed by indigenous feminism helps explains Dana's story and explores potential legal remedies for her experience. Trying to understand a case like Dana's using a feminist model that is not informed by colonization would fall short of explaining both her circumstances and her crime. Dana's experience as a member of a racial minority, for example, may not play nearly as significant a role in her life as the history of child removal in tribal communities. Considering colonization without gender is likewise problematic. Dana's experience as a Native mother is vastly different than that of Native men or fathers. In particular, in Dana's case, she bore the brunt of the child rearing and, therefore, also bore all the risk should her poverty, abuse, or trauma be used against her by the government. She simply had more on the line because of her position as a Native mother.

An indigenous feminist approach is simultaneously useful because it allows us to consider the history of the child protection system from the perspective of Native women. To understand Dana's experience more fully, we must also consider her experiences as a Native woman in the criminal justice system. Dana, like many women in the criminal justice system, arrived as a result of trauma.

How can a mother reach out for help from the legal or social systems about potential harm to her children? The professionals who have access to resources for help are typically also mandatory reporters—including social workers, medical care providers, and police officers. A woman who struggles to protect her children—from her partner, from poverty, or from her own mental illness—risks losing her children if she discloses the painful truth of her existence. If, for instance, she admits to a helping professional, "I am overwhelmed; I am not able to be a good parent right now" or "I am fearful that my children are in danger," she will likely be faced with potential removal of her children and/or criminal charges.

Native women have good reason to distrust state intervention. Before the death of her baby, Dana was genuinely afraid that disclosing the domestic violence would have threatened the existence of her family. Another compounding layer to all of this is the "extreme poverty and isolation" that Dana experienced, in particular, before the birth of Moses.[28]

Dana's story is no doubt similar to those of thousands of incarcerated Native women. She represents the ultimate intersectional example of oppression. She was a victim. She was poor. She was Native. She was a mother. The system honored none of those identities. When Moses died, she became a criminal. She is a Native mother who experienced individual and historical trauma without effective intervention—and this trauma had horrific results in her life.

The Sentencing Disparity:
Proof That Colonization Matters

In 2014 I worked with Dana and her family to file a petition for executive clemency, requesting an early merciful release so that she could return to her family, care for her ailing mother, and guide her daughters into young adulthood. Executive clemency, an extremely rare remedy, can only be granted by the president, but Dana has received support from hundreds of people who have written letters on her behalf and signed a petition requesting her early release. As of this writing, Dana's petition is under review by the Office of the Pardon Attorney.[29]

A central component of the petition for clemency focuses on a stark sentencing disparity experienced by Native women compared to other races. As we consider how colonization and gendered violence have shaped both Dana's crime and prison sentence, it is telling to find instances in which such historical factors are absent and where the story has a remarkably different ending.

Dana's claim of sentencing disparity arises, in part, from another case of neonaticide. In April 2008, just a few months before Moses's birth, a twenty-year-old woman named Laura gave birth in the bathroom of her sorority house at North Dakota State University (across the state from Fort Berthold) after struggling to conceal her pregnancy for several months. Like Dana, Laura fatally neglected her newborn and told no one about the birth or death. Like Dana, Laura concealed the body of her infant. Like Dana, Laura was experiencing great psychological distress at the time she gave birth. Like Dana, Laura initially told authorities her baby was stillborn. Like Dana, Laura was charged with a crime.

Unlike Dana, however, Laura was a young white woman attending a university. Unlike Dana, she was charged in state (not federal) court. Most significantly, unlike Dana, Laura received a one-year suspended sentence and three years of probation.[30] *She did not serve any time in jail.* Dana, a mother of three, having experienced a lifetime of hardship and trauma, who behaved in substantially the same way, is serving a decade behind bars. While the cases were decided in separate jurisdictions, the outcomes are telling and require us to think critically about how the American legal system fails Native women. Several questions emerge from this critique. Is Dana more dangerous to society than Laura? What do we expect women in Dana's position to do? And, as Judge Bright of the Eighth Circuit Court asks in his brilliant dissent, "Where were the government and social agencies during the many instances of physical, verbal, and sexual abuse suffered by Ms. Deegan as a child and young adult, as well as her younger sisters and mother?"[31] Answering these questions will no doubt stimulate ideas for improving the lives of all Native women.

Despite her circumstances, Dana continues to have a positive attitude, although it is difficult to be a mother from behind bars.

She truly wants to make things right with the universe. I close with her own words from the clemency petition because they tell the story much better than I:

> I apologize to my son's father, our daughters, our families, relatives and the tribal community who adopted and buried my son, Moses. We have cried and prayed for healing, forgiveness, and understanding of how abuse, violence and addiction have affected our lives for generations. I am stating "we" because through all of the separation and despair to my daughters' lives and family, we have struggled to stay together as a family—but we do, through healing, honesty and support for one another. We have ongoing discussions about what has happened, and why. My own healing and rehabilitation provides clarification and understanding of the cycle of violence. Drug and alcohol addiction, plus physical and sexual abuse have affected my life and the lives of my family on every level.

Dana's continued incarceration provides safety for no one—and the men who have brutalized her still walk free. I look forward to the release of my friend. She has taught me hard truths about the criminal justice system that I had been unwilling to face. Mvto, Dana.

SEVEN

The Enigma of Federal Reform

The Tribal Law and Order Act
and the Violence Against Women Act

NEAR THE END OF HIS LIFE, my grandfather had a bumper sticker that he liked so much he placed it on the car body rather than the bumper so that more people would see it. I remember pulling into his driveway and chuckling to myself when I saw it plastered on the front hood of his pickup truck. It was a common bumper sticker that you can still find for sale at powwows and other Native events. It read, "Trust the government? Ask an Indian!" He would drive around small towns in rural conservative Kansas where he lived and enjoyed the various reactions he got from the locals. But my grandfather was far from an anti-government Indian. He was elected to the Kansas legislature four times between 1953 and 1960 and volunteered for the Army Reserves from 1955 to 1959, earning the rank of master sergeant. His lifelong dedication was education; he taught American history to thousands of high school students and encouraged patriotic activities at school and sporting events as a public school superintendent. He hardly eschewed the federal government as something to distain or denounce.

So how do I make sense of that bumper sticker? I think Grandpa was a little cantankerous later in life, but I also think he was always a healthy skeptic of anything having to do with the federal government. However, his distrust, from an Indian perspective, was not grounds for complete disengagement and rejection of federal government. Moreover, his lifelong dedication to education and politics was largely rooted in the belief that most people will do the right thing once they have the right information. Although Grandpa never shared these sentiments with me explicitly, I credit him with encouraging me to consider that *some* kinds of political compromise can be valuable.

Grandpa died in 2009. Within three years of his death, I was privileged to attend two different presidential signing ceremonies for legislation that I helped develop. To be honest, there were many times during those three years that I felt conflicted about whether federal legislative reform could ever truly lead to change, but in the end I think great things were accomplished. The Native women who have championed this legislation are heroes of the highest order; no one thought it could be done. Personally, thinking about Grandpa's work in the state legislature was one of the reasons I didn't give up. I think he would have liked his bumper sticker to read, "Trust the government? With extreme caution."

This chapter examines the murky, convoluted, and controversial process of engaging with the federal government to seek remedies and solutions to problems caused by colonization. It may seem odd to devote an entire chapter to federal law in a book intended to focus on the resurgence and strengthening of tribal law. However, two federal laws have become part of the national dialogue about rape in Indian country and Alaska villages and have specific relevance to tribal legal reform. The Tribal Law and Order Act (2010) and the Violence Against Women Act reauthorization (2013) are the focus of this chapter.

TLOA and VAWA represent a complete shift in federal policy—and neither law would exist without the efforts of Native women. The grassroots movement to end violence against Native women has demonstrated that significant Indian law reform at the national level is possible—something that many had written off as impossible. The hard work of Native grassroots to make these changes is deserving of particular attention.[1] National and grassroots activism regarding VAWA is chronicled in detail in Jacqueline Agtuca, *Safety for Native Women: VAWA and American Indian Tribes*, a highly recommended text for comprehensive legislative history.[2]

This chapter offers a summary of the specific major changes in federal law that affects Native victims of rape. Some of these changes provide an opportunity for tribal governments to consider reform at the tribal level, particularly in the area of criminal justice. The summaries are intended to provide readers with the knowledge to celebrate and/or critique what these laws have to offer. I explore the continuing gaps in the system that will need future attention.

The Politics and Pitfalls of Federal Reform

Engaging with federal legislative reform efforts can be an inherently risky endeavor from a tribal perspective. On a practical level, members of Congress often fail to accurately remedy identified problems, or, worse, enact new anti-sovereignty legislation, which further limits the recognition of tribal authority.

This dynamic became a cogent reality in 2006, when Congress passed the Sex Offender Registration and Notification Act (SORNA). Commonly known as the Adam Walsh Child Protection and Safety Act,[3] the legislation unfortunately ended up pitting tribal sovereignty against mainstream political efforts to require all convicted sex offenders to be tracked in a national database. While sex offender registration and notification laws seem, at first glance, to be benevolent, serious due process concerns have arisen in response to such legislation—and there is no clear evidence that such laws effectively prevent sex crimes. But the tribal connection to SORNA became even more complicated.

The 2006 SORNA legislation raised fundamental concerns about sovereignty because it unilaterally authorized states to exercise civil regulatory authority (to register and track offenders) in Indian country, extending state authority into an unprecedented realm. Tribal leaders were not consulted about the SORNA, and the ignorance of the politicians who championed the law did not recognize the grave long-term implications of this intrusion. Tribal nations affected by PL 280 were particularly affected, as lawyers Virginia Davis and Kevin Washburn explain:

> Congress created state regulatory authority that had not previously existed on some Public Law 280 reservations and arguably created state criminal authority where it did not previously exist in non-PL 280 jurisdictions. For tribes in the latter category, SORNA constitutes the only delegation of authority to states on reservations,

dramatically undermining longstanding federal legal principles providing that Indians on reservations are subject to tribal or federal, but never state authority.[4]

SORNA imposed requirements on all tribes, not just those in PL 280 states. Tribal nations were forced to operate pursuant to an arbitrary time frame during which they could "assert" their sovereignty to undertake registration (with no guaranteed access to funding to make it happen). The law thus abruptly started the clock before most tribal leaders knew it existed. Tribal leaders had to scramble to preserve their nations' sovereignty.[5] This means that tribes had to develop fully compliant sex offender laws and accompanying infrastructure to implement them—and some of these tribal governments had never even prosecuted rape in their contemporary systems.

Objection to the law put tribal leaders and advocates in the uncomfortable position of challenging a law that was, on the surface, intended to protect innocent children from sexual predators (and had a great deal of bipartisan political support). When tribal leaders resisted state regulatory authority based on the precedent it could establish in other realms, some journalists unfairly characterized tribes as providing jurisdictional "shields" for sex offenders.[6] Moreover, tribal governments that had not actively been prosecuting rape were suddenly tasked with creating a sophisticated computerized registration system or surrender such authority (presumably forever) to state governments.

Registries and civil commitment (in which sex offenders who have served their punitive sentences in prison are remanded by the state, sometimes indefinitely, because the state believes they are still a threat) have fallen out of favor with many victim advocates and social change organizations. Registration and civil commitment laws actually run counter to most feminist theories, because they are inspired by the stereotypical "real rape" scenario that feminists have fought so hard to challenge. In truth, sex offender registration and notification laws were developed as a conservative political response to sexual abuse as experienced by white children who were assaulted by strangers—harking back to a day when the legal definition of rape required victims to be innocent and chaste to be worthy of protection. There is little evidence that registration and commitment laws are effective. Most rapists are never caught and prosecuted and so do not appear on these lists.

The legacy of SORNA should give pause to those who expect that engaging with the federal government will lead to tribal-centric solutions. And it leads me to ask a difficult question. Do tribal nations compromise or weaken their own sovereignty by the mere process of seeking federal legislative reform? I recognize a fundamental problem with federal law reform, because it requires a tribe to petition the colonizing government to ask for help for a problem that the colonizer created, to ask for a solution that will be on the colonizer's terms. The federal government is the source of the problem, so why would we expect it to be the source of the solution? Depending on a foreign government, especially a government established and created by colonizers, is not the solution to violent crimes committed upon Native women. Yet tribes find themselves in a catch-22. As the AWA/SORNA fiasco demonstrates, failing to engage with the federal system can be dangerous because Congress may pass laws that infringe on tribal sovereignty without consulting or even considering the sovereignty of tribal nations.

One school of thought to undoing this catch-22 argues that the federal government can never hold the answers. That it is simply a waste of time to fight for sovereignty in the halls of Congress. One could argue that energy might be better spent in building strong communities and tribal nations, revitalizing traditions and languages and focusing on elders, children, and those with disabilities and other special needs. In addition, engaging with the federal government may signal a form of surrender to federal dominion over tribal nations. Is it the same as consenting to jurisdiction in a courtroom? We show up; therefore we agree with the framework?

The legislative process itself can be patronizing and paternalistic. A case in point: the tribal provisions of the 2013 VAWA were initially introduced by Senator Daniel Akaka (D–Hawai'i] as the "SAVE Native Women Act" (the Stand Against Violence and Empower Native Women Act). I have no doubt that Senator Akaka was well intentioned, but the presentation of the legislation left much to be desired. Native women do not need to be "saved" by Senator Akaka, or any federal government official for that matter. *We are saving ourselves.*

Another fundamental challenge with federal reform is the risk of increasing federal presence and punishment on tribal lands. Both laws that I discuss in this chapter provide for more punitive measures in federal and tribal court, which may continue to feed into the cycle of high incarceration rates. The activism and scholarship of feminists of color have been particularly instructive with regards to critiquing the direction federal reform has on social justice issues generally. Any federal legislation, by definition, institutionalizes and endorses the United States as a protector of women—and this is a cession that some are not willing to make.

Contemporary Realities:
The Argument for Engagement

Despite the potential downsides to federal reform, the damage done to sovereignty today is done largely through rape. Any legitimate efforts to address this systemic crisis and provide justice and support for victims is worth considering, including partnerships with neighboring jurisdictions to ensure that rape victims have access to justice. I realize that this is a provocative claim, because there are many threats to tribal existence. But use of rape is widespread and is intended to terrorize and destroy the psyche of communities.

Rape is more of a fundamental threat to self-determination of tribal nations than the drawbacks federal reform could ever be. Rape and child sexual abuse are directly related to most of the social challenges tribal nations face, and when people are hurting, they cannot effectively govern themselves or provide guidance and support for the children in the community. Legal scholar and Grand Traverse citizen Matthew L. M. Fletcher reminds us that "tribal sovereignty is not a claim to power and authority for their own sake, but a tool to preserve the culture and traditions of Indian people."[7] The damage being done to sovereignty through sexual violence is so deep and significant that other tribal sovereignty efforts will continue to fail because people are hurting.

Western medicine has finally confirmed what many Native people have known for centuries—that psychological trauma is directly linked to long-term physical health problems. A long-range multi-faceted study commonly referred to as ACEs (Adverse Childhood

Experience) has provided the evidence that Native spiritual healers and medicine people have known for millennia—namely, that there is no formal separation between mind and body; trauma affects not just psychological but physical well-being.[8] The ACEs study has helped Western medicine understand that experiencing abuse is correlated with long-term chronic health problems that Western medicine has long dismissed as biologically unrelated.

The long-term health problems ACEs has linked to childhood trauma are all elevated in tribal communities, including heart disease, diabetes, obesity, and liver disease. The study shows that such health consequences are elevated for trauma victims—even controlling for external factors such as cigarette smoking. The authors also note that

> many of our most intractable public health problems are the result of attempted personal solutions to problems caused by traumatic childhood experiences, which are lost in time and concealed by shame, secrecy, and social taboo against the exploration of certain topics.[9]

Social harms, such as suicide and addiction, also have a direct connection to trauma. Chronic health conditions such as diabetes and obesity can be triggered or aggravated by unresolved psychological trauma. Many survivors of child sexual abuse have described a phenomenon of wanting to be sexually unattractive to avoid attention from predators—leading to eating disorders and agoraphobia. This philosophy is illustrated by training materials from several Native organizations—sustaining strong nations is simply not possible when most of the women in your community have been denied justice.

Challenges with the Scope of Federal Reform

Once a decision has been made to engage with federal reform, the next question invariably becomes "what can we politically accomplish" as opposed to "what is truly needed?" Are incremental changes enough? It is a fantasy, for example, to think that Congress will completely decolonize Indian law overnight. Politically, it is not possible to impose such a radical departure and recognize tribal nations as sovereign entities with no restrictions in one fell swoop. The incremental changes may seem frustrating, but also offer hope that Native voices have been heard.

I do not believe those of us who advocate for federal reform are under the impression that the Violence Against Women Act and the Tribal Law and Order Act of 2010 are the ultimate solutions to ending rape in tribal nations. Federal legal reform is only a small aspect in legal reform for tribal nations. So TLOA and VAWA, and laws to come, are and should be the subject of rigorous debate and intensive critique. The American government nearly destroyed tribal legal systems and replaced them with substandard systems that were designed to control Native people; not respect them. Little wonder that many tribal leaders are skeptical of federal efforts to improve the lives of Native people.

Organizations like the National Congress of American Indians and several tribal embassies in Washington, D.C., have established a physical presence in the nation's capital. It is becoming more and more difficult for Congress to move on legislation without hearing from at least one tribal organization about concerns. This was not the case until very recently, so perhaps the successes of TLOA and VAWA are a window into the future.

Hearings and Letters:
The Precursors to Federal Reform

Hard work for truly changing the landscape of tribal criminal authority began in 2004 when the Senate Committee on Indian Affairs (SCIA) began to hold hearings about the high rates of crime in tribal communities. Tribal leaders and victim advocates were invited to testify in front of Congress about the hardships and triumphs and thus communicated directly with Congress about the need for reform. Native women's and children's organizations as well as the National Congress of American Indians raised national awareness about the high crime rates—and specific legislation was proposed to restore authority to tribal courts and provide funding for victim advocacy. Leverage was hard to come by, however. It was hard to grab the attention of lawmakers except through the House and Senate committees on Indian affairs. That trend started to change when Amnesty International released a human rights report titled *Maze of Injustice: The Failure to Protect Indigenous Women from Sexual Violence in the USA* in April 2007. My colleagues at the Tribal Law and Policy Institute in St. Paul, Minnesota, and I consulted closely with Amnesty International in the development of the report, but I never expected the document to become a major player on Capitol Hill. As it turns out, *Maze of Injustice* was invaluable because congressional staffers had an external analysis of the problem that helped them convince colleagues of the incredible need for reform. *Maze of Injustice* provided a human face for the stark, dehumanizing statistics that had been released eight years earlier by the Department of Justice. The pictures and personal stories in the report raised the profile of the crisis and captured the attention of national news media, such as the *New York Times*. Suddenly, things began to move quickly. The Senate Committee on Indian Affairs began to circulate various proposals for federal reform in 2008. Senator Byron Dorgan (D–North Dakota) championed most of the proposals. The efforts resulted in two major acts—the Tribal Law and Order Act and the Violence Against Women Act reauthorization in 2013.

The Tribal Law and Order Act of 2010

Congress passed the Tribal Law and Order Act in 2010 and President Obama signed the law in a public ceremony held at the White House on July 29. Much of the law is concerned with federal reform, and this chapter has focused specifically on a subset of the reforms that directly affect tribal jurisdiction. TLOA had three main purposes, as outlined in a report from the Indian Law and Order Commission:

> First, the Act was intended to make Federal departments and agencies more accountable for serving Native people and lands. Second, TLOA was designed to provide greater freedom for Indian tribes and nations to design and run their own justice systems. This includes Tribal court systems generally, along with those communities that are subject to full or partial State criminal jurisdiction under P.L. 83-280. Third, the Act sought to enhance cooperation among Tribal, Federal, and State officials in key areas such as law enforcement training, interoperability, and access to criminal justice information.[10]

Here, I will focus on the second purpose, which has to do with tribal justice systems. As chapter 3 explained, the Indian Civil Rights Act (ICRA) imposed a cap on the sentencing authority of tribal courts. The original act, passed in 1968, capped tribal sentences at six months' incarceration and/or a $500 fine. Amendments in 1986 allowed for up to one year's incarceration and/or a $5,000 fine. Under TLOA, the cap has been lifted slightly—tribal nations may sentence an offender to three years incarceration sentence per offense. However, several strings are attached (discussed later).

The basic judicial authority change TLOA made to tribal jurisdiction from a rape survivor's perspective is as follows: tribal courts, if certain requirements are met, can now punish a rapist by sentencing him to jail for a maximum of three to nine years and fining him up to $15,000. Before TLOA, the relative caps were one to three years maximum and a fine of up to $5,000. This sentencing increase may seem negligible until one considers the perspective of a survivor—who can perhaps feel safer knowing that the perpetrator will not be able to return to the community for three to nine years.

VAWA 2013 and the Quest for an Oliphant Fix

The Violence Against Women Act was originally passed by Congress in 1994 and has been amended and reauthorized three times, most recently in 2013. VAWA is a comprehensive federal law that approaches violence in a multifaceted way, including funding, programming, and criminal justice system reform.[11] The funding streams have included targeted resources for tribal domestic violence and sexual abuse, which also resulted in the development of tribal nonprofit coalitions.

Beginning with the reauthorization effort of 2005, many Native women's advocates began to press for additional changes in the Violence Against Women Act to better meet the needs of Native women.[12] The result has been a "Tribal Title" (Title IX) in VAWA that addresses a variety of issues pertaining to Native women living in Indian country.[13]

When the VAWA was up for renewal in 2011, new provisions were proposed by advocates at the local and national level to address the crisis of violence against women in Indian country. The needed reforms went too far for some politicians, though, because the eighteen-year-old bipartisan energy of VAWA quickly dissipated when the proposed legislation added "controversial" provisions about Native women, immigrants, and the LGBTQ community.[14]

While there were several additions and changes to Title IX in what ultimately became the 2013 version, the most controversial change was the restoration of tribal jurisdiction over non-Indians who commit acts of domestic violence on tribal lands. This legislation has been framed as a "partial Oliphant fix" because it alters the legal rule imposed by the U.S. Supreme Court in the 1978 decision *Oliphant v. Suquamish*.

No one had attempted an "Oliphant fix" for quite some time. I remember someone on Capitol Hill commenting that pursuing an Oliphant fix was the "third rail" in Indian politics because it seemed like a fruitless endeavor and a waste of resources. But when the interracial statistics of attackers against Native women received more national and international coverage, the political winds shifted. President Obama's 2008 election probably didn't hurt either, because the president had actually crafted a policy statement on Indian issues that included the recognition that criminal justice in Indian country needed serious reform.

Speaking Truth: Native Women Fight Back

As the legislation stalled because of Republican discomfort about expanding the reach of VAWA, Native women began to home in on the message about non-Indian offenders, repeatedly emphasizing the high rates of interracial violence.

Native women have been telling their personal stories of survival in many circumstances over many years. However, a turning point in VAWA activism came in 2012, when Deborah Parker, who was at that time the vice chairwoman of the Tulalip Tribes in Washington State, decided during an unrelated trip to Washington, D.C., to speak out in favor of the tribal provisions in VAWA. Her remarks were broadcast and shared via YouTube. After describing her personal experience as a survivor of child sexual abuse at a press conference organized by VAWA sponsor Senator Patty Murray (D–Washington), Vice Chairwoman Parker turned her attention to Congress, directly asking

> Why did you not protect me or my family? Why is my life and the life of so many other Native American women less important? It is now 2012; I am urging Congress to uphold the U.S. Constitution.

And honor U.S. treaty agreements: to provide protection, education, health, and safety of our indigenous men and women of this
country.[15]

As far as I know, no members of the VAWA opposition ever directly
responded to Deborah Parker's basic questions. Instead, rhetoric
on the Hill took a bizarre turn.

Anti-VAWA Rhetoric and Settler Anxiety

As Capitol Hill energy ramped up in 2012, many politicians told
lies about the tribal provisions of the VAWA bill. Several Republi-
cans in Congress made sweeping, broad generalizations about the
inferiority of tribal courts. Some of the particularly vocal oppo-
nents engaged with civil rights rhetoric, with unfounded concerns
about tribal courts violating civil rights. Pro-VAWA Native activists,
then, had to confront this opposition by defending the credibility
of tribal courts using Anglo-American standards. In that sense, it
has been difficult to articulate a decolonized perspective of tribal
response to crime.

The concern about the rights of non-Native defendants in tribal
courts should VAWA pass with the tribal provisions reached a
fevered pitch in late 2012, mostly generated by Republican con-
gressmen who had never before made civil rights or civil liberties a
priority issue in any context. Some of the 2012–2013 rhetoric from
the opposition dehumanized Native people but it also exposed anti-
sovereignty sentiments and racist assumptions about Native people.

For example, Senator Chuck Grassley (R–Iowa) proclaimed in
his opposition to the bill that "on an Indian reservation, [a jury is]
going to be made up of Indians, right? So the non-Indian doesn't
get a fair trial."[16] In his haste to claim that Native people are somehow morally deficient, Senator Grassley failed to mention that tribal
nations that wish to take advantage of the restored criminal jurisdiction must actually ensure that no one is excluded from a tribal
jury based on race. (This, incidentally, will be one of the most difficult requirements for tribal nations to meet because of the difficult question of whether tribes have authority to subpoena nonciti-
zens to sit on juries. Some tribal governments have been doing it
for years, but it is a difficult system to set up and requires changes

to tribal criminal procedure.) Senator Grassley's objections how-ever, were not just about his concerns that Indians don't play fair. On the floor of the Senate in February 2013, he went even further by boldly declaring that "unlike a State, a tribe is not a sovereign entity";[17] Representative Richard "Doc" Hastings (R–Washington) made a similar series of statements during the same period, claim-ing, for example, that "tribal self-government is therefore not a gen-eral government power equivalent to that of a state."[18]

Representative Tom Cole (R-Oklahoma), a member of the Chick-asaw Nation, ultimately played a critical role in persuading his peers that Native governments should be recognized to protect their peo-ple. He explained to his Republican colleagues that he was the only person in Congress who could be held accountable for beating a woman on an Indian reservation.

Fortunately, the stalemate broke in March, thanks to Cole's efforts, and President Obama signed the restored jurisdiction in a ceremony at the Department of the Interior on March 7, 2013—exactly thirty-five years and one day after Justice William Rehnquist delivered the opinion in *Oliphant*. It had taken a genera-tion to begin to fix the harm that *Oliphant* had done.

Since the law was passed in 2013, many journalists have asked me *why* the Republican Party raised such opposition to the spe-cial domestic violence criminal jurisdiction provision. Republican staffers who attended meetings tended to claim, almost invariably, that the law was "unconstitutional." When pressed, however, these same staffers could not articulate *how* the legislation violated the constitution. While I think the full explanation of opposition has yet to emerge, it seems that most of the opposition was grounded in ignorance and racism.

Prosecuting Non-Indians: How Special Domestic Violence Criminal Jurisdiction Works

The most radical shift in VAWA 2013 is known as "special domes-tic violence criminal jurisdiction" (SDVCJ). The federal language recognizes the authority of a tribal government to prosecute a non-Indian who commits an act of domestic violence against a Native woman on tribal land. The terms concerning the tribal nation are explicitly limiting: the tribe may prosecute non-Indians for certain domestic violence with "sufficient ties" to the tribe.

VAWA 2013 thus does not extend to cases of rape outside the context of domestic violence. If a victim does not have an intimate relationship with the perpetrator, the non-Indian is still exempt from tribal criminal authority pursuant to *Oliphant*. The confusion about the scope of the restoration arises from the conflation of the terms "domestic violence" and "sexual assault" that I described in the introduction. In early conversations and papers, Senator Dorgan noted that reform needed to include restoration of tribal jurisdiction over all violent crimes, including rape and child abuse, committed on tribal lands. In the end, though, only domestic violence was included in VAWA 2013. The removal of other crimes was necessary in order to achieve passage: key congressional allies were willing to support the prosecution of a man who had married into the tribe, but balked when asked to support the prosecution of people who may not have ties to the reservation.

The exclusion of rape means that tribes still lack jurisdiction over most acquaintance rape, all child sexual abuse, and all stranger rape committed by non-Indians. The only sexual assault that can be covered is that committed by an intimate partner (spouse, dating partner, parent of a child in common). Politically, Congress simply didn't have the willpower to overturn all of *Oliphant,* so it started by restoring jurisdiction over abusers who have become part of the community by entering into relationships with Native women.

All tribal nations can exercise SDVCJ as of March 2015, but three tribes were selected for a pilot project—the Tulalip Tribes, the Confederated Tribes of Umatilla, and the Pascua Yaqui Tribe— and began exercising the restored jurisdiction in 2013. This limited application conveys an air of paternalism that has been part of the "approval" project for the pilot program for tribes, but given the sovereignty issues at stake, it is important that jurisdiction is exercised in a careful and deliberate way. Tribal governments and the Department of Justice will be called upon to defend the law in federal courts when a non-Indian defendant files a writ of habeas corpus as is his right under the law. If tribal governments are successful in these cases, then perhaps that will pacify some of the critics who perceive tribal courts as inferior. In 2014 the Pascua

Yaqui Tribe became the first tribal nation since 1978 to prosecute a non-Indian for beating his intimate partner. Despite all of the anti-VAWA rhetoric suggesting that tribal courts would not be fair, the Pascua Yaqui jury acquitted.

Conclusion

TLOA and VAWA are built on the blood, sweat, and tears of Native women and their allies, and these laws prove that change can come on the national level. While much of the legislation is focused on the relationship between the federal government and tribal nations, it has brought about significant changes to tribal authority that have immense symbolic value and great potential for practical safety for Native women. Much more remains to be done, however. VAWA and TLOA do not go far enough. To truly end rape in Native America, Congress needs to return full jurisdiction to tribal governments and support the infrastructure of tribal governments to provide justice for rape survivors.

EIGHT

Toward an Indigenous Jurisprudence of Rape

But to speak, at whatever the cost, is to become empowered rather than victimized by destruction. In our tribal cultures the power of language to heal, to regenerate, and to create is understood.

—Joy Harjo, *Reinventing the Enemy's Language*

SUPPOSE A CONGRESSIONAL MIRACLE OCCURRED, and in an instant, complete tribal jurisdiction was restored to its precolonial status with no restrictions. Tribal nations suddenly had the power and resources to respond effectively to rape. What would these systems look like? Would they mirror the state and federal systems? It is one thing to identify and quantify rape as a problem and pinpoint its origin and the extent of its harm. It is quite another thing to craft a system that does not perpetuate the weaknesses of the system it is seeking to replace. Tribal leaders and advocates have long expressed concern over the lack of response to rape, but we have not done enough to develop our own strategies for responding to this violence.

In this chapter, I explore the potential for tribal law to transcend the harmful shackles of American rape law. I am particularly interested in developing theoretical foundations that would underpin an indigenous jurisprudence of rape. I do not suggest we strive for a utopian, rape-free world where rape never happens, but rather a world in which rape is taken seriously, perpetrators are held accountable, and victims are made whole. To develop a contemporary system that meets the needs of today's tribal nations, we must fundamentally interrogate the crime of rape as an indigenous legal concept. A legal theory provides a foundation for a system's legal responses because it explains *why* the act itself is wrong.[1] In the past, the tribal approaches to justice have been ignored, dismissed, defamed, or even outlawed. So as Native people think about rape as a legal wrong, we may unearth some powerful truths. This chapter has two goals: to focus on the shortcomings of existing rape theories and to present an alternate theoretical approach that could serve as a starting point for developing a tribal-specific approach to thinking about legal theory in the context of particular language, culture, and traditions. Native women need community awareness and accountability for sexual violence at the local level, preferably framed in a culturally relevant way. Some tribal nations do not currently have written rape laws, for example. For all nations, defining and executing laws to protect women and children are central to the conception of sovereignty. The issue involves more than protecting individuals from harm; at stake are the safety and well-being of the entire community. The strength of the anti-rape sentiment in a tribal government will illuminate the strength and resolve of the entire community.

There is a certain degree of freedom in drafting a new criminal law from scratch. States started with extremely patriarchal rape laws in the nineteenth century and did not begin true reform until the 1970s. Reform has been a slow process, requiring a lot of political capital for even nominal improvements in the law. State and federal anti-rape policy efforts almost always include advocating for a legislative change in criminal law, which suggests that the process of fixing the law is not yet complete. Questions have even been asked about whether the American rape law reform movement has actually improved the system for the better.[2] Instead of reforming a dysfunctional existing law, a tribal nation is in the position of crafting an entirely new approach because of its independent sovereign status. It is through this process of thinking "outside the box" that tribal nations may actually be in the position of truly implementing some of the most radical changes in the world. Tribal law thus can have something to teach all legal systems about how to approach the issue of rape. While I'm not suggesting that non-Natives appropriate ceremonial or cultural property of tribal nations, there may be some universal aspects of the legal terminology we use along with emerging medical topics such as the neurobiology of trauma that could inspire changes in a much broader sense. As historian Sylvana Tomaselli explains, "We must *think* our own way to the end of rape, without a legacy, be it utopian or reformist, to draw from."[3]

To develop an effective contemporary response to rape at the tribal level, it is first necessary to deconstruct the American definitions of rape and develop an independent legal framework to address sexual violence. Native people need to develop an independent construction of legal wrongs as well as culturally appropriate sanctions. The resulting statutory construction may look significantly different from the American model, insofar as it frames the issue from a particular Native community's perspective. There will not be a singular response to sexual violence; instead, each tribal government must develop its own unique response to the crime of rape, although dialogue among tribal nations may be helpful in this regard.

Building a culturally specific response to rape may require starting from scratch. It is not enough to take a non-Native curriculum or legal structure and "tribalize" it. Programs should ideally start from a tribal-centric perspective. What did our ancestors do to honor women? What kind of impact has history had on the treatment of women in our community? How has colonization affected the kinship relations in this community? Ultimately, it is impossible to separate theories about indigenous self-determination from theories about rape jurisprudence.

Why Is Rape Wrong?

I think it is actually worthwhile to begin with the question "why is rape wrong?" It may seem like an obvious question to ask, perhaps even a dangerous question to ask. What sane, rational person would even consider this a matter for debate? If we ask why rape is wrong, we usually think immediately upon the harm that the crime does to its victims. Rape is wrong because a perpetrator attacks a woman or child at her core identity as a human being. Rapists treat victims with disregard and disrespect by committing violent, terrifying, humiliating attacks. But rape is also an attack on the community. If rape were merely an individual experience, then perhaps a simple civil remedy would suffice. Criminal justice systems are predicated on harm to the larger society. Taking this principle seriously means that we have to ask difficult questions about why rape harms everyone.

By acknowledging and integrating historical trauma into contemporary legal responses, tribal governments can better mete out justice for survivors. This chapter sets forth some preliminary issues and perspectives for the development of indigenous models of rape jurisprudence and visions for the development of a contemporary jurisprudence of rape for indigenous nations. Because I advocate for an indigenous theory of rape, I provide more connections and parallels between colonization and rape in this chapter.

However, a more foundational reason exists for critiquing the status quo response to rape in Indian country. State and federal governments cannot address the unique spiritual and emotional issues that arise in the context of rape. A woman's ability to seek justice in her own community can facilitate healing and emotional wellness, and this is why it is important to develop independent legal remedies. It is clear that Native women are particularly vulnerable to rape in contemporary society, and this vulnerability has a significant negative impact on women's lives and Native communities. Therefore, the lack of an effective response is actually feeding into the cycle of repeat offenders and victims. Contemporary tribal laws and policies do not necessarily reflect strong anti-rape sentiment, and much work will need to be done to reclaim the legal philosophy that once served to protect and honor women. Developing legal theory that is grounded in indigenous women's perspectives will lay the foundation for establishing widespread social change in tribal nations.

Unfortunately, legal scholarship has not kept up with the emerging needs of communities and indigenous anti-violence advocates and activists who are working daily to address the crisis in their local communities. The academic community has certainly not neglected the subject of rape more generally—rape is the topic of hundreds of law review articles. Historians have published lengthy volumes examining rape in different cultures and eras. In recent years, more attention has been paid to the failure of the federal system in responding to rape. However, very little has been written about the *tribal* legal response to rape.[4]

The legal academy does not adequately address the rape of Native women. In many ways, the legal response to the rape of Native women has been invisible in legal, social, and historical discourse. Native women have often been left out of many contemporary studies of the intersection of race or ethnicity and rape. Although feminist scholarship has provided critical theories for the analysis of rape law generally, it has not sufficiently addressed the experiences of Native women. On the other hand, indigenous legal scholarship often fails to address gendered violence in a substantive way. Legal discussions regarding the injustices and inequalities suffered by indigenous people rarely mention rape. There are dozens (perhaps hundreds) of articles and reports about historic mistreatment and federal policies that do not even mention women, gender, sexuality, or rape; articles and reports that detail the atrocities against Native people focus on slavery, ethnocide, land theft, forced removal, and genocide yet fail to mention rape. Until recently, most of the scholarship about tribal law never mentioned gendered crime. We must employ a dual analysis in both disciplines because rape is deeply embedded in colonizing and genocidal policies.

Scrutinizing Contemporary Tribal Law

Tribal leaders and tribal justice systems have a central role to play in responding to rape. To adequately address community needs, an indigenous response to rape should reflect the historical context of rape as well as the contemporary realities of tribal court systems and rates of violence. A review of historical, anthropological, and sociological records may provide some foundations for beginning the important discussion regarding why and how contemporary indigenous nations should respond to rape.

Some tribal nations do not have written rape laws, for example. Therefore, there is a certain degree of freedom and liberation in drafting a new law. Rather than "copy and paste" a dysfunctional existing statute from state or federal law, a tribal nation is in the position of crafting an entirely new approach. Such fundamental reform is nearly impossible at the state level, where change can only be achieved in incremental steps; it is unusual for a state government to engage in wholesale reform of criminal code.

We cannot re-create the past, and it would be a mistake to think that precolonial systems of support and respect will organically emerge from the restoration of jurisdiction. Reaching back five hundred years for systemic solutions is futile in both form and substance. Rather, the efforts should be grounded in a contemporary understanding of the crime, informed and contextualized by historical analysis. I agree with Osage scholar Robert Warrior, who explains that the source of indigenous survival "has always been predicated not upon a set of uniform, unchanging beliefs, but rather upon a commitment to the groups and the groups' futures."[5] Some tribal traditions simply do not fit in today's world (such as corporal punishment meted out to rapists among the Mvskoke people in 1825) and will need to be fundamentally restructured.

The Relevance of Colonialism

For Native survivors of rape, the individual experience must be understood in the historical context of colonialism and conquest.[6] The power of women's sexuality, because of its potential to affect reproduction and identity, is often a target of those seeking to destroy a people.[7] Rape is often linked to conquest and genocide precisely because of its effect on reproduction.[8] The role of a woman as a mother was often a critical component of identity within most indigenous communities.[9] The history of colonization in America includes numerous references to the motherhood of indigenous women. Widespread rape also affected fertility and birthrates. Priests and missionaries recorded that Native women chose to induce abortions or otherwise restrict their fertility in communities where rape had become commonplace. Sarah Winnemucca, a Paiute leader, wrote in 1883, "My people have been so unhappy for a long time they wish now to disincrease, instead of multiply. The mothers are afraid to have more children, for fear they shall have daughters, who are not safe even in their mother's presence."[10]

It is within this context that tribal nations must respond to rape—with a balance of historical insight and contemporary presentation. This legacy of rape must be explored and documented in order to reclaim authority and understanding about the contemporary context in which rape occurs.

The impact of rape on an individual can be compounded by the influence of this historical trauma, and the survivor may experience a rape as part of a larger policy to silence, disempower, and ultimately destroy her nation.[11] Because rape has been used as a tool of genocide, the psychological impact can be one of ultimate destruction—even if the perpetrator is Native as well. For a Native survivor, then, relying on an external jurisdiction to provide a resource for healing and justice may feed into that sense of destruction. The pursuit of justice might only be appropriate and logical in the context of her own people and traditions. The harm done by rape is a microcosm of the harm done by colonization. Because of the sense of possession and displacement, the psychological impact of rape can parallel the psychological impact of colonization. Thus, developing a contemporary tribal response to rape can be essential to the process of decolonization.

Framing an Indigenous Perspective

An effective rape response in Indian country will not originate from a simple blending of tribal law with feminist theory. Given the unique nature and structure of tribal legal systems, and the unique relationship between colonization and sexual violence, developing an indigenous jurisprudence of rape requires deconstructing the male-centered, colonial, American model. Palestinian criminologist Nadera Shalhoub-Kevorkian offers some helpful guidance in this regard, noting that "copying models of intervention without in-depth examination of their applicability to a given social setting might not only inflict additional pain and problems, but might also imprison helpers in unrealistic and non-applicable theories and methods."[12] Simply replicating the American model without serious debate will fail to address the unique nature and context of rape as experienced by Native women. In other words, if tribal governments rely on American legal conceptions of rape as a model, the crisis may actually be exacerbated rather than alleviated. Therefore, we must avoid the development of new institutions that value and thrive on trauma as opposed to justice.

Reshaping and reclaiming tribal responses to rape will necessitate an exploration of two areas—substantive rape law (defining and criminalizing rape) and procedural law. In the substantive arena, an indigenous response to rape may require development and reform of contemporary tribal rape laws. In addition, tribal governments may wish to reevaluate the process and methods through which rape cases are adjudicated. Before the more specific statutory and procedural issues can be approached, however, it is important to establish a legal "theory" of rape that forms the basis of the response.

Legal philosopher Keith Burgess-Jackson has identified three contemporary legal theories of sexual assault: conservative, liberal, and radical.[13] The conservative theory, which is reflected in historic English and early American rape law, analogizes rape to a kind of "trespass to chattels," wherein the perpetrator (usually a man) appropriates and uses the property (usually a woman or girl) of another male.[14] The liberal theory constructs rape as a kind of "battery," wherein the perpetrator offends another person with unlawful touching.[15] The radical theory views rape as an illegal "degradation," wherein the perpetrator causes a lowering in the victim's status as a person in the larger society.[16]

While these theories are helpful in classifying most of the existing legal scholarship on rape, none of these theories is necessarily comprehensive in its explanation of the experience of rape victims. A new theory of rape is needed to fully articulate and honor the experiences of survivors.[17] Philosopher Laura Hengehold notes that

> the act of "defining" rape necessarily raises difficult questions, including . . . whether and how the individual's search for a "just" recovery should mirror a movement's hope for wider forms of social justice, and what conception of the traumatic event enables feminists to link the level of the political and that of the existential without assuming the role of "expert discourse" vis-à-vis the women they hope to empower.[18]

With these thoughts in mind, there is a need to consider a fourth category of rape law theory: an indigenous theory of rape. This indigenous theory transcends the limitations of the nonindigenous theories by conceiving of rape as an unlawful "invasion" of the body, mind, and spirit. This theory allows the resulting legal system to address the crime of sexual violence holistically—that is, as a crime against a person in the context of her entire self. Therefore, the theory could conceivably apply to any survivor of sexual violence—not just indigenous survivors. Where the liberal theory concentrates solely on the physical (body) aspect of the crime, and the radical theory concentrates solely on the social (political) aspect of the crime, this indigenous model allows the entire experience of the victim to be acknowledged. In short, rape is conceived of as a violation of a person's humanity.

As survivors of invasion on a massive and extended scale, tribal nations are in a unique position to develop this theory of rape in contemporary legal thought. As "survivors" of invasion, tribal legal systems can conceptualize the experience of survivors of rape in a way that would be difficult for the dominant legal system to do. Additionally, indigenous legal theory generally brings a more holistic approach to jurisprudence, compared to the American system, which compartmentalizes human experience.

An indigenous theory of rape will manifest itself differently for each tribal nation—therefore the accurate term would be indigenous "theories." Using unique history, language, and government structure, each nation may conceive of rape in slightly different ways. Identifying sources and foundations for building a discourse about the indigenous theories of rape is critical. The following section explores several possibilities for starting points in development of indigenous theories.

Tools for Developing a Tribalcentric Response to Rape

Contemporary tribal rape law will be most effective if rooted in tradition and grounded by a uniquely indigenous philosophy that understands the experience of rape on both a micro (individual) and macro (community) level. Many tribal nations have an abundance of resources from which to draw in developing a theory of rape. These resources include stories, history, language, and the shared experiences of community members. Below I discuss six possible resources for research and discussion by individual tribal nations attempting to address the appropriate response to rape.

Stories of Survivors

Seneca scholar Mishuana Goeman has written that that "stories are a narrative tool that must be part of Native feminisms."[19] These same stories are tools that must be part of rape reform. It is difficult to overstate the power of individual women's stories of surviving rape. Indeed, there are accounts of the power of a single woman's story to effect change within her tribal government.[20] Reclaiming and understanding these stories are critical in developing a meaningful legal structure that is responsive to the real experiences of contemporary indigenous women. The stories of survivors are stories of despair and pain but also of strength and survival.

Tribal legislatures interested in crafting new legislation about sexual assault may wish to convene a panel of survivors of sexual assault from the community. This panel can describe for tribal lawmakers how the current system(s) responded to the crime (if at all), and whether the current system is providing true justice. In addition, survivors could provide guidance to lawmakers regarding how the legal response can be developed in a victim-sensitive way. Keeping in mind that most tribal nations' constitutions provide Western-style protections for defendants, tribal nations should work with survivors and advocates to assure that victims' privacy, rights, and well-being are protected during any law reform efforts.

Native women's stories carry the truths about rape in Indian country. Rape is a theme found in poetry,[21] fiction,[22] and nonfiction written by Native women. The voices of women who have survived sexual violence can form the foundation of contemporary tribal responses to rape. Grounded in the reality of the individual horrors of the crime, Native women who choose to describe their experience and survival provide significant information about the appropriate legal response. These voices are continuations of the protests that began centuries ago. Listening to women's stories is in keeping with the ancient tradition of considering a woman's perspective as a separate entity. This school of thought does not deny that men can be victims of sexual violence, but it does acknowledge the value of learning and teaching from a gendered perspective. Given that women in many tribal cultures have unique and specific roles, it follows that they may have unique and specific legal knowledge about rape. It is not unusual for women to have particular unique knowledge that is specific to the experiences of women.[23]

A point of caution: women should not feel pressured or obligated to share their story in a public forum unless and until they are ready. At times, the American anti-rape movement has suggested that survivors must "break the silence" or that they otherwise have political obligations to pursue justice for all rape victims. Given that many Native women have chosen silence as a true means to survival, the choice not to speak out must be honored as much as the choice to speak out. Rape is the manifestation of removing choice and should not be perpetuated in the quest for justice. Stories are the intellectual property of the survivors.

Historical Anti-Rape Activism

Contemporary tribal nations can also draw upon the strengths of historical leaders who have spoken out in protest against rape. Records of indigenous perspectives on sexual assault are found in the writings and speeches of historical figures such as Sarah Winnemucca and Yankton Dakota Chief Struck-the-Ree.

Sarah Winnemucca was a Paiute activist in the late nineteenth century. In her 1883 autobiography, *Life among the Piutes,* Winnemucca wrote about specific instances of sexual violence against women in her community. This book is the first nonfiction work published by a Native woman in the United States and is a compelling documentation of the experience of Paiute people in the mid- to late nineteenth century. In no uncertain terms, Winnemucca blamed ugly and sinister colonial brutality for the widespread occurrence of rape in her community. For example, in one passage about her childhood, Winnemucca recounts an experience in which her mother and aunt actually buried her in the dirt and covered her with plants to hide her from violent settlers. "Oh," she wrote, "can any one in this world ever imagine what were my feelings when I was dug up by my poor mother and father?"[24]

While Winnemucca was not focused solely on the issue of rape but colonialism more generally, it is worth noting that frank and graphic discussions of sexuality were almost unheard of in mainstream American society at the time her book was published. Winnemucca shared these horrific experiences with the world in the Victorian era when no one—even white women's rights advocates—was safe to discuss matters related to sexuality. In that sense, Winnemucca's bravery and honesty are inspirational. Winnemucca's story is one reason I bristle when I hear presenters say that anti-rape activism in the United States started in the 1970s.

Winnemucca's story is well known and accessible because her words were documented by a mainstream publisher. No doubt stories of bravery like that of Sarah Winnemucca are accessible via oral tradition or tribal archives at the local level throughout Indian country. Inquiring as to the history of this kind of activism by Native women provides two tools for developing an indigenous jurisprudence of rape. First, these histories can provide encouragement and solace to those engaged in the very hard work of responding to sexual assault. Second, they offer a glimpse at how tribal nations were forced to respond to violence as it happened, using tools that might be relevant today. Native men have also played a role in responding to rape, and those stories also deserve to be uncovered and retold. One example is Yankton Dakota leader Struck-by-the-Ree, who testified in front of Congress in 1867 about how U.S. soldiers were forcing the women of his nation to provide sexual favors for food and clothing.[25]

These historical figures provide contemporary tribal nations with a sense of continuity and leadership in the resistance to sexual violence. Clearly, for leaders such as Winnemucca and Struck-by-the-Ree, rape was not acceptable or tolerable in any form. Each indigenous culture has its own historical figures, legends, or writings that can be incorporated into the contemporary understanding. There is ample evidence that rape has traditionally been defined as criminal behavior by tribal nations. Many tribal nations, though, are struggling with the incorporation and codification of traditional beliefs into the contemporary legal systems.[26] One method of incorporating traditional beliefs into the contemporary context is to engage in a rigorous examination of tribal oral histories, anthropological and linguistic studies, and interviews with tribal elders.[27]

Traditional Beliefs and Oral Traditions

Stories, ceremonies, and spiritual teachings have always played a central role in indigenous responses to crime.[28] When determining the best way for any particular community to respond to sexual violence, it may be beneficial to revisit some of these stories and beliefs. For example, many cultural beliefs include strong social sanctions against certain kinds of sexual behavior, such as incest. Shame and ostracism often are associated with perpetrating sexual crimes, such as the philosophy among the Apache that a rapist "does not even deserve to be called a man, a human being."[29] Traditionally, women passed on information concerning sexual matters through stories, ceremonies, and songs. The loss of these practices (through criminalization of tribal spiritual and cultural practices) has meant a greater vulnerability to exploitation and victimization. Sexually explicit stories often addressed issues of inappropriate, abusive, or criminal conduct, and may still have value today. Written records and/or English translations are not often recommended as valid sources of information. In many tribal cultures, the most sacred laws are passed down through oral traditions in the tribal language, and it would be inappropriate to condense them to written words or to render them into other languages. Sometime the traditional response to rape was quite simple and straightforward: "The Clan mother explained that traditionally a violator of women would have suffered severe consequences for his crime. This punishment would have been carried out by the women of the community."[30]

Accounts of rape and the traditional response can be found in numerous oral traditions and histories; sometimes they are not obvious and may not be apparent to legal theorists or contemporary tribal attorneys. The following examples are but a few of the accounts I have discovered in researching the issue of rape in indigenous thought. I do not presume to articulate a fully accurate interpretation of these accounts; rather I provide them as examples of how research and dialogue can happen within each tribal community as the governments reclaim their jurisdiction over crimes of sexual violence against women.

ANI-KUTANI (CHEROKEE)

Cherokee traditions describe the Ani-Kutani as a class or clan made up of very powerful individuals from an ancient era of theocracy.[31] It is not clear exactly when the Ani-Kutani existed, but they are almost always described as a family or clan that exerted great spiritual power and control over others. Most accounts of the Ani-Kutani refer to an incident or incidents of sexual impropriety against one woman or several women in the community. This inappropriate sexual behavior instigated a revolt against everyone who was associated with Ani-Kutani. Every last member of the Ani-Kutani was slain, and today the clan or group is extinct.

The story of the Ani-Kutani may provide powerful lessons and guidance for indigenous nations today. First, there is a clear understanding that rape stems from an abuse of power and dominance. The clan members, who were once revered leaders, began to abuse and manipulate their power for personal gain. Second, the extermination of the Ani-Kutani provides a warning and lesson for those who would commit such crimes; in violating women, the perpetrator jeopardizes not only his own life and liberty but also that of his clan. Depending on the particular interpretation and methodology, a story such as this could have profound influence on the development of contemporary sexual violence jurisprudence.

TALE OF THE RAPED MAIDEN (OJIBWE)

An Ojibwe tale, published in 1906 by an anthropologist, is an empowering story of the worth and value of women.[32] The story was told by an Ojibwe elder named Mrs. Chatfield in 1894. The main protagonist in the story, an Ojibwe woman, was raped by members of a warring tribe. In the aftermath of the rape, this woman becomes revered among her own people, becoming both a medicine woman and a warrior. She is clearly held up to be a strong and powerful woman.

This imagery of the survivor of rape in this story is in sharp contrast to many widely held Western beliefs about women who have been raped as stigmatized, shamed, or soiled. Building a legal response on the strengths and power that women survivors of sexual violence bring to their community will provide safety and accountability. It also addresses the profound shame and embarrassment that stems from an Anglo construction of rape law, in which a virgin is defiled. As one Ojibwe traditional healer noted, the dominant cultural view is that society needs to protect women because they are weak.[33] This story and other teachings demonstrate that the "Indian way is to protect women because they are strong."[34]

TAA'II' TI' AND THE RUSSIANS
(GWICH'IN ATHABASCAN)

This story originates from Alaska and was recorded by Johnny Frank in 1971; it was later transcribed, translated, and published by the Alaska Native Language Center at the University of Alaska

Fairbanks.[35] This story describes a tribal leader's response to rape perpetrated by outsiders, although it is not clear from the text when and where the incidents occurred. The story centers on the leader of the village, Taa'ii' Ti', and how he responded to the molestation of community women by Russian sailors. The Russians who sexually abused the women in the village were warned about their behavior, and when they continued, Taa'ii' Ti' killed all but four of the men. This story shows not only the gravity of the crime but also the immediate and swift response to the victims and the importance of strong leaders. The assertion of jurisdiction over the non-Indian Russians also shows the strong inherent sense of sovereignty—and the importance of authority over outsiders.

Beginning a Respectful Conversation

Articulating specific anti-rape sentiments will be difficult and challenging for many communities. The intellectual exercise of developing a theory of jurisprudence of sexual assault is rational and unemotional—but the subject matter itself is intensely and overwhelmingly personal.[36] Because sexual violence has been so pervasive and yet so hidden in most tribal communities, initial attempts to construct a conversation about the appropriate response to rape may result in highly emotional and painful discussions. This phenomenon, I contend, is absolutely vital and necessary to a long-term plan for the development of a contemporary response to rape. Beginning the conversation in communities where silence has been the norm for more than a century may raise such painful feelings among members of the community that old addiction and/or suicidal thoughts are triggered. This reality should be anticipated and there should be a plethora of victim advocates ready to provide confidential support.

For instance, the impact of rape is so damaging that even the drafters of a new tribal law on rape may have much processing and healing to do themselves before they can address the topic in a clear and empowering way. There is also the reality that perpetrators may also hold positions of leadership and influence.[37] Because of these circumstances, ceremonial and traditional healers may need to be at the forefront of the discussion about rape law reform at the tribal level.

In many tribal nations, it is likely that generations of rape survivors have remained silent about their experiences and that many perpetrators have gone unpunished. Denial and secrecy have incredible power over victims.[38] Therefore, it is critically important that local, indigenous grassroots women's advocates be a central part of the dialogue. Women's advocacy programs, especially those grounded in grassroots organization, can provide support and encouragement for survivors of rape, and a voice for those who cannot speak.

Women's advocates bring other skills to the table as well. For example, advocates have unique perspectives on the current legal response to rape and can give feedback about weaknesses in the system. They also may have more accurate statistics on rape in a particular community. It will be difficult, if not impossible, for tribal communities to address rape head-on without the inclusion and leadership of such advocacy programs.

Conclusion

Protecting and supporting the citizenry is a central component of sovereignty. Native women cannot depend on external systems of justice to provide justice and accountability for the high rates of rape they experience. Therefore, tribal governments must make efforts to restore and strengthen their ability to address these crimes. Contemporary indigenous leaders have worked tirelessly to reclaim and redefine what it means to be a sovereign nation, but the pervasiveness and destructive power of sexual violence against Native women continue unabated. Perhaps it is at the intersection of federal Indian law and rape law reform that community solutions will become better illuminated. Part of decolonizing the mind and body is to send a message that as tribal nations we will no longer tolerate the invasion of our communities through the violation of our grandmothers, our clan mothers, our life givers, our sisters, or our daughters—by outsiders or by those within our communities. As sovereign nations, we must look to our histories, beliefs, resources, and experiences to reclaim safety and empowerment for all women.

NINE

The Trouble with Peacemaking

False Dichotomies and the Politics
of Restorative Justice

Healing . . . is a dangerous thing to promise and a difficult thing to assess.
—Annalise Acorn, *Compulsory Compassion: A Critique of
Restorative Justice*

GIVEN THE MANY FAILURES of the American legal system to
provide justice for survivors of rape, it is not surprising that victims might seek alternatives to the criminal justice system. One
commonly referenced proposed solution to violent crime in Indian
country is to develop or revitalize traditional dispute resolution
forums to address criminal behavior. In this chapter, I deploy the
word *peacemaking* as a shorthand way to refer to a wide array of
dispute resolution processes that are based on tribal principles of
balance and harmony. Not all tribal governments refer to their process as "peacemaking" per se, but the term is a useful label for this
philosophical approach to resolving problems. There are a variety of models of tribal peacemaking in the United States, the best
known being the Navajo (Diné) Nation Peacemaking Courts. Diné
Peacekeeping jurisprudence is predicated on traditional Diné values, including specific teachings and ceremonies that are directed by
a "peacemaker"—someone with knowledge of cultural values and
stories that are used to instruct the parties on returning to balance.

Peacemaking offers a striking alternative to the American civil
legal system. Instead of relying on a zero-sum game with one winner and one loser, the peacemaking philosophy focuses on repairing

relationships through the airing of grievances and facilitated discussion. This approach is known in the American system as "alternative dispute resolution" and is often staffed by attorneys known as "mediators" or "neutrals." There is ample evidence that a non-adversarial approach is an appropriate and innovative avenue for seeking resolutions to disputes concerning child custody, employment or property, probate matters, and juvenile delinquency. The application of peacemaking or ADR to violent crimes such as rape is quite controversial, however.

We must be careful when applying peacemaking to rape. I have noticed a tendency to romanticize the peacemaking process as one that can "foster good relationships" and heal victims.[1] In this chapter, I critique some of the literature that describes the use of these methods in the context of rape. In doing so, I do not mean to conclude categorically that peacemaking can never provide justice for victims or accountability for perpetrators. Instead, I seek to offer cautionary notes on the assumption that replacing an adversarial system with a restorative system will yield guaranteed justice for survivors of rape. Sometimes, in a rush to reject the harms that have been inflicted by American justice, there is an understandable impulse to try something that seems more in line with tribal belief systems. There is no particular reason to assume, however, that restorative justice practices automatically honor women's experiences, and it would be a mistake to apply such practices to rape without rigorous interrogation.

Because an adversarial model and a restorative model seem, at first glance, incompatible, there may be a tendency to reject one approach in favor of the other. As I will explain later in this chapter, it may be possible to blend elements of the systems with a survivor-centric focus. Rape is more than a violent crime; it can be described as "soul murder." Extreme caution is warranted to ensure that a peacemaking or restorative approach does not replicate traditional Anglo-American constructs of victim blaming, shame, and secrecy. Any model that avoids naming and establishing rape as a political (or even gendered) crime will likely fail to fully address the inequities faced by contemporary Native women. One of the potential weaknesses of an approach like restoration/restorative justice is the assumption of some degree of preexisting equality between the parties—and clearly a rape survivor and her perpetrator are at unequal places. Moreover, since the goal of Navajo Peacemaking is "reconciliation of the parties in dispute," a victim of sexual assault may feel as though she has failed if she has not "made peace" with her rapist.[2]

The Perils of Applying Peacemaking to Accusations of Rape

Many restorative justice scholars and practitioners have concluded that peacemaking and other restorative models are never appropriate in cases of gendered violence.[3] However, the book *Navajo Nation Peacemaking* (2005) describes the use of peacemaking approaches to respond to rape that lack a victim-centered perspective. I quote these passages at length because they highlight some serious concerns about using this system in response to rape.

> An Indian Health Service (IHS) psychologist who specialized in the treatment of sex offenders called the Office of the Chief Justice for assistance. He explained that he operated a special program for sex offenders and that a Navajo abuser had reported himself to it. The man had dropped his denial, and the IHS official felt that peacemaking would be an effective means of dealing with his sexual abuse. Arrangements were made for a referral to peacemaking, with protections of confidentiality, given the likelihood that the Federal Bureau of Investigation did not know about the underlying crime.[4]

From a rape survivor's perspective, there are at least two significant problems with this account. First, there is no evidence that the man's victim (or victims) were willing or able to go to Peacemaking. (Note that the victims are not even mentioned in this passage.) Second, while bypassing law enforcement may benefit the offender, the lack of accountability for perpetrating rape may endanger both the victim and the community at large. This tendency to protect the offender from the "white man's system" without an alternative response is dangerous, as it can lead to further victimization. The passage in *Navajo Nation Peacemaking* regarding sex offenses continues:

> This [using peacemaking methods in sexual abuse cases] is a controversial subject that is clouded by the anger that sex offenses generate,

leading to a lack of focus on solutions. While James W. Zion, one of the co-editors of this book, was teaching a Navajo common law course, a student who was a lawyer asked his opinion about a case in which the child was being sexually abused but the lawyer did not know if the abuser was the child's father or maternal grandmother. He asked how peacemaking would address such a case. Zion explained that he had seen a similar case in which the family, with the assistance of the peacemaker, had put the problem on the table in the hope that the ensuing discussion would prompt a confession. The lawyer then asked what would happen if neither admitted it. In the case that Zion was citing, the family isolated the child from both people and made sure the child was never alone with either. The lawyer expressed his amazement at the simplicity of the approach and said that he has been so focused on the notion of identifying and punishing the wrongdoer that he had not thought about simply protecting the child in the future.[5]

Again, this passage has several alarming aspects. First, the child's victimization is framed as a family conflict instead of a violent crime. There is no evidence that the isolation approach acknowledges the psychological harm suffered by the child, and simply isolating suspected sex offenders from a child does not directly address the underlying criminal behavior. Perpetrators of sexual assault are not limited to physical abuse but often exert emotional, intellectual, and spiritual power over their victims. The physical isolation proposed as a solution in this scenario does not address these fundamental violations because there is no enforcement mechanism in place to prevent future harm. Furthermore, because the offender is not held accountable by the community, he or she is apparently free to commit offenses on other children. Keeping the crime a secret within the family hardly seems like a victim-centered response.

The second passage quoted also suggests that "anger" is somehow misplaced and inappropriate in regard to these cases (anger "clouds" the subject). While a thoughtful and deliberate approach to addressing rape is necessary and valuable, it is a disservice to survivors and their advocates to suggest that anger (not rape) is the real problem. From a survivor-centric perspective, emotions can and should be part of the process of reforming the system because anger after rape is justified, and with support from community members, anger can be channeled in productive ways. Consider the role of ceremony and poetry of Native rape survivors, such as Connie Fife (Cree):

> i am the one who was raped by
> my father then my uncle
> and spent years hiding then decided
> to change it all
> and used all my rage to castrate my
> memory of them
> and healed myself with love/
> I am the one who late at night screams and howls
> And hears voices answer/
> I am the one whose death was intended
> And didn't die[6]

It is disrespectful to the narrator of this poem to dismiss her anger as irrelevant or misplaced. Restorative justice is purportedly interested in the needs and rights of survivors; I submit that the expression of anger and rage is a valid contribution to the process. The expression of anger can conflict with the end goal of most tribal peacemaking programs, which is to restore relationships and mend the community. But survivors with legitimate anger may not be interested in having a relationship with their rapist. In that regard, it is important to consider the potential drawbacks to engaging in a relationship-building or relationship-repairing exercise.

Critics of using restorative practices in the context of violence against women point to several categories of concern, including safety, coercion, accommodation of offender's needs at the expense of the survivor's, and recidivism. These problems, of course, are also common features of the adversarial American criminal justice system, but replicating these problems using traditional approaches does not improve the experience of survivors. Therefore, each of these potential drawbacks merits separate and serious consideration, for collectively they can create an atmosphere that can ultimately lead to revictimizing a survivor of rape, as well as excusing the rapist's behavior, thus aggravating the vicious circle of victimization in tribal communities.

Dismissing Legitimate Fear

Rape survivors have a continuum of needs in the aftermath of assault, and each survivor's experience is different. A commonly expressed need, however, is the desire for safety. Safety (protection) provides a foundation for rebuilding a life with confidence that the danger has dissipated. Survivors may feel unsafe for a variety of reasons. Many survivors, for example, have well-justified fears about revictimization or retaliation, perhaps because they have been directly threatened with future harm. Physical safety is not the only concern; some survivors describe fear of the offender as implicating psychic and spiritual safety. If a peacemaking system is too informal or relaxed, it has the potential to replicate some of the troubling dynamics from the adversarial system (such as requiring the victim and perpetrator to sit in the same room as the crime is described in detail). Without establishing specific measures to provide some degree of separation between the victim and the defendant, peacemaking risks revictimizing the survivor by placing her in direct communication with the defendant. Requiring survivors to face their perpetrator in an informal, relaxed setting could trigger new trauma. Resolving the violence, if that is possible, is not only a matter of stopping future occurrences but also one of victim healing. If a crime victim does not feel safe in the forum, then the forum itself runs a risk of exacerbating the harm that has already been done.

A well-known Canadian model of using restorative justice for intrafamily sexual abuse, the Hollow Water model, has been the subject of much praise in the restorative justice literature. Hollow Water is a small Indian reserve in Manitoba with approximately 1,200 members. In the 1980s, several initiatives were launched to deal with the alarming rate of sexual abuse in the community and the corresponding high rates of alcoholism and incarceration. After numerous conversations about the high rates of sexual abuse in the community, local organizers created a system that would avoid or delay incarceration for offenders in favor of a restorative process. The formal thirteen-step protocol is known today as "Community Holistic Circle Healing" and involves a series of talking circles and ceremonies.[7]

One article indicates that Hollow Water operates on the premise that the only way an abused person can rebuild his or her life is to "expose his or her pain in the abuser's presence . . . [so that] the abuser actually feels the pain that he or she created."[8] This premise suggests that a survivor's well-being is predicated on the perpetrator's ability to empathize, a notion that could put tremendous pressure on a survivor. Not only must she describe the violation that happened to her but she is also, at some level, responsible for her perpetrator's response. In this regard, a survivor could experience some of the same dynamics as she would in an Anglo-American criminal trial—an exposure of the graphic, intimate details of a horrific experience without any guarantee of justice.[9] The Hollow Water model literature describes extensive support for the victim(s)—before, during, and after the Healing Contract.[10] However, this ultimatum ("your healing is dependent upon the offender's response") may still present a variety of safety issues. Since the process is oriented toward offenders and the focus is on avoiding incarceration, a survivor of rape may experience the system as flawed. These concerns about safety are closely linked to another aspect of revictimization—coercion.

Coercion and Shame

Because a peacemaking system may be deemed to be more "indigenous" than the American system, Native survivors may feel coerced into participating even if the system feels unsafe. Coercion is not always explicit; within the Navajo Peacemaking system, for example, all parties to a dispute must formally consent to the process. Presumably, a victim could decline to consent. There can be unofficial methods of pressuring and coercing a survivor to participate, however. Donna Coker, in her examination of Navajo Peacemaking as applied in domestic violence cases, writes that there have been "problems of coerced participation and inadequate attention to the victim's safety."[11] Mohawk scholar Dawn Martin-Hill explains how a traditional legal system can protect perpetrators:

> In a Haudenosaunee community, a woman's daughter was raped at a party. There were witnesses, and her mother sought justice for her

daughter, only to be approached by the local Peacekeepers and told not to go to the police. The Peacemakers told her that they would "handle it" and that if she went to the police, she would be a traitor to her Nation. When she inquired how they planned to deal with it, they told her that their solution was to put the perpetrator in a Sweat Lodge, "to teach him how to respect women." When she protested that this was not punishment for his crime, they told her, "It's not our way to punish, we much teach him."[12]

This focus on the offender's issues is a common problem embedded in restorative justice literature. In the Hollow Water model, each person (including, presumably, the victim) is required to "sign on" to the process.[13] This "Healing Contract" then binds the signers to a two- to five-year process. The literature does not indicate whether the victims have the opportunity to withdraw from the process. At the conclusion of the "Healing Contract," the "Cleansing Ceremony" is held to "honor the victimizer."[14] In my critique of this approach, I do not mean to insinuate that survivors of rape can never find solace in such a process. Certainly, the individual needs of survivors vary dramatically. Instead, I raise the concern that survivors may be pressured to participate in this healing process, which may put them in direct contact with the person who raped, terrorized, and humiliated them.

Pressure to participate in the "Healing Contract" may be implicit or explicit, but the literature indicates that the "alternatives are either looking the other way on rampant sexual abuse or having their people sent off to prison, which is another form of genocide."[15] The message to survivors, then, could be construed as "either participate in this process or send dad/grandpa/uncle to prison and participate in genocide." After researching a form of restorative justice in Canada known as "circle sentencing," Canadian scholar Charlene Levis has concluded that "determining whether the victim is really a willing participant is more problematic than we can know."[16] We must be cautious about manipulating victims to be "traditional."

The notion of "closure" may also present problems. Although the Hollow Water literature emphasizes that the process takes several years, there is a clear goal for a concluding ceremony. Many victims, however, continue to experience "new" symptoms as they age and go through different stages of life—and something could trigger a painful memory that needs to be addressed. Consider the experience of a twelve-year-old girl who has been raped by an uncle. Applying the Hollow Water philosophy and model, her uncle is brought before the circle and the process of making peace begins. The process ends when she is seventeen. Perhaps at that point the survivor feels satisfied and comforted that she and her family have experienced justice. However, just three years later, she becomes a mother for the first time. Attending a family reunion or ceremony, she suddenly has newfound fears and shame when she sees her uncle. She remembers the terror, but now from a mother's perspective. It is not clear that the Hollow Water model would allow a return to the process that had been ceremonially closed. Thus, the uncle may benefit from the ceremonial closure, but his victim's sense of justice may not necessarily be resolved. Rape is a violent act, not a mere dispute or misunderstanding. Accountability and responsibility are key elements of resolution—if a peacemaking system approaches violence with acceptance and compromise it may fail to provide true justice.

Eclipsing Accountability

Most peacemaking models are predicated on the notion that conflict is resolved through compromise, which is a logical approach to nonviolent disagreements about money, property, or employment. It is less clear that a compromise model is appropriate in the context of rape, which is much more damaging than a civil disagreement. A compromise model begins with an assumption that both parties share responsibility (if not for the crime, then for its resolution). Framing rape as an interpersonal conflict circumvents the larger issues of hierarchical power and control and therefore does not contribute to social change. Rape is not a matter of disagreement between sexual partners. It has been used as a means to control and subjugate women. Minimizing this reality benefits no one.

However, a focus on the macro problem in place of the micro problem will not always adequately address the larger context in which Native women experience rape. A tribal prosecutor once asked me, "Why would we have a traditional response to a nontraditional crime?" Rape does not happen in a vacuum; it is an individualized manifestation of a larger societal problem. The challenge, then, is to decolonize rape law by acknowledging this history without allowing perpetrators to minimize personal responsibility.

If peacemaking resembles mediation or negotiation, it has the potential to provide leniency in rape cases, providing excuses for a rapist's behavior. For example, if a rapist was mistreated as a child or has an alcohol and/or drug problem, he may be able to manipulate the peacemaking system into allowing him to excuse or mitigate his behavior. Many people are mistreated as children, however, but do not become rapists. Therefore, these excuses cannot and should not be tolerated in a contemporary tribal response.

Moreover, a mediation-like approach may open the door for the exploration of a particular victim's "culpability" in a rape case. For example, if the victim had substance abuse problems that the perpetrator exploited, a macro-level analysis runs the risk of framing the victim's "bad behavior" (alcoholism) and the perpetrator's "bad behavior" (rape) as equally undesirable products of colonization. In other words, we are all victims of colonization in the same way—perpetrators and victims alike. In this regard, an indigenous feminist analysis can provide some important jurisprudential distinctions that elevate rape above other social ills without abandoning the historical analysis. As Plains Cree Métis scholar Emma LaRocque notes, "Political oppression does not preclude the mandate to live with personal and moral responsibility within human communities."[17] All of us have experienced colonization; not all of us rape.

Recidivism—When the Rapist Reoffends

Restorative justice models also run the risk of avoiding the topic of recidivism—repeat crimes or cyclical patterns in the lives of offenders. One central question is whether a system is truly able to respond to reoffenders—especially if there has been a public acknowledgment or ceremony to respond to an earlier rape. For example, if peacemaking "fails"—and the rapist strikes again (with the same or a different victim), does the system have the capacity to do something differently to address the repeat offender? Consider the painful experience a victim might have if her perpetrator rapes again after a peacemaking process. Her disclosure that this person has continued to violate women and children has the potential to disrupt not only her life but also the entire community that may have supported the offender's reintegration. This scenario could be exacerbated if the process were closely intertwined with spiritual or ceremonial benchmarks.

The Fatal Flaw of Peacemaking: Confronting Denial

A lingering fatal flaw in applying peacemaking models in response to rape is that there is typically "no fact-finding mechanism in restorative justice."[18]

Most restorative justice models do not hold themselves out to be fact finders—indeed, quite the opposite. The peacemaking system is therefore based on confession of some kind. Victims of perpetrators who categorically deny any wrongdoing will not see accountability. The premise of the adversarial justice system is admittedly problematic for myriad reasons, including the focus on hierarchical power structures and the inevitability of winner versus loser outcomes. Proving the rape happened in the face of absolute denial sometimes requires a review of scientific evidence, eyewitness reports, and law enforcement testimony, and restorative justice does not accommodate such disputes. I have found that very few studies about restorative justice have adequately confronted the problem of fact-finding. The process cannot work without some level of acknowledgment by the accused; especially since the denial in some tribal communities runs deep.

The Perils of Applying Western Law to Accusations of Rape

My critique of tribal peacemaking should not be confused with an endorsement of the American adversarial criminal justice system. The American approach to gendered crime has been wholly inadequate, and its forced application in tribal communities has resulted in dysfunction and distrust of the legal system more generally.

As noted in chapter 2, American rape law has its roots in European property law. In this construct, women were conceived as the "property" of men—and rape was merely a trespass to chattels. Even today, the narrative and direction of a rape case in American law are dictated by the government, not the voices of the victimized women. Women's truths about rape are often lost in the American criminal justice system, a reality somberly described by political scientist Kristin Bumiller: "Even as stories unfold in the courtroom, the value of the 'facts' the court will call evidence has been predetermined by the social mechanisms that privilege certain forms of communication."[19] The American legal system has not been kind to white rape victims—much less women of color. Native women, by the nature of their marginalized status, will probably always struggle to find justice in a legal system that was originally designed to destroy their lives. The American criminal justice system certainly can never incorporate tribal customary (or "common") law that reflects Native values.

The American criminal justice system also relies heavily on incarceration as a response to violent crime. While removing a violent perpetrator from a community may be necessary to achieve immediate safety, many indigenous people are rightly concerned that long-term incarceration with no possibility of rehabilitation is not the solution to violent crime in Indian country. Native people—both women and men—are incarcerated at significantly disproportionate rates in the United States. It is also worth noting that the federal government rarely prosecutes rape unless it is committed on an Indian reservation (most rape cases are adjudicated at the state level). As a result, most of the sex offenders in federal prisons are Native, and there is little to no access to sex offender treatment programs in the federal prison system.[20] Offenders can be released from prison, free to return to their communities, and they may have become more dangerous during their time behind bars, especially when no treatment or rehabilitation programs are available in the prison system. This reservation-to-prison pipeline has done nothing to address the widespread trauma, and so we must think outside the law-and-order framework.

Transcending the Existing Models

Since rape can be conceived of as an individualized manifestation of colonization, perhaps tribal governments can address rape in the same way they approach the colonial process in general. Tribal nations have been coerced to adopt the legal methodology and philosophy of the colonial state in responding to violence. Taiaiake Alfred and Jeff Corntassel explain that indigenous people have been put in the untenable position of mimicking coercive practices of the colonial government, which results in "disconnection, dependency and dispossession."[21]

Instead of being trapped by a false dichotomy of choosing between the American adversarial model and the mediation-like peacemaking model, I want to encourage the restoration or revitalization of responses to rape that include elements of both retribution and restoration. Incorporating a unique indigenous vision for justice, tribal nations can develop a model that transcends both the male-dominated adversarial model of justice and the male-dominated peacemaking model. A long-term vision for radical change requires both immediate measures to address rape and a forward-looking effort to dismantle the culture of rape that has infiltrated tribal nations.

Social change work is central to the future of tribal nations. In a society in which at least one-third of Native women experience rape, only committed activism and action will lead to a reversal of this devastating trend. One of the principal sources of strength for Native women survivors of violence today is found within relationships and kinship circles. Historian Karen Anderson writes, "Women's power [traditionally] derived in large part from the actual structure of kin relations and residence patterns."[22] Reinstilling the importance of clan and family in the legal process will empower survivors and lessen the isolation and shame that so often accompany sexual violence. Integrating family responses to rape will necessarily result in social change. It should be noted, however, that family responses must be informed by Native women. Paula Gunn Allen describes one such scenario in her book *Off the Reservation:*

> Having failed to persuade the governing body to enact and enforce regulations combating violence against women, a number of older women banded together. When abuse of a woman occurred, the "aunties" confronted the abuser, chastised him, shamed him by making him aware that his mother, grandmother, aunts, nieces, and daughters knew about and condemned the abuse. In other words, the women of the community took total responsibility for ending

the crime that they recognized was directed against them all. They held men to the standard set by women, and by making community life woman-centered, their safety and that of the entire community was ensured. I hear that violence against women doesn't occur there anymore.[23]

Allen's description is at once both romantic and practical. It suggests a path that transcends the existing restorative model—a potential remedy for a community with a history of failed legal intervention. The perspective of rape survivors should be clearly articulated in any justice system purporting to offer justice to survivors of rape. These voices can and will guide communities in developing appropriate responses that take into account both safety and dignity for survivors. This is why community activism, survivor panels, and public education will continue to be part of responding to sexual violence. I encourage tribal communities that are contemplating, implementing, or revitalizing an alternative to the adversarial process to approach rape (and other forms of gendered violence) with particular caution. Some perpetrators are notorious for their ability to manipulate systems of accountability in their favor—and some are even able to convince the community that they have changed their ways in believable and sincere ways, only to continue perpetration at the same time. A reactionary approach to justice carries with it the same burdens as the problematic system itself. To adopt peacemaking for rape cases simply because the American system doesn't work falls short of true justice. Rape threatens the very existence of our nations. Responding to sexual violence is central to restoring and maintaining sovereignty as indigenous nations. Integrating ceremony, song, and stories into the legal process will encompass both safety and sovereignty, ultimately restoring the respect and dignity that rape has attempted to destroy.

TEN

"Righting" Tribal Rape Law
Proposals for Reform

SO FAR, this book has focused on two important themes: the harm of rape and the need for reform. This chapter is focused on practical nuts-and-bolts changes to written tribal law that should be considered when developing and revitalizing tribal rape law. Despite the barriers and restrictions on tribal authority imposed by federal law, tribal governments continue to have a responsibility to create and cultivate systems that respect and honor survivors of rape. Accountability for offenders can be a more difficult question because of the nature of many tribal belief systems regarding punishment, rehabilitation, and community responsibility. Nonetheless, it is evident that the federal and state systems (even if much improved) will not serve as the ultimate foundation for liberating tribal nations from the legacy of rape. Tribal laws themselves, grounded in the voices of survivors, will serve as the point of social change because true justice and healing are only possible when victims can seek accountability within their own judicial systems.

Using foundational theories such as the indigenous theory of rape discussed in chapter 8, tribal governments can make changes to their laws and policies to enhance the likelihood that survivors will feel safe and respected in coming forward. Maximizing sovereign authority by establishing a variety of legal remedies for rape will ideally provide victims of rape with a much wider array of options for achieving justice. Rape is the antithesis of choice and safety; justice is the restoration of choice and safety. The goal of reform is to develop a system in which survivors are believed, advocacy is readily available, and perpetrators are held accountable. In many ways, tribal governments have the capacity to draft and implement the most progressive and comprehensive laws in the world, in part because they are not necessarily limited by the precedent and the incremental reform that is usually required at the state and federal level.

I had the opportunity to develop some of the ideas in this chapter when I worked at the Tribal Law and Policy Institute between 2002 and 2008. During that time, I had a chance to learn about Hopi common law from Pat Sekaquaptewa, one of the cofounders of TLPI. She and the TLPI executive director, Jerry Gardner, had developed a process for helping tribal nations recognize and revitalize tribal solutions to social problems. Instead of starting with a state statute as a template, we encouraged tribal nations to spend time deliberately thinking about the kinds of laws they truly needed. We were invited to travel to tribal nations and spend a few intensive days of training and code development on a variety of issues, including child protection and family law. Together with my colleague and mentor Bonnie Clairmont, we developed TLPI "workbooks" for tribes seeking to draft or revise tribal laws and policies on gendered violence. The result was a series of workbooks that cover various topics, including rape and domestic violence (both civil and criminal remedies) that can be downloaded from the TLPI website (http://www.tlpi.org).

The information in this chapter builds on the content of those workbooks to establish a starting point for potential legal reform projects pertaining to rape. The suggestions will be applicable to every tribal government. It will be necessary to consider what reform projects will have the most impact. For example, if a tribal nation is not currently exercising criminal jurisdiction, it will make more sense to forgo criminal reforms in favor of civil reforms. This chapter includes recommended reforms to criminal law, civil law, and family law—and also has a section designed to facilitate compliance with the requirements of the 2010 Tribal Law and Order Act and the 2013 reauthorization of the Violence Against Women Act.

Reforming Tribal Criminal Rape Law

Responding to rape in the mainstream American legal system almost always concerns criminal justice, with arrest, prosecution, and conviction often forming the default vision of justice for victims. Statutory reform in the criminal context is an excellent starting point for tribal rape reform efforts because writing criminal law is one of the purest ways to present a tribal government's official definition of the behavior it seeks to address. Defining the crime sends a clear message about the expectations for respectful behavior in the community. Even survivors who choose not to engage with the criminal justice system can benefit from a clear directive in tribal law that defines their experience as a crime. It can be validating for a woman to know that the harm she has experienced is considered to be criminal behavior.

Although I have used the term *rape* throughout this book to encourage readers to think of all forms of sexual assault through a particular sociolegal lens, identifying the various actions I mean to capture by *rape* will likely require distinct definitions of the various crimes that run the continuum of sexual violence. For example, there may need to be separate statutory schemes for victims who are adults and victims who are children. The comprehensive set of definitions may also include a wide range of crimes such as indecent exposure, obscene phone calls/texts, and contemporary acts such as "revenge sexting"—sharing nude pictures of ex-girlfriends as a means to humiliate.

Rape prosecution in tribal courts is becoming more frequent and thus many tribal governments already have criminal statutes prohibiting a wide range of sexual crimes. Unfortunately, some of these tribal laws mirror language from state rape laws of the early to mid-twentieth century. Criminal provisions in many contemporary tribal codes date back to the Indian Reorganization Act[1] era, in which many federally recognized tribal governments adopted constitutions and laws that were heavily influenced by the American system via the Bureau of Indian Affairs. Many contemporary tribal criminal laws were adopted in the time of "boilerplate" or "model tribal codes"—wherein a generic law was simply adopted by a tribal council without modification. In the 1970s the Bureau of

Indian Affairs developed the "Model Code for the Administration of Justice by Courts of Indian Offenses," which was "nothing more than a redraft of the old Bureau regulations."[2] These problematic tribal codes are rarely inclusive of traditional tribal values and can present obstacles for a tribal prosecutor who is seeking to charge and prosecute sexual violence.

Moreover, some of the rape law reforms at the state level throughout the 1970s and 1980s have not yet been incorporated into the tribal rape laws.[3] One of the reasons these laws may not have been updated is that very few tribal nations actively prosecute sexual assault cases. While we are reforming federal law we also have to reform tribal law so that we can put the control back into the hands of the tribal governments in a very practical way. If jurisdiction is restored to tribal governments, tribes must be able to effectively prosecute those crimes, or very little changes for the lives of victims.

Common Weaknesses in Tribal Rape Law

The American legal model for rape (like all crimes) originated in English common law. In the American Model Penal Code, for example, rape is narrowly defined as "carnal knowledge of a woman, not one's wife, by force and against her will."[4] There are numerous problems with this approach, which resulted in an entirely flawed legal system that more often than not has blamed victims for the violence they suffered. First, the crime was gendered—only women could be victims; only men could be perpetrators, thus eliminating criminal protection for male victims and essentially legalizing sex crimes perpetrated by women.

This limiting language is still found today in some tribal rape laws, meaning that there is no recourse for male victims. In addition, laws written this way do not allow for accountability for female perpetrators, which is a relatively less common occurrence but still warrants criminalization. These gendered laws are particularly complicated in the context of Two-Spirit/LGBTQ tribal citizens who may experience sexual abuse from their partners but have no recourse under criminal law.

Second, the historical definition did not criminalize the rape of one's spouse. At common law, it was assumed that a wife, by virtue of marriage, had no legal standing to object to sexual behavior. It wasn't until the late 1980s that all fifty states criminalized spousal rape. Even today, some states continue to differentiate between spousal rape and other categories of rape, requiring a higher standard of proof in the marital rape context. Because many tribal laws were transplanted before the spousal rape law reform, some tribal rape laws today still contain a blanket spousal exemption, which prevents a tribal prosecutor from charging a man who rapes his wife.

Third, the historical definition, by requiring "carnal knowledge," limited its coverage to cases involving penile–vaginal penetration, which is a reinforcement of the gendered framework but also avoids the application of criminal law to acts other than sexual intercourse. This problem has largely been remedied in state laws that now define "sexual contact" or "sexual conduct" to include a wide range of acts in addition to penetration.

Fourth, and probably most important, the historical definition provided an almost insurmountable burden for the prosecution by requiring proof of force. In this antiquated framework, prosecutors (and victims) had to demonstrate extreme physical force, which usually required proof of extreme physical resistance. For example, the 1980 Texas rape law required that the victim "resist to the utmost" or with "such earnest resistance as might reasonably be expected under the circumstances." It was common for juries to acquit alleged rapists because the victim was not sufficiently injured, determining that she could not truly have been forced if she did not fight back. Physical force is, of course, uncommon in cases of sexual assault. Perpetrators generally use other kinds of nonphysical force, such as coercion and threats. In some tribal codes, there remains a requirement that the tribal prosecutor show physical force in order to secure conviction. Most states have reformed rape law such that lack of consent is sufficient to prove rape. So tribal laws that include a physical force requirement are really replicating antiquated Anglo-American rape law.

Suggested Definitional Reforms

As a tribal government considers reforming rape law, it may help to begin by brainstorming a list of specific behaviors it wishes to criminalize. Advocates and survivors are a critical part of this painful conversation—again, survivors are the experts in how the laws have or have not protected them. After the rape laws have been revised, revisit this list of behaviors and consider whether the draft has been written broadly enough to encompass each of the behaviors described on the list.

There is no such thing as the perfect rape law. There are, however, important conversations that can lead to a customized tribalcentric law that provides protection for a wide range of victims. In thinking about the burden of proof for a crime of sexual violence, the trend among victim-centered organizations is to focus on consent (or lack thereof). Focusing on nonconsent as an element of the crime will broaden the coverage of the law to include a variety of behaviors that are inconsistent with tribal principles. For example, consider the following situations in the context of "consent" and describe what a prosecutor should have to prove to secure a conviction.

- The victim is unconscious, drunk, stoned, or sleeping.
- The perpetrator is a boss, a police officer, a teacher, or a "so-called" or "self-described" spiritual leader[5] (or other person in authority).
- The victim doesn't actually say "no" but implies "no" through other words or behavior.
- Two people are engaged in sexual activity, but one person changes his or her mind and wants to stop or limit the extent of the activity.
- The victim is too young to consent.

These sample scenarios usually provide enough information to draft a rape law based on nonconsent. It can be difficult and emotional to hammer out the details, but the result can be a tremendous improvement over the standard boilerplate language.

Tribal legislation can also include purpose statements and findings preceding the language of the law that declare, in the strongest terms, the tribe's official position on rape. Consider the following: Rape has deeply damaged our nation. Rape is contrary to our tribal culture and traditions, and has always been treated as a significant violation of body and spirit. This rape law is intended to send the strongest message to our community that all rape charges are taken seriously and that survivors are honored and respected.

Criminal Penalties for Rape

This section is probably the most difficult and controversial section of the book. What do we do with men who have been convicted of rape? Native people will need to engage in an ongoing conversation about real-world consequences for those who rape women and children. Incarceration and fines have often been the focal point of tribal punishment because they are the most common sanctions imposed by the Anglo-American system—and limited by the Indian Civil Rights Act of 1968 (as explained in chapter 3). However, one of the most salient critiques of the American criminal justice system is the overreliance on punitive measures that are designed to ostracize and stigmatize offenders, leading to high rates of recidivism.

We also must acknowledge that many of the perpetrators who live in our communities had serious adverse occurrences in their childhoods. While their behavior may be partly explained by such experiences, they cannot serve as blanket excuses. I submit that appropriate punitive measures should be considered in the effort to break the cycle. If people are not truly held accountable through some kind of punitive system, it sends a strong message to future generations that the penalty for behaving in sexually abusive ways is counseling and ceremony. Survivors will be reluctant to come forward if the system does not seem to be sending a strong message that sexual abuse will be treated as a serious violation of the law. It is not punishment for the sake of punishment, but punishment for the sake of the well-being of the community and the safety of survivors.

It is very challenging to impose accountability on offenders— accountability that sends a strong message about a nation's intolerance for rape. The sad truth is that there are people who are walking around tribal communities with a history of brutal behavior that has never been addressed. Some of these offenders present a real threat to the community simply by being present—and they continue to damage the hearts of victims and their families. Unaddressed rape ostracizes and stigmatizes survivors in some circumstances; Native women have fled their reservation or village to escape the sights and sounds of abusers with power. Children have grown up without access to their sacred sites and traditional practices because it has been too dangerous for their mothers to stay.

Thus, stigmatization burdens both perpetrators and victims. A legal system grounded in nonviolence might seek to lessen stigmatization for victims and enhance stigmatization for offenders. This ostracisim/stigma for people who rape is not retribution for the sake of retribution. It is a way for a tribal government to proclaim its ultimate goal—which is to decrease rape. Anti-rape scholar Peggy Reeves Sanday notes that "as long as men are not accountable for their actions, women will be sexually abused." Emma LaRocque's writings explain this maxim in the Native context: "As long as offenders are defended in the name of culture, they will continue to avoid taking any personal responsibility for their actions. And this will only perpetuate the problem."[6]

INCARCERATION

Should tribal governments imprison sex offenders? Incarceration is a controversial approach to crime in most communities of color, for good reason. The prison system in the United States disproportionately imprisons people of color and has nearly destroyed some tribal nations through mass incarceration.[7] Is that a system we want to replicate? Moreover, there is little to no evidence of formal systems of incarceration in North American prior to European contact. Other sanctions were used to punish offenders and protect victims. The notion of incarceration is largely a foreign concept, only taking hold in tribal communities in the late nineteenth or early twentieth century, usually as a result of federal law enforcement agencies that were set up to punish Native people who practiced traditional ways. As tribal correctional facilities developed during the past century, they mimicked the problems of contemporary non-Native prisons and jails. A September 2004 report from the Bureau of Indian Affairs' Office of the Inspector General found serious safety concerns, as well as human rights violations, in multiple tribal jails.[8]

If incarceration is not a long-term solution, it may still be worth considering as a short-term solution for particularly dangerous offenders. But the broader question is whether such jails can ever be appropriate places for Native sexual assault offenders. Ideally, tribal jails could be reformed in such a way that they provide safety for communities, as well as accountability and rehabilitation for offenders. Tribal governments have only entered into the prison-industrial complex in the past few decades. There may still be time to rethink how containment can provide both safety and accountability. Some believe, however, that sex offenders cannot be rehabilitated. If this is the case, then tribal governments will have to continue to wrestle with the question of what to do once a sex offender has been identified and convicted.

BANISHMENT

Many tribal nations traditionally banished rapists from the communities. Sometimes banishment decrees were permanent, others were temporary (months or years). Many banishment orders were lifted after the offender complied with certain requirements. In contemporary settings, however, banishment does not carry the same significance as it once did. A rapist or pedophile who is "banished" may simply move to a new community and continue to perpetrate on other victims. A Native feminist model of justice must address the long-term consequences of sexual violence, keeping in mind the nature of predatory behavior and the likelihood of recidivism.

The Sac and Fox Tribe of the Mississippi in Iowa has devised a banishment law that covers a plethora of criminal activity:

Sac and Fox Tribe of the Mississippi in Iowa

Sec. 13–8202 Grounds for Banishment; Automatic Banishment

Any person shall be automatically banished, and the Tribal Council shall issue a banishment decree, upon conviction for knowingly or intentionally killing, or attempting to kill, a member of the Tribe, employee of the Tribe, or any person on the Settlement. A person may be banished by the Tribe for:

(a) Upon conviction for recklessly killing or attempting to kill a member of the Tribe, employee of the Tribe, or any person on the Settlement;

(b) *Upon conviction of raping or attempting to rape a member of the Tribe, employee of the Tribe, or any person on the Settlement;*

(c) Upon conviction of having sexual contact with, or attempting to have sexual contact with, a member of the Tribe or person on the Settlement who is less than 16 years old;

(d) Stealing or unlawfully retaining possession of tribal records or destroying tribal records without authorization;

(e) Upon conviction for manufacturing or distributing illegal drugs;

(f) Desecration of Meskwaki cultural or religious sites or artifacts;

(g) Repeatedly engaging in assault intended to inflict serious bodily harm, or which does inflict serious bodily harm to a member of the Tribe, employee of the Tribe, or any person on the Settlement, or repeatedly engaging in aggravated assault of a member of the Tribe, employee of the Tribe, or any person on the Settlement; or

(h) Conspiring with others to commit any of the acts stated above.

There are a number of issues to consider before settling on banishment as a remedy for rape. How will the banishment order be enforced? Will neighboring governments help to enforce the banishment order? Will there be ways to warn other tribes about the individual? Today's banishment looks quite different than it did in the nineteenth century—and the implementation of such sanctions will need to be carefully considered.

MEN'S REEDUCATION PROGRAMS

A common intervention for domestic violence in Indian country is to require offenders to participate in a batterer intervention program that is often customized to be relevant for tribal cultural beliefs. A BIP is a court-ordered intervention for men who are convicted of domestic violence; or sometimes required as part of a protection order, but a BIP is not a type of "treatment" program—perpetrators are taught to see substance abuse issues as independent from their violent behavior. The BIP is sometimes called a "men's reeducation program" because abusers are learning about healthy gender roles and the role of colonization in the lives of Native people. For example, a Native Hawaiian program known as Ke Ala Lōkahi (Pathway to Harmony) is a curriculum based on Native Hawaiian values, beliefs, and practices.

The curriculum is composed of twenty-four weekly, two-hour sessions with a culminating

48-hour session held at a cultural site. The curriculum is divided into four units or *mokuna*, each guided by a theme. The overall theme of the Natural Order of Balance is the binding force that holds each *mokuna* together. The curriculum uses cultural metaphors as the primary teaching method through which Hawaiian values and practices are imparted and connections made to non-violent, healthy behaviors. Program activities include Hawaiian crafts, chants, genealogy, ceremonies and visits to sacred places as the learning medium through which alternatives to domestic violence might emerge and evolve.[9]

A major challenge to developing tribal-centric intervention programs is the lack of available funding. Federal funding, for example, usually requires a focus on victim services. Perhaps new funding streams need to be made available to develop these reeducation programs.

ALTERNATIVES TO INCARCERATION

I have tried to consider tribal court penalties from the perspective of a Native woman who has been raped. What do survivors need and deserve, and what can courts be prepared to offer? There are a number of potential remedies that do not require expensive incarceration but could still provide a measure of safety and security to victims. For example, a tribal court might be authorized to issue lifetime/permanent orders of protection. These orders would require a perpetrator to stay away from his victim (and her family) under penalty of arrest.

While financial restitution to a rape victim may seem futile in many impoverished communities (it is not helpful for a victim to be "awarded" restitution from a man who will never be able to pay it), there may be more creative forms of restitution that tribal courts could impose. For example, the tribal court could require a perpetrator to provide material goods to the victim and her family, such as wood, meat, or fish. The principle of restitution is to restore the victim to her position prior to the rape. Given the trauma that victims and their family experience, there may be extra ceremonial needs that require attention, and this may interfere with subsistence hunting or other day-to-day necessities. Victims and their families need time to mend and adjust in the aftermath of rape. It makes sense that the attacker would bear at least part of that burden.

Rapists can be punished in ways that do not necessarily involve incapacitation. These penalties are admittedly retributive at some level, but would help send a message that rape is unacceptable.

For example, a system could cancel licenses and land assignments for those who violate the law. A more controversial proposal is to cancel per capita payments for convicted rapists; in the few tribal nations that have enjoyed financial success through gaming enterprises, such a law would certainly catch the attention of would-be predators.

Tribal laws might also address the status of offenders as inconsistent with leadership roles. A tribal law could be developed that automatically removed an elected leader from office for a rape conviction, and this rule could even be expanded to include all government jobs. A tribal nation can send a strong message that it will not employ people convicted of rape.

Public Defenders: A Critical Component of Rape Law Reform

Some mechanical provisions in the Tribal Law and Order Act and the Violence Against Women Act will require many tribal governments to amend their codes to provide explicit protection for defendants' rights. For example, to exercise jurisdiction in TLOA and sentence an offender to more than one year's incarceration, the tribal court must provide the following:

- Effective assistance of counsel
- Free, appointed, licensed attorneys for indigent defendants
- Law-trained judges who are also licensed to practice law
- Publicly available tribal criminal law and rules
- Recorded criminal proceedings

To exercise jurisdiction over a non-Indian who commits an act of domestic violence (SDVCJ), the tribal court must comply with the preceding provisions of TLOA as well as:

- Protect the rights of defendants under the Indian Civil Rights Act, which largely tracks some of the U.S. Bill of Rights, including the right to due process
- Include a fair cross-section of the community in jury pools and not systemically exclude non-Indians.
- Inform defendants ordered detained by a tribal court of their right to file a federal habeas corpus petition.

It may seem demeaning to have a foreign government demand certain things of tribes. However, it does no good for a victim to find vindication in a system that mimics some of the same harms done in the American adjudicatory system by denying the right for the accused to have a fair trial. Professor Barbara Creel (Pueblo of Jemez), a former federal public defender, has eloquently written that "declining to provide counsel for defendants may be an act of tribal sovereignty, but it may come at the expense of the same sovereign power."[10] Like it or not, tribal courts will be under more scrutiny in the future. In terms of culturally appropriate responses, I have never come across a tribal tradition that involves imposing a punishment without allowing a defendant an opportunity to speak and have support from another person. In addition, nothing in the legislation prohibits a tribe from providing an advocate for every victim; in fact, this approach would be an improvement over the state and federal systems.

Civil Law: Expanding Remedies for Rape Survivors

Criminal justice is not the only area of tribal legal reform to consider. Civil remedies have an advantage from a survivor's perspective because the legal mechanism is initiated and controlled by the survivor herself as a plaintiff. This section focuses on two potential avenues for reform outside the criminal justice context—civil protection orders and tort reform.

Civil Protection Orders for Rape Survivors

Protection order statutes are designed to provide a civil legal remedy for victims of violence, namely, a legal order to prohibit further abuse and even contact. However, many current tribal protection order statutes are limited to domestic violence. Tribal governments can provide an option for sexual assault survivors by enacting new ordinances that allow them to file for an order of protection. Protection orders have a variety of labels in different systems (including orders for protection, domestic violence orders, restraining orders, and harassment orders). When issued, these protection orders require a perpetrator to comply with certain conditions, such as not contacting the victim or coming within a certain distance from the victim. These orders are most commonly understood in the context of domestic violence.

Protection orders have become increasingly used in tribal courts as tools for women victimized by their partners in cases of domestic violence. Depending on the laws of the particular tribe, a protection order can stipulate that the named individual stop committing violent acts, stay away from the victim and her family, stop contacting the victim, and fulfill other requirements designed to ensure the safety of the victim. However, most tribal statutes do not allow a victim of rape to file for or obtain a protection order because her relationship to the perpetrator does not fall within the definition of the statute. Survivors of rape who do not have a history of intimacy with their assailant may not be eligible for a protection order.

In recent years, significant attention has been given to the issue of domestic violence and the improvement of contemporary tribal justice systems in responding to intimate partner violence.[11] Because of the reform of tribal statutory law and changes in tribal procedural rules, Native women survivors of domestic violence have increasingly been able to obtain orders of protection in tribal courts.[12] Many tribal codes outlining protection order statutes are specific to domestic violence, requiring that the petitioner have a history of (presumably consensual) intimacy with the respondent.[13]

If a survivor of rape has no "intimate partner" relationship, she probably will not qualify for a protection order despite the fact that she has justifiable fears for her safety. Most rapes are committed by acquaintances, not strangers; therefore, a survivor (especially in a small, isolated family) may be constantly on the alert for her attacker, with no real legal remedy that she can control.

Some tribal codes do include provisions for generic civil "restraining orders" or "injunctions." These are usually distinct from (and sometimes predate) domestic violence protection orders, and there are several reasons why these options may not provide adequate relief. Most civil restraining order statutes are not designed with victimization and healing in mind. First, there is often a filing fee or court costs associated with obtaining a restraining order. Second, provisions for emergency orders (also known as "ex parte" orders) are lacking, which may leave a survivor vulnerable to violence in the immediate aftermath of a crime. Third, the restraining orders may offer only injunctive relief against actions such as trespassing and may not reflect victims' safety and security needs. Many generic tribal restraining order codes require that the petitioner show irreparable harm if the order is not granted.

The goal of any new protection order statute for rape survivors should be to provide for at least four important components: safety, accountability, prevention, and healing. Safety should be the paramount goal in any protection order system. Studies indicate that almost half of all women survivors of sexual assault report that they feared severe bodily injury or death during the assault.[14] The pain and trauma associated with sexual assault are such that women can relive the mental anguish of the assault whenever they encounter the perpetrator. Repeated exposure to the perpetrator, even without additional physical violence, can compound the trauma. Protection orders can provide survivors of violence with a sense of security and safety. A protection order may offer some degree of control over the survivor's life, particularly for a survivor who believes her perpetrator will continue to present a danger to her. Because she will not have to wait until an additional assault occurs to contact law enforcement authorities, a court order can provide peace of mind and a sense of safety. A sexual assault protection order should, at a minimum, require the perpetrator to stay away from the survivor's person, residence, school, place of employment, or other location.

The civil nature of protection orders provides more options for survivors who do not want to involve the criminal justice system. A civil proceeding offers more control to the survivor because she is making her decision independent of the criminal justice system. The criminal justice system puts control of the case in the hands of the prosecutor. Many women do not want to relinquish control of their story. For many survivors, the opportunity to tell their story of survival to a judge may be integral to their healing and reintegration into the community. Storytelling can be a powerful experience for survivors of rape.[15] A protection order hearing can serve as a forum for the stories of survivors, and offers a formal setting in which survivors can ask the court for protection from further harm. Even though a protection order is not equivalent to a criminal conviction or a lengthy incarceration, it can provide a survivor with the knowledge that there is a public acknowledgment of her story.

A protection order is a public record of the reality of the need for protection, and it documents that the court believes the survivor.

However, protection orders are never a panacea for any survivor of violence and should only be one of the options (not *the* option) for victims. In a typical protection order process, the survivor is required to submit evidence that provides legal justification for the protection order. Should a respondent choose to challenge a protection order, he may be allowed to cross-examine the petitioner in a court hearing, either on his own behalf or through hired counsel. Many survivors of rape may not want to expose themselves to this kind of public questioning and scrutiny. The open forum of a tribal courtroom is not necessarily a comforting locale for someone who has been raped; and it is possible that survivors who are reluctant to report the assault to law enforcement out of shame or embarrassment will feel no differently about reporting the crime to a judge. In addition, not all survivors of rape will be able to utilize protection order statutes. Protection orders will also not be useful in cases of stranger rape, because the survivor does not have information necessary to file for a protection order against a particular person—nor will the tribal court have the ability to provide notice and service to an unknown party.

Protection orders generally have other weaknesses as well—regardless of whether they are issued in a case of domestic violence or of sexual assault. For the protection order approach to be useful to sexual assault survivors, law enforcement must be available to enforce the order. The civil protection order "solution" will not be practical in locations where there are not enough law enforcement officers. In addition, if a law enforcement officer raped a woman, she may not want to rely on law enforcement to protect her from further harm.[16]

Even if a protection order is granted, a court order cannot guarantee that a violent individual will stop posing a threat to a particular victim. However, the protection order will provide law enforcement with probable cause to arrest an individual who violates the order's provisions. Protection orders, then, afford an extra level of security beyond the status quo. Ultimately, the proposal to expand protection order statutes to include survivors of sexual assault is a matter of offering additional choices and options to survivors. The sense of empowerment and control that this additional choice and option gives is significant. In my experience working with survivors of sexual assault, even the decision to decline a particular course of action is preferable to having no options at all.

The question now arises about the logistics of expanding the tribal protection order process to include sexual assault survivors as eligible applicants. There is debate among activists and researchers in the field of violence against women as to whether existing domestic violence protection codes should be expanded to include the crime of sexual assault, or whether a separate and distinct sexual assault protection code (a "stand-alone" code) should be drafted. Tribal legislative bodies are not limited or controlled by state legislative approaches to sexual assault protection orders, but an examination of the issues addressed by state legislation can illuminate key issues to consider. Several state sexual assault coalitions that are attempting to address the issue at the state level have asserted that a stand-alone protection order to address sexual assault is the best method.[17] Other states have also expanded existing protection order statutes to include victims of rape and sexual assault as eligible for protection orders.[18]

The following are some of the key components for tribal legislatures to consider when drafting a stand-alone protection order statute for sexual assault survivors:

- There should be no charge for filing and/or registering a sexual assault protection order. There should also be no charge or penalty for dropping a protection order, if the survivor should later decide that the order is not in her best interest.[19]
- The protection orders should be available to any victim who alleges a single incident of nonconsensual sexual conduct or sexual penetration as defined by tribal law.[20]
- The language of the protection order statute should invoke a "rape shield law" or similar provision to protect the victim's privacy. Because a survivor's prior consensual sexual activity is irrelevant to an incident of sexual assault, the respondent should be prohibited from raising such matters in opposition to the protection order.
- The victim's eligibility for an order of protection should not be dependent upon reporting the sexual assault to law enforcement or participating actively in the criminal justice system.[21]

- The court should not require physical injury or medical/forensic examination of the victim in determining whether to issue a protection order.[22]

Full Faith and Credit of Tribal Protection Orders for Sexual Assault

Suppose a survivor of sexual assault successfully obtains a protection order against her assailant in tribal court, but then finds herself being stalked by her perpetrator when she is off the reservation. The full faith and credit provisions of the Violence Against Women Act include a very broad definition of "protection order," which includes protection orders for victims of sexual assault.[23] Nothing in 18 U.S.C. §2265 or 18 U.S.C. §2266 makes specific reference to domestic violence. Therefore, tribal nations that develop stand-alone protection order codes for sexual assault survivors (or include sexual assault victims in existing protection order codes) can assert that such protection orders must be enforced by other jurisdictions, including states and local governments.[24] Because most state protection order statutes do not allow survivors of sexual assault to obtain protection orders, tribal governments have a unique opportunity to provide a leading example to the nation in the field of sexual assault response. Given the strong traditional responses to sexual assault in tribal communities, it is only natural that tribal governments lead the way in addressing the needs of sexual assault survivors in the contemporary context.

Tort Law

Rape victims can sue their attackers under an Anglo-American legal principle known as "tort" (better known as personal injury). In a tort case, the victim files a lawsuit against her perpetrator—completely independent of the criminal justice system. If the perpetrator is found to be liable for the victim's injuries, the court can award relief (usually in the form of money damages). There are a number of reasons why this avenue may be beneficial for survivors. For example, a lawsuit may be one of the only avenues of redress for survivors in tribal nations that do not currently prosecute rape. In addition, the burden of proof in civil cases is lower than that in criminal cases—preponderance of the evidence as opposed to beyond a reasonable doubt. Therefore, even if the tribe does not have a codified rape law, it may be possible to address illegal behavior through the introduction of these traditional tort laws.

Civil remedies may be particularly useful in a case where the perpetrator has access to monetary resources. For example, a victim of sexual abuse by a parish priest filed a lawsuit against his perpetrator and the diocese in Navajo District Court in 2010.[25] Although the Navajo District Court initially dismissed the lawsuit, the Navajo Nation Supreme Court later issued a strongly worded decision about the statute of limitations in cases of child sexual abuse. The court used strong language to couch the issue of victimization as intersecting with colonizing policies. The nature of the abuse was of particular concern to the court:

> While the Navajo Nation is very tolerant of all religious traditions, it would be a cruel irony if the same authority figures who seek to replace our ancient holistic traditions are also harming our children in such unspeakable ways. Our courts have a duty, in parens patriae, to ensure allegations of harm to our children are fully heard and not dismissed on mere technicalities.

Additional Avenues of Legal Reform

Basic criminal and civil law reform is only the beginning. There are also at least two other significant ways in which a tribal government could assert its authority to protect women from rapists outside the context of the criminal justice system. If the perpetrator is an employee of the tribal nation or a tribal enterprise, the tribal government, depending on the tribal law, may have the ability to terminate his employment. At least one tribal court has ruled in favor of terminating the employment of a sex offender, based on the tribal government's authority to terminate employees who present safety and security concerns.[26]

The Sac and Fox Tribe of the Mississippi in Iowa has family law provisions that are designed to prevent sex offenders from successfully retaining custody of children. There are few legal barriers to developing laws and policies regarding education, prevention, and services for survivors of crime. Indigenous nations may wish to explore, for instance, developing statutory provisions that mandate sexual assault prevention programs in all tribal schools and programs.

Confidentiality

For survivors of rape to be truly safe, they must be able to trust that they have the protection of confidentiality from their supportive system; this can often be a matter of life or death.[27] This recommendation requires that the tribal law acknowledge trained advocates in the same category as doctors, psychologists, and ministers. To call a woman's advocate to the stand against her will—even once—has dangerous potential for the entire network of support that a victim is seeking. Trained and compassionate advocates who have some degree of independence from the tribal government are a central component of a strong rape response system. A more controversial matter concerns the categorization of advocates as mandatory reporters of child abuse and neglect. Mandatory reporting requirements often put advocates and attorneys in the unenviable position of "turning in" a battered mother. Tribal leaders should have frank discussions about this aspect of addressing child abuse.

Conclusion

Changes to the tribal response to rape should be grounded in the stories and voices of survivors and women's advocates, who are the true experts in shortcomings of the current system. If tribal courts can move toward offering a forum in which more women can be heard and believed, and in which the community takes responsibility for the protection of women who have been assaulted, there is a potential for lessening the amount of shame, self-blame, and humiliation experienced by survivors of sexual assault. One emerging school of thought among the international legal community is the potential efficacy of "specialized units in the justice system" to deal with violence against women, because such units are "more responsive and effective in enforcing laws or violence against women." The American legal system has experimented with specialized domestic violence courts, with mixed results. It may be appropriate for a tribal government to consider creating such a specialized unit if it were consistent with tribal culture and tradition.

Tribal governments have a strong tradition of providing protection and safety for their people. However, because of limitations imposed on modern tribal governments by the federal government, tribal nations have few options in protecting and honoring survivors of sexual assault and rape. By developing comprehensive codes and enforcement practices to protect all victims of rape, tribal governments have the opportunity not only to provide an additional legal remedy for survivors of sexual assault but also to set an example for state and local governments. In taking these actions, tribal governments can create a harbor of safety that does not exist in many nontribal communities. While it is important to critique the response to sexual assault of Native women by the state and federal systems, the ability to restore strength and dignity to the survivors of sexual assault in Native communities should be centered in the tribal justice system, because the restoration of power and dignity ultimately lies within the community. Tribal governments will be strengthened by the reconnection to traditional lifeways that promote and protect the safety and sovereignty of women.

The End of Rape in Native America

WHEN I STARTED as a rape crisis advocate at age twenty, I often felt helpless when victims seemed to be sinking right before my eyes. How can you help someone navigate a broken system? Is it enough that she is "just" surviving? Advocates for rape survivors do not have a perfect metric to know whether they are making a difference in the lives of victims. I remember that one of our community funders wanted our organization to track "outcomes" for our services, and I remember wondering what kinds of benchmarks would qualify as effective outcomes. How do you measure surviving?

Many tribal anti-rape programs are funded by entities that require proof of success. But the provided metrics do not adequately assess qualitative change. Federal grant programs, for example, ask tribal organizations to count the number of survivors served, trainings attended, and court cases closed. These questions may serve a bureaucratic purpose, but the responses to them provide little useful information to assess effectiveness. We need new metrics and we should develop them ourselves. Tribal nations certainly do not need permission or authorization from the federal government to initiate or sustain internal social and structural change. It follows, then, that tribal nations are in no way limited to federal or state standards when assessing progress toward justice for rape victims.

In this epilogue, I offer a series of questions aimed at challenging tribal governments to ensure that survivors of rape are believed and perpetrators are held accountable. Native women and tribal leaders might consider reflecting on these questions (or variations of them) to help determine whether or not social and structural change is taking place. Answering the following questions in narrative form will allow a tribal community to look critically beyond the numbers and consider the qualitative nature of how rape survivors experience (or do not experience) justice. The questions will need to be customized for each community and are designed to be used by survivors, advocates, leaders, and community members to begin to develop tribal-centric metrics that will help document the journey to justice.

1. Are local conversations about rape happening?

Are there safe places to talk about rape? Social change sometimes starts slow—if there is at least one place (such as in a support group) where it is safe to talk about rape, that can be a start.

2. Do people who are victimized know where they can go for support?

Conversations about rape will invariably trigger memories and emotions for some survivors who may have repressed or otherwise emotionally distanced themselves from the crime(s). Confidential advocacy programs provide crucial, lifesaving services when such painful emotions rise to the surface. It can be unsafe to begin widespread community education and outreach about rape without twenty-four-hour access to confidential advocates. Native women have always had systems of communication for keeping each other informed of safe places to go. Consistent, compassionate information circulating throughout a community can go a long way. Even if a formal organization does not exist, people should know where to turn for help if feelings become overwhelming.

3. Does our tribal nation support or partner with independent Native women's organizations to provide confidential shelter and advocacy services?

The cultivation of independent Native women's anti-rape organizations is a crucial component of a strong tribal response to rape. Because of the danger many survivors experience, it is critical that

communications and services be offered in a confidential setting—
and, where possible, without direct oversight from law enforcement
or tribal government. Many tribal nations provide victim advocacy
through a program that seems intuitively connected to the needs
of rape survivors, such as mental health or social services. But such
governmental programs can present problems for confidentiality
and trust in cases where a politically powerful person is accused of
rape. Nonprofit organizations can be chartered by a tribal government, but the political separation will provide more protection to
women who come forward.

4. Does the tribal court system recognize an advocacy "privilege" that requires the protection of confidential communications between a survivor and her advocate?

This question is an extension of number 3. If there is not an explicit
recognition of advocate–victim privilege in tribal law, perpetrators
and their allies can disrupt these relationships by trying to subpoena records and documents that contain private, sacred information the survivor has shared. Advocate communications should be
placed in the same category as doctor–patient and attorney–client
privilege. Whenever possible, the privilege should be codified in
court rules or statutes.

5. What happens first when someone reports a rape in our nation?

There needs to be a plan. The plan should be flexible, but it should
provide victims with some semblance of organization. The most
common models are known as a sexual assault response team or a
multidisciplinary team—but at the very least, there should be an
agreement between law enforcement, health care providers, and
advocates about the protocol for responding to rape. The agreement
should provide a plan for how the various disciplines will communi-
cate with each other to ensure that survivors do not feel abandoned
at any point in the process.

6. *Do survivors in our community have access to a comprehensive health care response to rape, including access to emergency contraception?*

One of the most frustrating aspects of tribal rape law reform can be the lack of control the tribal nation has over the federal and/or state agencies tasked with responding to violence. Health care is one example of a service that is not always entirely under the control of the tribal leadership (Indian Health Service, a federal agency, provides health care on many reservations). However, advocates are continuing to press for comprehensive health care response to survivors of rape, which should include access to emergency contraception without interference. Emergency contraception prevents pregnancy after rape and should be available to any survivor of rape.

7. *Does our tribal legal system offer more than one option for victims seeking justice?*

The American legal system offers little flexibility, treating every violation of the law with the same type of response. But not all survivors have the same needs. Having different options and the agency to choose one of the options is a valuable remedy for the harm that rape does. Some survivors will not be interested in engaging even the most supportive criminal justice system. There may be valid reasons for not reporting a crime, but that same survivor may wish to get a protection order or file for employment protection.

8. *For survivors who report the crime to law enforcement, do the criminal justice agencies reliably follow up and follow through with investigation?*

As with health care, it is not always totally within tribal control whether law enforcement officials and prosecutors respond in a timely fashion. Since 2010 there has been considerable effort to educate federal partners and encourage collaboration. It may be many years, however, before change happens on the ground. In the meantime, do tribal officials have plans to pursue rape cases concurrently with the federal or state government?

9. Are rapists serving as elected tribal leaders, tribal employees, or designated as spiritual leaders?

Rape is an insidious phenomenon that infiltrates even the most sacred spheres of power. It is unacceptable for a rapist to hold a position of power or influence. When a rapist serves as a tribal leader (or inherits a hereditary title), the entire community suffers. Whenever possible, such perpetrators should be called out, exposed, impeached, and fired.

10. Do survivors have access to healing services outside the context of mental health care?

Western science has historically pathologized logical response to trauma. Behavior that may be a natural outgrowth of victimization (for example, hypervigilance) is framed as a deficiency or illness on the part of the survivor—and diagnoses of conditions like PTSD are common. In some tribal epistemologies, however, the behavior of a victim might be indicative of a gift or strength in the midst of horror. Certainly many survivors may wish to seek counseling, therapy, and pastoral care, but should have other options related to tribal identity and ceremony.

11. Are there mandatory education programs for teachers, leaders, employees to learn about rape?

Because rape has been shrouded in silence in many tribal communities, it is necessary to begin the conversations in a gentle but persistent way. Tribal nations can cultivate healthy discussions about rape by creating in-service training for government employees where tribal laws can be distributed and discussed.

12. Are perpetrators being held accountable?

This is probably the hardest question that can be presented to a tribal nation in regard to rape. The answer(s) can only be generated by honest, hard conversations that reflect the real, lived experiences of rape survivors in that particular community. If survivors feel threatened, humiliated, or shamed for someone else's actions, then the answer to this question is no. It may take years to be able to answer this question in the affirmative, but if the conversations do not start soon, the answer will never be yes. The end of rape in Native America will be directly tied to the accountability of federal, state, and tribal leaders who fail to intervene when Native women are raped.

HEALTHY TRIBAL NATIONS and survivors of rape share much in common:

We want to do more than just survive.

We seek nothing more than human dignity, and nothing less than justice.

We will not acquiesce until the end of rape arrives.

Epilogue

IN EARLY SEPTEMBER 2014, as I was working on this manuscript, I received "the" phone call from the John D. and Catherine T. MacArthur Foundation. The caller initially asked if I could speak privately. I wondered if someone was being a bit overzealous in checking a reference, but I dutifully closed my office door and picked up the phone again. I glanced at the clock, feeling a little frustrated that I was scheduled to teach a class in twenty minutes and wanted to finish preparing my lecture notes. The next words I heard were "We are calling to congratulate you. You have been selected as a 2014 MacArthur Fellow."

You might think a once-in-a-lifetime conversation would be etched into a person's memory, but I remember my emotion much more than the exact words. As the caller explained how I was selected and described the cash prize, my initial reaction was amazement and gratitude. I am rarely speechless, but "thank you" was the only thing I could think to say. At the most fundamental level, the MacArthur Fellowship represents opportunity—and that opportunity comes at a time when I'm ready to focus on next steps. In the coming years, I will continue to press for positive change at federal, state, and tribal levels to improve the lives of rape victims.

The MacArthur Fellowship and the completion of this manuscript mark a pivotal moment in my life. At this stage of my career, I have been writing about violence against Native women for a little more than ten years. I am a newly tenured faculty member and one of the only Native women law professors in the United States.

The MacArthur Fellowship has allowed me to reflect on my past decade of work and begin to think about new projects that will further the ability of Native women to end violence on our own terms. The completion of this book marks the end of one chapter of my life and the beginning of another.

I plan to continue teaching, writing, and contributing to ongoing reform efforts at the tribal and federal level. The opportunities provided by the Tribal Law and Order Act and the ongoing implementation of the Violence Against Women Act reforms are very exciting and provide opportunities to improve the lives of many victims of crime. Yet many victims continue to fall through the cracks of a broken legal system and deserve focused attention. I am thinking about Native women exploited in sex trafficking, the LGBTQ/Two Spirit population, missing and unsolved murders of Native people, and the all-encompassing link between environmental desecration and the lives and bodies of Native people. In my scholarship, I will continue to propose solutions that restore authority to tribal nations while encouraging the federal government to respect traditional practices and customary law. And we cannot forget about tribal legal reform. Restored authority means very little if it cannot be exercised in a thoughtful way.

In my future scholarship, I want to explore the role of language in shaping our experience of reality. A substantial body of anthropological and linguistic research concludes that language is fundamental to how we understand and structure reality generally and social relations specifically. I want to learn more about how Native languages shape legal concepts such as crime, violence, and justice. I am particularly interested in exploring how my tribe, the Mvskoke Nation, has constructed these concepts—and how these views might provide an alternative to the use of law as an instrument of oppression. For the past four summers, I have been traveling to Oklahoma to take lessons in Mvskoke, an endangered language with many gifts to offer the world. The MacArthur Fellowship may provide me with the opportunity to spend more time in Oklahoma as I begin the next phase of my learning.

In addition to studying the linguistics of Native peoples, I am interested in projects that build on the chapters in this book to elevate the voices of Native women who have developed solutions and interventions within their tribal nations. Journalists often refer to

MacArthur Fellowships as "genius" grants—a moniker that makes me uncomfortable for a variety of reasons, although I understand it is meant as a compliment. During the past decade, I have listened to countless testimonials from Native women about the brutal violence they have experienced. These women are the true "geniuses" because they have not just told stories about experiencing the pain and humiliation of rape but have used those stories to build a movement for radical change in the way our federal government has been treating tribal governments and Native women and children for centuries.

In all things, I seek to bridge scholarship and activism. The Fellowship and the publication of this book are a result of those efforts.

Acknowledgments

There are many people to thank. I cannot include everyone who has been generous to me with time and attention, but I offer here a special thanks to the following people. I must initially thank and acknowledge two coauthors who have enriched my life both personally and professionally: Carrie Martell Frias, who was the lead author of the previously published article that turned into chapter 2, and Joanna Woolman, who was the lead author of a longer version of chapter 6. Mvto for your wisdom and patience.

Two law professors in particular at the University of Kansas helped me navigate through three very long years of law school. A. Kimberley Dayton and Robert Odawi Porter (Seneca) allowed me to explore the intersection of feminist jurisprudence and federal Indian law with few restrictions. Although both have long since left Kansas, I still retain strong affinity for my education at the University of Kansas, where my consciousness about my life's work first developed. Relationships with fellow feminists on campus, like Connie Burk, rounded out my study with real lessons about organizing and activism.

Many mentors from the advocacy community have come in and out of my life since I began as a volunteer advocate in 1993. These mentors helped me shape my perspectives about justice for survivors of rape. Sarah Jane Russell, director of the Douglas County (Kansas) Rape-Victim Survivor Service (now known as GaDuGi Safe Center) for more than twenty-five years, was instrumental in my development as an advocate. She taught me that dignity, above all else, is the center point of justice for survivors of rape. Bonnie Clairmont (Ho-Chunk) has also been a true gift in my life. For most of her life she has worked to end rape and sexual abuse and has truly exemplified the model of a fearless advocate and truth teller. Other advocates who shaped my approach to this work are Charon Asetoyer (Comanche) and Lonna Stevens Hunter (Dakota/ Tlingit)—women who represent truth, strength, and integrity.

Several people have encouraged my writing and teaching over the years. Thank you to those who gently nudged me into teaching: Carole Goldberg, Douglas Keehn, Stacy Leeds, Pat Sekaquaptewa, Kelly Stoner, Melissa Tatum, Kevin Washburn, and all my fellow panelists at the April 2006 "Native Feminisms without Apology" event at the University of Illinois (a pivotal event for me): Jennifer Denetdale, Mishauna Goeman, Lisa Kahaleole Hall, J. Kēhaulani Kauanui, Lee Maracle, Renya Ramirez, Audra Simpson, and Andrea Smith. I have received support and encouragement from colleagues at other law schools, including Bethany Berger, Kirsten Matoy Carlson, Kristen Carpenter, Barbara Creel, Christine Zuni Cruz, Angelique Townsend Eaglewoman, Matthew L. M. Fletcher, Mary Jo Brooks Hunter, Sonia Katyal, Sarah Krakoff, John LaVelle, Frank Pommersheim, Angela Riley, Addie Rolnick, Wenona Singel, Alex Tallchief Skibine, Gloria Valencia-Weber, and Elizabeth Kronk Warner.

The staff and board at the Tribal Law and Policy Institute, where I worked from 2002 until 2008, deserve special acknowledgment. First, I thank the executive director, Jerry Gardner, for his wisdom and patience. So many of the staff from the early years are near to my heart—Elton Naswood, Diane Payne, and Lou Sgroi. The TLPI family has grown significantly since I left the organization. I am especially indebted to Heather Valdez Singleton, who has been instrumental to my continued relationship with TLPI, providing liaison work for the Tribal Legal Studies textbook series, along with my coauthors on the two first textbooks, *Introduction to Tribal Legal Studies* (with Justin B. Richland) and *Tribal Criminal Law and Procedure* (with Carrie Garrow). Maureen White Eagle came to TLPI while I was battling cancer in 2006 and has played an instrumental role in continuing the work of providing legal analysis and training on violence against Native women.

Since starting my academic career at William Mitchell College of Law in 2008, I have a new community to thank—first and foremost, my "partner in crime" Colette Routel, the codirector of the Indian Law Program at William Mitchell. Both of us are grateful for leadership and support from Lenor Scheffler, a Mitchell alumna and trustee who became the first enrolled member of any Minnesota Mdewakanton Dakota Tribe to become an attorney when she graduated in 1988. Our family of Indian law at Mitchell rounds out with adjunct professor of Advanced Indian Law, John Jacobson, a longtime friend to the William Mitchell Indian Law family. Lynette Fraction provides impeccable administrative support for the Indian Law program.

I offer thanks to all of my faculty colleagues for accepting me into their community with such warmth and collegiality. I am especially grateful for the mentorship and support offered by Phebe Haugen, Doug Heidenreich, Eric Janus, Ann Juergens, Raleigh Levine, David Prince, Neils Schaumann, Mike Steenson, and Nancy Ver Steegh.

The national movement to end violence against Native women is anchored by local and national organizations that spearhead reform at the national and international levels. Thank you for allowing me to be part of the work. A special thanks to the staff and board members of the National Indigenous Women's Resource Center (and its predecessor organizations), Native American Women's Health Education Resource Center, Mending the Sacred Hoop, and the Minnesota Indian Women's Sexual Assault Coalition. Shawn Partridge and the wonderful women at the Muscogee (Creek) Nation Family Prevention Program—you are the true warriors.

I have been blessed with amazing students during the past few years. The following students have been involved in the development of this manuscript: Courtney Allensworth, Steven Budke, Jeff Cormell, Aram Desteian, Cecilia Knapp, Rachel Kowarski, Amy Krupinski, Anna Light, Kelly McGinty, Sara McKlugell, Heather Monasky, Ella Phillips, Evangeline Stratton, Blue Bird Thomas, and Rachel Vesely. They have all gone on to bigger and better things than being my research assistants, but each one was an integral part of this journey.

I have learned so much about the work to end violence against Native women from people from all walks of life—federal officials, practitioners, tribal court judges, tribal leaders, tribal police officers, activists, artists—and all of these connections have enriched my knowledge. In no particular order, mvto to Victoria Ybanez, Patina

Park Zink, Jim Zion, Ronet Bachman, Peggy Bird, Deborah Parker, Eileen Hudon, Duane Champagne, David Avraham Voluck, Carma Corcoran, Christine Stark, Joy Harjo, April Russell, Jim Clairmont, Erik Stegman, Ed Reina, Karen Artichoker, Ada Deer, M. Brent Leonhard, Christina Entrekin, Radmilla Cody, Hallie Bongar White, Rachel Ward, Wende Gozan Brown, Peggy Flanagan, Olga Trujillo, Marcus Briggs-Cloud, Marina Colby, Marlin Mousseau, Rebecca St. George, Tammy Young, Eleanor Ned, Julie Johnston, Marmie Jotter, Dana Deegan, Sacheen Smith, Lauren Chief Elk, Kimberly Robertson, Jessica Danforth, Juskwa Burnett, Louisa Riley, Eli Grayson, Leslie Hagen, Margaret Chiara, Joye Frost, Kathleen Gless, and Shannon May. And many more.

I thank my Mvskoke language teacher and friend, Rosemary McCombs Maxey, and her entire family, who hosted my visits to Oklahoma for the past four years.

My parents, Jan and Montie Deer, have always pushed me to excel, and I would not be where I am today without their love and guidance. My late paternal grandparents, Isaac (Kelso) Deer and Wanda Lee Deer, both passed away during the development of this manuscript. I know they would be proud to see this book. Special thanks to my friends who have been so supportive over the years: Andy Birch, Brandon Clark, Marla Clark, Jennifer Farnham, Lisa Frank, Courtney Henry, Lia Kvatum, P. Nelson Le, Sarah Leonard, Michael-jon Pease, Catherine Rogers, David Sartorius, Christopher Taykalo, Kimberly Hefling Thomas, and Chris Wolf.

Thank you to everyone at the University of Minnesota Press, especially Jason Weidemann.

And finally I wish to thank Neal Axton, my spouse and the emotional rock of all that I do.

Mvto . . .

Notes

INTRODUCTION

1. Suzy Khimm, "The Violence Against Women Act Is on Life Support," *Washington Post*, Jan. 25, 2013, http://www.washingtonpost .com (citing the "epidemic of domestic violence among Native Americans"); Rebecca Solnit, "A Rape a Minute, a Thousand Corpses a Year," *Huffington Post*, Jan. 24, 2013, http://www.huffingtonpost.com/ ("Speaking of epidemics, one of three Native American women will be raped").

2. Sherene H. Razack, *Looking White People in the Eye: Gender, Race, and Culture in Courtrooms and Classrooms* (Toronto: University of Toronto Press, 1998), 59.

3. "NNEDV Honors and Celebrates the Legacy of Tillie Black Bear," July 25, 2014, http://nnedv.org.

4. See "Winnebago Tribe v. Bigfire," *Indian Law Reporter* 24 (Winnebago Tr. Ct. 1997) (noting court may consult with elders regarding tribal tradition or culture under Winnebago Code §1–).

5. Jack D. Forbes, *Columbus and Other Cannibals: The Wétiko Disease of Exploitation, Imperialism, and Terrorism* (New York: Seven Stories Press, 1992), 160.

6. Dian Million, *Therapeutic Nations: Healing in an Age of Indigenous Human Rights* (Tucson: University of Arizona Press, 2013).

7. This connection is informed by activist materials describing the parallels between sovereignty of nations and sovereignty of women. See, e.g., Brenda Hill, *Ending Violence Against Native Women from the Roots Up: An Overview of Shelter and Advocacy Program Development Supporting Women's Sovereignty* (Rapid City, S.Dak.: Sacred Circle, National Resource Center to End Violence against Native Women, 2009), 2.

8. Bonnie Clairmont, "Overview of Sexual Violence Perpetrated by Pur-

ported Indian Medicine Men," in *Sharing Our Stories of Survival: Native Women Surviving Violence*, ed. Sarah Deer et al. (Lanham, Md.: AltaMira Press, 2007), 226.

9. See Leslie E. Korn, "Community Trauma and Development," *Fourth World Journal* 5, no. 1 (2002): 1–9.

10. David Archard, "The Wrong of Rape," *Philosophical Quarterly* 57 (2007): 374.

11. Rose Corrigan, *Up Against a Wall: Rape Reform and the Failure of Success* (New York: New York University Press, 2013), 12.

12. Most rapists have multiple victims. See David Lisak and Paul M. Miller, "Repeat Rape and Multiple Offending among Undetected Rapists," *Violence and Victims* 17, no. 1 (2002): 73–84.

1. KNOWING THROUGH NUMBERS?

1. President Barack Obama, "Remarks by the President before Signing the Tribal Law and Order Act," July 29, 2010, http://www.whitehouse.gov.

2. See generally Eugene P. Ericksen, "Problems in Sampling the Native American and Alaska Native Population," *Population Research and Policy Review* 16 (1997): 43.

3. Lawrence A. Greenfeld and Steven K. Smith, *American Indians and Crime* (Washington, D.C.: U.S. Department of Justice, 1999), http://www.bjs .gov/content/pub/pdf/aic.pdf. The report was reissued in 2004 with updated data. Steven W. Perry, *American Indians and Crime: A BJS Statistical Profile, 1992–2002* (Washington, D.C.: U.S. Department of Justice, 2004), http://www.bjs.gov/content/pub/pdf/aic02.pdf.

4. University of Delaware criminologist Ronet Bachman is the leading statistician on violence against Native women in the United States. See Ronet Bachman et al., "Estimating the Magnitude of Rape and Sexual Assault against American Indian and Alaska Native (AIAN) Women," *Australian and New Zealand Journal of Criminology* 43, no. 2 (2010): 199. Other studies that support the prevalence findings include Shira Rutman et al., "Reproductive Health and Sexual Violence among Urban American Indian and Alaskan Native Young Women: Select Findings from the National Survey of Family Growth," *Maternal and Child Health Journal* 16, no. 2 (2012): 347; Danette Buskovick and Elizabeth A. Peterson, *Domestic Violence: Results from the 2008 Minnesota Crime Victim Survey* (St. Paul, Minn.: Department of Public Safety, 2009), https://dps .mn.gov.

5. Amnesty International, *Maze of Injustice: The Failure to Protect Indigenous Women from Sexual Violence in the USA* (New York: Amnesty International, 2007), https://www.amnestyusa.org/pdfs/MazeOfInjustice.pdf.

6. See, e.g., Jennifer L. Truman and Michael Planty, *Criminal Victimization,*

2011, Bureau of Justice Statistics Bulletin (Washington, D.C.: Department of Justice, 2012), 1, http://bjs.gov/content/pub/pdf/cv11.pdf; Lynn Langton et al., *Special Report: Victimizations Not Reported to the Police, 2006–2010* (Washington, D.C.: Department of Justice, 2012), http://bjs.gov/content/pub/pdf/vnrpo610.pdf; Janet L. Lauritsen et al., *Methods for Counting High-Frequency Repeat Victimizations in the National Crime Victimization Survey* (Washington, D.C.: Department of Justice, 2012), http://bjs.gov/content/pub/pdf/mchfrv.pdf.

7. See *Survey Methodology for Criminal Victimization in the United States*, http://www.bjs.gov/index.cfm?ty=dcdetail&iid=245#Methodology (last visited July 13, 2014).

8. See Ronet Bachman et al., "Violence against American Indian and Alaska Native Women and the Criminal Justice Response: What Is Known" (2008), 38, https://www.ncjrs.gov/pdffiles1/nij/grants/223691.pdf (hereafter "What Is Known").

9. Patricia Tjaden and Nancy Thoennes, *Full Report of the Prevalence, Incidence, and Consequences of Violence against Women* (Washington, D.C.: U.S. Department of Justice, 2000).

10. M. C. Black et al., *National Intimate Partner and Sexual Violence Survey 2010 Summary Report* (Atlanta: Centers for Disease Control and Prevention, 2011), 20.

11. Ronet Bachman et al., "Estimating the Magnitude of Rape and Sexual Assault against American Indian and Alaska Native (AIAN) Women," *Australian and New Zealand Journal of Criminology* 43, no. 2 (2010): 199–222.

12. Ibid.

13. Ibid.

14. Ibid.

15. Native American Women's Health Education Research Center, *Indigenous Women's Dialogue: Roundtable Report on the Accessibility of Plan B as an Over the Counter (OTC) within Indian Health Service*, Feb. 2012, 10, http://nativeshop.org/images/stories/media/pdfs/Plan-B-Report.pdf (emphasis added).

16. Chris Cunneen and Simone Rowe, "Changing Narratives: Colonised Peoples, Criminology and Social Work," *International Journal for Crime, Justice and Social Democracy* 3, no. 1 (2014): 58.

17. Greenfeld and Smith, *American Indians and Crime.*

18. Ibid.

19. Ibid.

20. Bachman et al., "What Is Known."

21. Oliphant v. Suquamish Indian Tribe, 435 U.S. 191, 212 (1978) (holding that tribes lack criminal jurisdiction over non-Indians by way of implied divestiture).

22. See, e.g., Larry Long et al., "Understanding Contextual Differences in American Indian Criminal Justice," *American Indian Culture and Research Journal* 32, no. 4 (2008): 41–65; Scott Seaborne, op-ed., "Crime Data Misrepresented to Serve Hidden Tribal Agenda," *Indian Country Today*, June 14, 2012, http://indiancountrytodaymedianetwork.com. But see Carole Goldberg and Kevin Washburn, op-ed., "Lies, Damn Lies, and Crime Statistics," *Indian Country Today*, July 25, 2008, http://indian countrytodaymedianetwork.com.

23. Christine Crossland, Jane Palmer, and Alison Brooks, "Program of Research on Violence Against American Indian and Alaska Native Women," *Violence Against Women* 19, no. 6 (2013): 774.

24. "Indian country" is a legal term of art defined at 18 U.S.C. § 1151 and includes reservations, dependent Indian communities, and allotments. Tribes have criminal jurisdiction over crimes perpetrated by Indians within Indian country. When a crime occurs outside "Indian Country," even if a tribal member is a defendant, the tribe lacks criminal jurisdiction.

25. See generally Andrea Smith, *Conquest: Sexual Violence and American Indian Genocide* (Boston: South End Press, 2005) (providing a full discussion of how this dynamic has developed in the United States).

26. Deborah A. Miranda, "'Saying the Padre Had Grabbed Her': Rape Is the Weapon, Story Is the Cure," *Intertexts* 14, no. 2 (2010): 96.

27. Bachman et al., "What Is Known."

28. Zainab Amadahy, "The Healing Power of Women's Voices," in *Strong Women Stories: Native Vision and Community Survival*, ed. Kim Anderson and Bonita Lawrence (Toronto: Sumach Press, 2003), 144, 152.

29. Minnesota Indian Women's Sexual Assault Coalition, Barrette Project description, http://miwsac.org.

30. Rebecca St. George and Sterling Harris, *Safety and Accountability Audit of the Response to Native Women Who Report Sexual Assault in Duluth Minnesota, 2006–2008* (Duluth: Mending the Sacred Hoop and Program to Aid Victims of Sexual Assault, 2008).

31. Claudia Card, "Rape as a Weapon of War," *Hypatia* 11, no. 4 (1996): 6.

32. Lynne N. Henderson, "What Makes Rape a Crime," *Berkeley Women's Law Journal* 3 (1987): 225.

33. Robin L. West, "Legitimating the Illegitimate: A Comment on *Beyond Rape*," *Columbia Law Review* 93 (1993): 1448.

34. See Sarah E. Ullman and Henrietta H. Filipas, "Correlates of Formal and Informal Support Seeking in Sexual Assault Victims," *Journal of Interpersonal Violence* 16, no. 10 (2001): 1028–47.

35. Judith Lewis Herman, *Trauma and Recovery: The Aftermath of Violence—from Domestic Abuse to Political Terror* (New York: Basic Books, 1992), 211.

36. Susan J. Brison, "Surviving Sexual Violence: A Philosophical Perspective," *Journal of Social Philosophy* 24, no. 1 (1993): 13.
37. See, e.g., Rebecca Campbell, *Mental Health Services for Rape Survivors: Current Issues in Therapeutic Practice* (2001), http://www.mincava.umn .edu.
38. Elsie B. RedBird, "Honouring Native Women: The Backbone of Native Sovereignty," in *Popular Justice and Community Regeneration: Pathways of Indigenous Reform*, ed. Kayleen M. Hazelhurst (Westport, Conn.: Praeger, 1995), 121.
39. See, e.g., Venida S. Chenault, *Weaving Strength, Weaving Power: Violence and Abuse against Indigenous Women* (Durham, N.C.: Carolina Academic Press, 2011).
40. Ariel Levin, Sunrise Black Bull, and Summer Lunderman, *Not Our Tradition: A Report on Violence on the Rosebud Reservation* (2013), http://www.wbcws.org/media/wbcwsorg/adultsurveyreport%20(1)%20(2).pdf; Ariel Levin, Sunrise Black Bull, and Summer Lunderman, *Report on Results of Youth Victimization Survey for the Rosebud Reservation* (2013), http://www.wbcws.org/media/wbcwsorg/youthsurveyreport.pdf.
41. Levin, Black Bull, and Lunderman, *Not Our Tradition*.
42. Dian Million, "Felt Theory," *American Quarterly* 60, no. 2 (2008): 267–72.
43. Linda Tuhiwai Smith, *Decolonizing Methodologies: Research and Indigenous Peoples*, 2nd ed. (London: Zed Books, 2012), 26 (explaining that "one of the supposed characteristics of primitive peoples was that we could not use our minds or intellects").
44. Ibid.

2. WHAT SHE SAY IT BE LAW

1. Antonio J. Waring, ed., *Laws of the Creek Nation* (Athens: University of Georgia Press, 1960), 24.
2. Cassia C. Spohn, "The Rape Reform Movement: The Traditional Common Law and Rape Law Reforms," *Juremetrics* 39, no. 2 (1999): 129 (reflecting historical American legal approaches to rape, wherein women are often revictimized in court).
3. Merril D. Smith, ed., introduction to *Sex without Consent: Rape and Sexual Coercion in America* (New York: New York University Press, 2001), 5; Roy Porter, "Rape—Does It Have a Historical Meaning?," in Tomaselli and Porter, *Rape*, 216, 217.
4. Ohland Morton, "The Government of the Creek Indians," *Chronicles of Oklahoma* 8, no. 1 (1930): 42, 54.
5. Emma LaRocque, "Violence in Aboriginal Communities," in *The Path to Healing: Report of the National Round Table on Aboriginal Health and Social Issues* (Ottawa: Royal Commission on Aboriginal Peoples, 1993).

6. Jean Chaudhuri and Joyotpaul Chaudhuri, *A Sacred Path: The Way of the Muscogee Creeks* (Los Angeles: UCLA American Indian Studies Center, 2001), 48.

7. Anne Waters, "Language Matters: Nondiscrete Nonbinary Dualism," *American Indian Thought: Philosophical Essays,* ed. Anne Waters (Malden, Mass.: Wiley-Blackwell, 2004), 103.

8. Ibid.

9. See generally Sylvia Marcos, "The Borders Within: The Indigenous Women's Movement and Feminism in Mexico," in *Dialogue and Difference: Feminisms Challenge Globalization,* ed. Marguerite Waller and Sylvia Marcos (New York: Palgrave Macmillan, 2005), 87–88 (discussing the shifting balances in concepts of equality between men and women after feminist groups came into the Chiapas area of Mexico). Marcos also discusses how in indigenous Mexican women's movements in the mid-1990s, women "crossed over" between so-called traditional women's roles and that of insurgents or "soldado."

10. Jennifer Denetdale, "Carving Navajo National Boundaries: Patriotism, Tradition, and the Diné Marriage Act of 2005," *American Quarterly* 60, no. 2 (2008): 293.

11. Mark St. Pierre and Tilda Long Soldier, *Walking in the Sacred Manner: Healers, Dreamers, and Pipe Carriers—Medicine Women of the Plains* (New York: Touchstone, 1995), 81.

12. Diron D'Artaguiette, "Journal of Diron D'Artaguiette, 1722–1723," in *Travels in the American Colonies: 1670–1744,* ed. Newton D. Merenes (New York: Macmillan, 1916), 73.

13. Carol Devens, "Separate Confrontations: Gender as a Factor in Indian Adaptation to European Colonization in New France," *American Quarterly* 38, no. 3 (1986): 467–68.

14. Tarrell Awe Agahe Portman and Roger D. Herring, "Debunking the Pocahontas Paradox: The Need for a Humanistic Perspective," *Journal of Humanistic Counseling, Education and Development* 40, no. 2 (2001): 185–89.

15. See generally Karen Anderson, *Chain Her by One Foot: The Subjugation of Women in Seventeenth-Century New France* (New York: Routledge, 1991); Carol Devens, *Countering Colonization: Native American Women and Great Lakes Missions, 1630–1900* (Berkeley: University of California Press, 1992); Lisa J. Udel, "Revision and Resistance: The Politics of Native Women's Motherwork," *Frontiers: A Journal of Women Studies* 2, no. 2 (2001): 43–62.

16. See generally, James Axtell, *The White Indians of Colonial America* (n.p.: Ye Galleon Press, 1979).

17. Laurel Thatcher Ulrich, *Good Wives: Image and Reality in the Lives of Women in Northern New England, 1650–1750* (New York: Vintage, 1982), 97.

18. David R. Wrone and Russell S. Nelson, eds., *Who's the Savage?* (1973; repr., New York: Fawcett, 1982), 17.

19. James Axtell, *The European and the Indian* (New York: Oxford University Press, 1981), 182.

20. See, e.g., "Complementary but Equal: Gender Status in the Plateau," in *Women and Power in Native North America,* ed. Laura F. Klein and Lillian A. Ackerman (Norman: University of Oklahoma Press, 1995), 87.

21. See, e.g., Gloria Valencia-Weber and Christine P. Zuni, "Domestic Violence and Tribal Protection of Indigenous Women in the United States," *St. John's Law Review* 69, no. 1 (1995): 69–170.

22. Lisa M. Poupart, "The Familiar Face of Genocide: Internalized Oppression among American Indians," *Hypatia* 18, no. 2 (2003): 86.

23. Ibid.; Paula Gunn Allen, *The Sacred Hoop: Recovering the Feminine in American Indian Tradition* (Boston: Beacon Press, 1986).

24. Douglas E. Beloof, *Victims in Criminal Procedure* (Durham, N.C.: Carolina Academic Press, 2006).

25. Gloria Lee, "Defining Traditional Healing," in *Justice as Healing: Indigenous Ways,* ed. Wanda D. McCaslin (n.p.: Living Justice Press, 2005), 98.

26. Inés Hernandez-Avila, "In Praise of Insubordination," in *Transforming a Rape Culture,* ed. Emilie Buchwald et al. (Minneapolis: Milkweed Editions, 1993).

27. Elizabeth Cook-Lynn, "The Big Pipe Case," in *Why I Can't Read Wallace Stegner and Other Essays: A Tribal Voice* (Madison: University of Wisconsin Press, 1996), 115.

28. Sally Roesch Wagner, *Sisters in the Spirit: Haudenoasaunee (Iroquois) Influence on Early American Feminists* (Summertown, Tenn.: Native Voices, 2001), 67.

29. English Lord Chief Justice Matthew Hale is given considerable credit for the development of modern American common law rape jurisprudence, importing significant European patriarchal misogyny. Lord Hale is credited with originating the jury instruction that rape is "easy to charge and hard to prove" and the common-law rule that a woman cannot be raped by her husband. Matthew Hale, *The History of the Pleas of the Crown,* ed. Sollom Emlyn (Am. ed. 1778), 634.

30. Virginia Marie Bouvier, *Women and the Conquest of California, 1542–1840: Codes of Silence* (Tucson: University of Arizona Press, 2001), 12.

31. Roy Porter, "Rape—Does it Have a Historical Meaning?," in Tomaselli and Porter, *Rape,* 216, 217.

32. Michelle J. Anderson, "Women Do Not Report the Violence They Suffer: Violence against Women and the State Action Doctrine," *Villanova Law Review* 46, no. 5 (2001): 924–25.

33. See generally Sherene H. Razack, "Gendered Racial Violence and Spatialized Justice: The Murder of Pamela George," *Canadian Journal of Law and Society* 15, no. 2 (2000): 91–130.

34. Congressional Record 2596 (1909), quoted in Shirley R. Bysiewicz and Ruth E. Van de Mark, "The Legal Status of the Dakota Indian Woman," *American Indian Law Review* 3, no. 2 (1975): 255–312.

35. Gray v. United States, 394 F. 2d 96, 101 (9th Cir. 1968).

36. "Recent Case, Constitutional Law—Equal Protection of the Laws—Federal Statute Imposing Less Severe Penalty upon American Indian Who Rapes an Indian Woman Than upon Other Rapists Is Constitutional," *Harvard Law Review* 82 (1969): 697–702.

37. Hilary N. Weaver, "The Colonial Context of Violence: Reflections on Violence in the Lives of Native American Women," *Journal of Interpersonal Violence* 24, no. 9 (2008): 1552–63 (describing the colonial context of gender roles and violence against Indian women). See generally Bethany Ruth Berger, "After Pocahontas: Indian Women and the Law, 1830–1934," *American Indian Law Review* 21, no. 1 (1997): 1–62 (outlining the historical trends experienced by Native women).

38. *Indian Law Reporter* 13 (Sitka Community Association Trial Court, Apr. 7, 1986): 6011–19.

39. Ibid., 6016 (quoting the Court of Elders decision).

40. In re J.J.S., *Indian Law Reporter* 11 (Navajo District Window Rock, Nov. 4, 1983): 6031.

41. Ibid.

42. Ibid., 6032.

43. Ibid.

44. *Indian Law Reporter* 24 (Navajo Nation Supreme Court, May 28, 1997): 6252, 6153.

45. Ibid., 6152.

46. *Indian Law Reporter* 20 (Rosebud Sioux Court of Appeals, June 16, 1993): 6074.

47. Ibid., 6075.

48. *Indian Law Reporter* 25 (Winnebago Tribal Court, June 19, 1997): 6232.

49. Ibid., 6233.

50. Fort Peck Tribes v. Martell, http://indianlaw.mt.gov/content/fortpeck/decisions/000s/090.pdf (1990).

3. AT THE MERCY OF THE STATE

1. Robert B. Porter, "The Meaning of Indigenous Nation Sovereignty," *Arizona State Law Journal* 34 (2002): 75–112.

2. Michele de Cuneo, "Letter to a Friend," in *The Discovery of America and*

Other Myths: A New World Reader, ed. Thomas Christensen and Carol Christensen (San Francisco: Chronicle Books, 1992), 129.

3. Albert L. Hurtado, "When Strangers Met: Sex and Gender on Three Frontiers," in *Writing the Range: Race, Class and Culture in The Women's West,* ed. Elizabeth Jameson and Susan Armitage (Norman: University of Oklahoma Press, 1997), 136.

4. Gary Clayton Anderson and Alan R. Woolworth, eds., *Through Dakota Eyes: Narrative Accounts of the Minnesota Indian War of 1862* (St. Paul: Minnesota Historical Society Press, 1988), 24.

5. Albert L. Hurtado, *The Destruction of California Indians,* ed. Robert F. Heizer (Lincoln, Neb.: Bison Books 1993), v, xv.

6. 18 U.S.C. § 1153 (2004).

7. Act of August 15, 1953, ch. 505, 67 Stat. 588–590 (1953) (codified as 18 U.S.C. §1162, 25 U.S.C. §1360 and other scattered sections in chapters 18 and 28 of United States Code).

8. 25 U.S.C. §§ 1301-1303 (2000).

9. 435 U.S. 191 (1978).

10. Philip P. Frickey, "Domesticating Federal Indian Law," *Minnesota Law Review* 81, no. 1 (1996): 31–96.

11. B. J. Jones, "Jurisdiction and Violence against Native Women," in Deer et al., *Sharing Our Stories of Survival,* 233–47.

12. 109 U.S. 556 (1883).

13. Sidney L. Harring, *Crow Dog's Case: American Indian Sovereignty, Tribal Law, and United States Law in the Nineteenth Century* (Cambridge: Cambridge University Press, 1994).

14. B. J. Jones and Christopher J. Ironroad, "Addressing Sentencing Disparities for Tribal Citizens in the Dakotas: A Tribal Sovereignty Approach," *North Dakota Law Review* 89 (2013): 65.

15. Larry EchoHawk, "Child Sexual Abuse in Indian Country: Is the Guardian Keeping in Mind the Seventh Generation?," *NYU Journal of Legislation and Public Policy* 5 (2001): 83–127.

16. See Harring, *Crow Dog's Case.*

17. Robert N. Clinton, Carole E. Goldberg, and Rebecca Tsosie, *American Indian Law: Native Nations and the Federal System,* 4th ed. (n.p.: Lexis-Nexis, 2003).

18. See Westit v. Stafne, 44 F.3d 823, 825 (9th Cir. 1995) (ruling that tribes retain inherent sovereignty to prosecute Indians who commit crimes enumerated by Major Crimes Act).

19. Ada Pecos Melton and Jerry Gardner, "Public Law 280: Issues and Concerns for Victims of Crime in Indian Country," http://www.tribal-institute.org/articles/gardner1.htm.

20. See generally Duane Champagne and Carole Goldberg, *Captured Justice:*

Native Nations and Public Law 280 (Durham, N.C.: Carolina Academic Press, 2012).

21. Soo C. Song and Vanessa J. Jimenez, "Concurrent Tribal and State Jurisdiction Under Public Law 280," *American University Law Review* 47, no. 6 (1998): 1627–1707.

22. Elizabeth Ann Kronk, "Tightening the Perceived 'Loophole': Reexamining ICRA's Limitation on Tribal Court Punishment Authority," in *The Indian Civil Rights Act at Forty*, ed. Kristen A. Carpenter, Matthew L. M. Fletcher, and Angela R. Riley (Los Angeles: UCLA American Indian Studies Center, 2012).

23. 25 U.S.C. § 1302(7) (1968).

24. Pub. L. No. 99–570, tit. IV, § 4217, 100 Stat. 3207–146 (1986).

25. 435 U.S. 191, 195 (1978).

26. Matthew L. M. Fletcher, "Sawnawgezewog: 'The Indian Problem' and the Lost Art of Survival," *American Indian Law Review* 28 (2004): 35–105.

27. See Stephen D. Easton, "Native American Crime Victims Deserve Justice: A Response to Jensen and Rosenquist," *North Dakota Law Review* 69 (1993): 939; Andrea Smith, "Sexual Violence and American Indian Genocide," *Journal of Religion and Abuse* 1, no. 2 (1999): 31–52.

28. John V. Butcher, "Federal Courts and the Native American Sex Offender," *Federal Sentencing Reporter* 13, no. 2 (2000): 85–89 (establishing majority of defendants in federal sexual abuse cases as Native American).

29. Catherine Baker Stetson, "Decriminalizing Tribal Codes: A Response to *Oliphant*," *American Indian Law Review* 9, no. 4 (1981): 62.

30. See generally U.S. Commission on Civil Rights, *A Quiet Crisis: Federal Funding and Unmet Needs in Indian Country* (2004), http://www.usccr.gov/pubs/na0703/na0204.pdf.

31. Ibid.

32. See United States v. Lester, 992 F.2d 174, 174 (8th Cir. 1993) (acknowledging defendant convicted of rape and simple assault by Standing Rock Sioux Tribal Court).

33. Michael Edmund O'Neill, "When Prosecutors Don't: Trends in Federal Prosecutorial Declinations," *Notre Dame Law Review* 79, no. 1 (2003): 224.

34. Michelle J. Anderson, "Women Do Not Report the Violence They Suffer: Violence against Women and State Action Doctrine," *Villanova Law Review* 46 (2001): 907.

35. United States Government Accountability Office, *U.S. Department of Justice Declinations of Indian Country Criminal Matters* (2010), http://www.gao.gov/new.items/d11167r.pdf.

4. ALL APOLOGIES

1. This type of apology has been documented in some sex offenders. Diana Scully and Joseph Marolla, "Convicted Rapists' Vocabulary of Motive: Excuses and Justifications," in *Social Deviance: Readings in Theory and Research*, ed. Henry N. Pontell (Upper Saddle River, N.J.: McGraw-Hill, 2005).

2. Chris Cunneen and Simone Rowe, "Decolonising Indigenous Victimisation," *Crime, Victims and Policy* 1, 7 (2014), http://ssrn.com/abstract=2438503.

3. Larry EchoHawk, "Child Sexual Abuse in Indian Country: Is the Guardian Keeping in Mind the Seventh Generation?," *New York University Review of Legislation and Public Policy* 5, no. 1 (2001): 99.

4. Bonnie Burstow, "Toward a Radical Understanding of Trauma and Trauma Work," *Violence Against Women* 9, no. 11 (2003): 1314.

5. William Bradford, "'With a Very Great Blame on Our Hearts': Reparations, Reconciliation, and an American Indian Plea for Peace with Justice," *American Indian Law Review* 27 (2003): 1–175.

6. Brent T. White, "Say You're Sorry: Court-Ordered Apologies as a Civil Rights Remedy," *Cornell Law Review* 91, no. 6 (2006): 1286.

7. See Christopher Buck, "'Never Again': Kevin Gover's Apology for the Bureau of Indian Affairs," *Wicazo Sa Review* 21 (2006): 97.

8. Rebecca Tsosie, "The BIA's Apology to Native Americans: An Essay on Collective Memory and Collective Conscience," in *Taking Wrongs Seriously: Apologies and Reconciliation*, ed. Elazar Barkan and Alexander Karn (Stanford, Calif.: Stanford University Press, 2006).

9. Melissa Nobles, *The Politics of Official Apologies* (Cambridge: Cambridge University Press, 2008), 86.

10. Roy L. Brooks, ed., introduction to *When Sorry Isn't Enough: The Controversy over Apologies and Reparations for Human Injustice* (New York: New York University Press, 1999).

11. Matthew F. Bokovoy, "Humanist Sentiment, Modern Spanish Heritage, and California Mission Commemoration, 1769–1915," *Journal of San Diego History* 48, no. 3 (2002), available at http://www.sandiegohistory.org/journal/2002-3/humanist.htm; see also Dee Brown, *Bury My Heart at Wounded Knee* (1971; New York: Henry Holt, 1991), 38–39.

12. Antonia I. Castañeda, "Sexual Violence in the Politics and Policies of Conquest: Amerindian Women and the Spanish Conquest of Alta California," in *Building with our Hands: New Directions in Chicana Studies*, ed. Adela de la Torre and Beatríz M. Pesquera (Berkeley: University of California Press, 1993).

13. Bouvier, *Women and the Conquest of California, 1542–1840*.

14. James A. Sandos, "Between Crucifix and Lance: Indian-White Relations in California, 1769–1848," in *Contested Eden: California Before the Gold Rush,* ed. Ramón A. Guitérrez and Richard J. Orsi (Berkeley: University of California Press, 1998), 206.

15. Rose Stremlau, "Rape Narratives on the Northern Paiute Frontier: Sarah Winnemucca, Sexual Sovereignty, and Economic Autonomy, 1844–1891," in *Portraits of Women in the American West,* ed. Dee Garceau-Hagen (New York: Routledge, 2005).

16. Ibid.

17. Albert L. Hurtado, "When Strangers Met: Sex and Gender on Three Frontiers," *Frontiers* 17 (1996): 59.

18. See John Demos, *The Tried and the True: Native American Women Confronting Colonization* (New York: Oxford University Press, 1995), 89; Carolyn Ross Johnston, *Cherokee Women in Crisis: Trail of Tears, Civil War, and Allotment, 1838–1907* (Tuscaloosa: University of Alabama Press, 2003), 57.

19. David Roberts, "The Long Walk to Bosque Redondo," *Smithsonian,* Dec. 1, 1997.

20. See, e.g., Angie Debo, *A History of the Indians of the United States* (Norman: University of Oklahoma Press, 1976), 159 (quoting General George Crook: "It was of no unfrequent occurrence for an Indian to be shot down in cold blood, or a squaw to be raped by some brute. Such a thing as a white man being punished for outraging an Indian was unheard of").

21. Leslie E. Korn, "Community Trauma and Development," *Fourth World Journal,* 5, no. 1 (2002): 4.

22. Amerigo Vespucci, "Mundus Novus," in Christensen and Christensen, *The Discovery of America and Other Myths,* 14.

23. Paula Gunn Allen, *Off the Reservation: Reflections on Boundary-Busting, Border-Crossing Loose Cannons* (Boston: Beacon Press, 1998), 66.

24. Robert B. Porter, "Strengthening Tribal Sovereignty through Peacemaking: How the Anglo-American Legal Tradition Destroys Indigenous Societies," *Columbia Human Rights Law Review* 28 (1997): 235.

25. Dolores Subia Bigfoot, *History of Victimization in Native Communities* (Washington, D.C.: Department of Justice, 2000).

26. Katy McColl, "If Two White Girls Had Been Butchered, There Would've Been Arrests That Night," *JANE Magazine,* March 2004, 136; Pete Yost, "FBI Whistle-blower in Sept. 11 Matter Seeks New Probe," Associated Press, Nov. 6, 2003; Dian Million, "Policing the Rez: Keeping No Peace in Indian Country," *Social Justice* 27, no. 3 (2000): 101–19.

27. Lisa M. Poupart, "Crime and Justice in American Indian Communities," *Social Justice* 29, nos. 1–2 (2002): 144–59.

28. Beth E. Richie, *Arrested Justice: Black Women, Violence, and America's Prison Nation* (New York: New York University Press, 2012), 51.

29. S. Rep. No. 101–60 (1990).

30. See Matt Kelley, "At Least 118 Federal Doctors Punished for Wrongdoing," Associated Press, Apr. 14, 2002.

31. Daugherty v. Thompson, 322 F.3d 1249 (10th Cir. 2003).

32. "Doctor Surrenders Medical License," *Shawnee News-Star*, Oct. 9, 1997.

33. "Family Doctor Admits to Shipping Child Porn," *Albuquerque Journal*, May 15, 1998, B3.

34. "BIA Agent Found Guilty of Sex Assault," *Billings Gazette*, July 30, 1998.

35. "Four Workers Put on Leave after Teen Dies at Indian School," Associated Press, Dec. 26, 2003.

36. "IHS Doctor Charged with Battery," *Farmington Daily News*, March 17, 2004.

37. "Ex-FBI Official Admits Sex Assaults," Associated Press, Feb. 18, 2004.

38. Dennis Wagner, "Whiteriver Serial Rapist Investigation Failed, Files Show," *Arizona Republic*, Sept. 12, 2010, http://www.azcentral.com.

39. "Jailer Charged with Sexual Abuse of a Ward," *Bismarck Tribune*, July 20, 2010.

40. "BIA Officer for Spirit Lake Charged in Stabbing," Associated Press, Aug. 15, 2010.

41. Scott Waltman, "Man Pleads Guilty to Child Porn Charges," *Aberdeen News*, May 5, 2012.

42. Allen J. Beck et al., *Sexual Victimization in Prisons and Jails Reported by Inmates, 2011–12* (Washington, D.C.: Department of Justice, 2013).

43. Meg Warner, "Ex-HHS Cyber Security Chief Sentenced to 25 Years in Prison for Child Porn," *New York Daily News*, Jan. 6, 2015.

44. 42 C.F.R. 136.416.

45. Federal Tort Claims Act, 28 U.S.C. § 2671 et seq.

46. Jack W. Massey, "A Proposal to Narrow the Assault and Battery Exception to the Federal Tort Claims Act," *Texas Law Review* 82, no. 6 (2004): 1651.

47. Lavetta Elk v. United States, 87 Fed. Cl. 70 (2009).

48. "A Bad Man Is Hard to Find," *Harvard Law Review* 127 (2014): 2521.

49. Lillian Marquez, "Making 'Bad Men' Pay: Recovering Pain and Suffering Damages for Torts on Indian Reservations Under the Bad Men Clause," *Federal Circuit Bar Journal* 20 (2011): 609–31.

50. Fort Laramie 1868 Treaty. 15 Stat. 635, ratified Feb. 16, 1869, proclaimed by President Andrew Johnson on Feb. 29, 1869.

51. Marquez, "Making 'Bad Men' Pay."

52. Elk, 87 Fed. Cl. 70, 82.

53. Ibid., 87.

54. Carey N. Vicenti, "The Social Structures of Legal Neocolonialism in Native America," *Kansas Journal of Law and Public Policy* 20 (2000): 529.

5. RELOCATION REVISITED

1. Barbara B. Covell, "An Unforgotten Legacy[:] Yachats Commemorates the History of the Amanda's Trail," *South Lincoln County News*, Aug. 4, 2009, http://www.southlincolncountynews.com/V2_news_articles .php?page=72&story_id=989.
2. Jessica Musicar, "Blood and Tears," *World*, July 20, 2009, http://theworldlink.com/news/local/blood-and-tears/article_aa6c2c24-20df-5a9e-aa18-57c38c0b9c52.html.
3. Covell, "An Unforgotten Legacy."
4. Musicar, "Blood and Tears."
5. Covell, "An Unforgotten Legacy."
6. See David Peterson Del Mar, *Beaten Down: A History of Interpersonal Violence in the West* (Seattle: University of Washington Press, 2002), 29.
7. Trafficking Victims Protection Act, 22 U.S.C. § 7101 (2006) (amended 2008).
8. See, e.g., Tracey Kyckelhahn, Allen J. Beck, and Thomas H. Cohen, *Characteristics of Suspected Human Trafficking Incidents, 2007–08* (Washington, D.C.: U.S. Department of Justice, 2009) (describing the number and characteristics of suspected human trafficking investigations and their outcomes in the United States); Janice G. Raymond and Donna M. Hughes, *Sex Trafficking of Women in the United States* (New York: Coalition against Trafficking in Women, 2001) (discussing both international and domestic trafficking of women for sexual exploitation in the United States).
9. See, e.g., *Assessment of U.S. Government Efforts to Combat Trafficking in Persons in Fiscal Year 2005* (Washington, D.C.: U.S. Department of Justice et al., 2006), 1 (claiming that "the United States is among the nations leading the fight against this terrible crime").
10. Ibid., 34 (quoting Attorney General Alberto Gonzales: "Today, its victims are usually aliens"). Some articles and reports provide a list of the common countries of origin, which usually include nations that "tend to be relatively unstable politically or economically disadvantaged." David R. Hodge, "Sexual Trafficking in the United States: A Domestic Problem with Transnational Dimensions," *Social Work* 53, no. 2 (2008): 145.
11. Hodge, in "Sexual Trafficking in the United States," writes that "trends in international trafficking are easier to estimate than trends in domestic trafficking."
12. Desyllas writes, "Countries holding power and privilege have domi-

neering policies and imperialistic frameworks and ideologies that are imposed upon the rest of the world." Moshoula Capous Desyllas, "A Critique of the Global Trafficking Discourse and U.S. Policy," *Journal of Sociology and Social Welfare* 34 (2007): 58.

13. Vine Deloria Jr., *Custer Died for Your Sins: An Indian Manifesto* (New York: Macmillan, 1969), 57.

14. 1850 Cal. Stat. 408–10 (cited in Chauncey Shafter Goodrich, "The Legal Status of the California Indian," *California Law Review* 14 [1926]: 93). See also Vanessa Ann Gunther, *Ambiguous Justice: Native Americans and the Legal System in Southern California, 1848–1890* (East Lansing: Michigan State University Press, 2006), 26.

15. See Goodrich, "The Legal Status of the California Indian."

16. Jean Allain, "The Definition of Slavery in International Law," *Howard Law Journal* 52, no. 2 (2009): 240–41.

17. See Adrienne Davis, " 'Don't Let Nobody Bother Yo' Principle': The Sexual Economy of American Slavery," in *Sister Circle: Black Women and Work*, ed. Sharon Harley (New Brunswick, N.J.: Rutgers University Press, 2002), 107. Davis also provides the example of an 1859 Mississippi case, in which the defendant (an enslaved man accused of raping an enslaved girl) had his conviction overturned, in part, based on the argument that "sexual intercourse [of slaves] is left to be regulated by their owners." Ibid., 113 (referencing State v. George, 37 Miss. 316 [1859]). Although this case (and Davis's chapter generally) focuses on the enslavement of enslaved persons of African descent, this legal conception of slavery and sexuality was applied in the same way to Native slaves.

18. As abolitionist William Goodell explained in 1853, under American slavery, "slaves, as Property, may be used, absolutely by their owners at will, for their own profit or pleasure. . . . Nothing, therefore, can prevent the master from putting [the slave] to any use he pleases." William Goodell, *The American Slave Code in Theory and Practice: Its Distinctive Features Shown by Its Statutes, Judicial Decisions, and Illustrative Facts* (New York: American and Foreign Anti-Slavery Society, 1853), available at http://www.unz.org/Pub/GoodellWilliam-1853.

19. Bethany R. Berger, "Indian Policy and the Imagined Indian Woman," *Kansas Journal of Law and Public Policy* 14 (2004): 103–20.

20. Rose Stremlau, " 'To Domesticate and Civilize Wild Indians': Allotment and the Campaign to Reform Indian Families, 1875–1887," *Journal of Family History* 30, no. 3 (2005): 273–74.

21. Francis Paul Prucha, *American Indian Policy in the Formative Years* (Cambridge, Mass.: Harvard University Press, 1962), 199.

22. Lawrence M. Friedman, *Crime and Punishment in American History* (New York: Basic Books, 1993), 215.

23. Even in contemporary settings, police may collude with traffickers. See Hodge, "Sexual Trafficking in the United States," 144 ("Indeed, in some nations, police collude with traffickers, returning those who escape to their former exploiters in the sex or prostitution industry").

24. David T. Courtwright, *Violent Land: Single Men and Social Disorder from the Frontier to the Inner City* (Cambridge, Mass.: Harvard University Press, 1996), 64.

25. Anne M. Butler, *Daughters of Joy, Sisters of Misery: Prostitutes in the American West, 1865–90* (Champaign: University of Illinois Press, 1985), 10 (quoting W. L. Lincoln, Report of the U.S. Indian Agent, Montana, in Office of Indian Affairs, *1885 Commissioner Indian Affairs Annual Report* [Washington, D.C.: Department of the Interior, 1885], 130). In 1870 a Colorado Indian agent reported that "the whole tribe is infected with syphilis. I do not believe there is a single squaw who is not suffering from this disease." Office of Indian Affairs, *1870 Commissioner Indian Affairs Annual Report* (Washington, D.C.: Department of the Interior, 1870), 129. The agent also reported that an eight-year-old Indian girl died of syphilis and noted that he had heard of other children of that age who had been "used for improper purposes." Office of Indian Affairs, *1870 Commissioner Indian Affairs Annual Report*, 129–30.

26. Mark Diedrich, *Old Betsey: The Life and Times of a Famous Dakota Woman and Her Family* (Rochester, Minn.: Coyote Books, 1995), 34 (quoting William B. Hennessey).

27. Fay Yarbrough, "Legislating Women's Sexuality: Cherokee Marriage Laws in the Nineteenth Century," *Journal of Society History* 38, no. 2 (2005): 388.

28. 51st Cong., 1st Sess. 295 (report of Thomas Priestley, Yakima Agency, Aug. 16, 1889) (reporting that "the white men who marry Indian women for purposes of getting a home on an Indian reservation are not of the better class").

29. "Dusky Maidens Are in Demand," *Oklahoman*, Dec. 11, 1910, 21.

30. Rennard Strickland, "Osage Oil: Mineral Law, Murder, Mayhem, and Manipulation," *Natural Resources and Environment* 10, no. 1 (1995), 39 (describing the "Osage Reign of Terror").

31. Maureen Trudelle Schwarz, "Unraveling the Anchoring Cord: Navajo Relocation, 1974 to 1996," *American Anthropologist* 99, no. 1 (1997): 50.

32. William M. Osborn, *The Wild Frontier* (New York: Random House, 2000), 203 ("The land and the slaves were packaged together").

33. California Genealogy and History Archives, History of Humboldt County, https://archive.org/details/historyofhumboldooirvi (last visited July 14, 2014).

34. Ibid.

35. Lucy (T'tcetsa) Young, "Out of the Past: Lucy's Story," in *No Rooms of*

Their Own: Women Writers of Early California, ed. Ida Rae Egli (Berkeley, Calif.: Heyday Books, 1992), 49.

36. Ibid.

37. Ibid.

38. Ibid., 52–58.

39. See, e.g., T. S. Twibell, "Rethinking Johnson v. M'Intosh (1823): The Root of the Continued Forced Displacement of American Indians despite Cobell v. Norton (2001)," *Georgetown Immigration Law Journal* 23, no. 1 (2008): 150.

40. Indian Removal Act, Pub. L. No. 148, §1, 4 Stat. 411 (1830).

41. See, e.g., Maria Yellow Horse Brave Heart and Lemyra M. DeBruyn, "The American Indian Holocaust: Healing Historical Unresolved Grief," *American Indian and Alaska Native Mental Health Research* 8, no. 2 (1998): 62.

42. Laura Tohe, "Hwéeldi Bééhániih: Remembering the Long Walk," *Wicazo Sa Review* 22, no. 1 (2007): 77–82.

43. See, e.g., Berger, "Indian Policy and the Imagined Indian Woman," 110n41 (citing Lynn R. Bailey, *Bosque Redondo: The Navajo Internment at Fort Sumner, New Mexico, 1863–1868* [Tucson: Westernlore Press, 1998], 145 [describing "hog farms," as brothels were called, that arose in Fort Sumner]).

44. See Tohe, "Hwéeldi Bééhániih," 79.

45. Elizabeth Sullivan, *Indian Legends of the Trail of Tears and Other Creek Stories* (Tulsa, Okla.: Giant Services, 1974), 2.

46. Congressional debates from 1871 provide some evidence that Congress moved tribes to reservations rather than exterminating them, in part because doing so was less expensive than continued warfare. Cong. Globe, 41st Cong., 3d Sess. 733 (1871) (statement of Sen. Beck).

47. See David Wallace Adams, *Education for Extinction: American Indians and the Boarding School Experience 1875–1928* (Lawrence: University Press of Kansas, 1995), 95–163 (arguing that the goal of boarding Indian children was to remove them from their savage surroundings and to place them in a purified environment in order to learn to look, act, and think like their white counterparts); Sandra Del Valle, *Language Rights and the Law in the United States: Finding Our Voices* (Tonawanda, N.Y.: Multilingual Matters, 2003), 276–85 (discussing the prohibition on children speaking their native Indian languages in boarding schools and how this helped stigmatize and destroy Indian culture); Amelia V. Katanski, *Learning to Write "Indian": The Boarding-School Experience and American Indian Literature* (Norman: University of Oklahoma Press, 2007), 133–34 (discussing how boarding schools changed Indian self-identity through an examination of Indian children's writing at boarding schools); Kathleen Malley-Morrison and Denise A. Hines, *Family*

Violence in a Cultural Perspective: Defining, Understanding, and Combating Abuse (Thousand Oaks, Calif.: Sage, 2004), 70–72 (asserting that adult Natives could not be influenced to assimilate into white civilization, and thus Native children were targeted through education in boarding schools so that they would abandon Native culture); Barbara Perry, *Silent Victims: Hate Crimes against Native Americans* (Tucson: University of Arizona Press, 2008), 31–33 (discussing the violence against Indian children in government-sponsored boarding schools, as well as the violence against their culture); Andrea Smith, *Conquest: Sexual Violence and American Indian Genocide* (Boston: South End Press, 2005), 35 (exploring the establishment and subsequent history of Grant's Peace Policy of 1869, which gave administrative power of Indian reservations to Christian denominations to erect and run schools); Clifford E. Trafzer, Jean A. Keller, and Lorene Sisquoc, eds., "Introduction: Origin and Development of the American Indian Boarding School System," in *Boarding School Blues: Revisiting American Indian Educational Experiences* (Lincoln: University of Nebraska Press, 2006), 13–19 (discussing the establishment of the first government-sponsored boarding schools and the literal stripping-away of any and all semblances of the Indian children's culture).

48. See generally Andrea Smith, "Soul Wound: The Legacy of Native American Schools" (2003) at http://www.amnestyusa.org/node/87342.

49. Ibid.; see also Charles Horejsi, "Reactions by Native American Parents to Child Protection Agencies: Cultural and Community Factors," *Child Welfare* 71 (1992): 330.

50. See Robert A. Trennert, "Victorian Morality and the Supervision of Indian Women Working in Phoenix, 1906–1930," *Journal of Social History* 22, no. 1 (1988): 113–28.

51. Janelle F. Palacios and Carmen J. Portillo, "Understanding Native Women's Health: Historical Legacies," *Journal of Transcultural Nursing* 20, no. 1 (2009): 21.

52. Adams, *Education for Extinction*, 98 (describing several documented accounts of the "final farewells").

53. In 1892, Commissioner of Indian Affairs Thomas J. Morgan issued a rule that Indians who attempted to "prevent the attendance of children at school" were guilty of an offense and subject to imprisonment "for not less than ten days." Subsequent offenses could be punished by as much as six months of incarceration. H.R. Doc. No. 52–1, pt. 5, at 28–31 (1892), reprinted in Thomas J. Morgan, "Rules for Indian Courts," in *Americanizing the American Indians: Writings by the "Friends of the Indian," 1880–1900*, ed. Francis Paul Prucha (Cambridge, Mass.: Harvard University Press, 1973), 300. See also Adams, *Education for Extinction*, 209–14

(discussing the various ways parents would attempt to keep their children from being taken to the schools and the reasons why they would do so).

54. K. Tsianina Lomawaima, *They Called It Prairie Light: The Story of Chilocco Indian School* (Lincoln: University of Nebraska Press, 1994), 36. See also Frank Wilson Blackmar, "The Socialization of the American Indian," *American Journal of Sociology* 34, no. 4 (1929), 658 (noting that the reluctance of Indian parents to send their children away "kept the agents busy running over the country and gathering in their students").

55. Lomawaima, *They Called It Prairie Light*, xiv.

56. Bethany Ruth Berger, "After Pocahontas: Indian Women and the Law, 1830–1934," *American Indian Law Review* 21, no. 1 (1997): 49 ("To ensure that the female pupils would not backslide into Indian ways, the girls were 'placed out' during vacation to give them experience with a non-Indian family").

57. Robert A. Trennert, "Victorian Morality and the Supervision of Indian Women Working in Phoenix, 1906–1930," *Journal of Social History* 2, no. 1 (1998): 115.

58. Ibid. See also Margaret D. Jacobs, "Working on the Domestic Frontier," *Frontiers* 28, nos. 1–2 (2007): 165 (discussing the experiences of Indian girls working in white households in the San Francisco Bay area).

59. Trennert, "Victorian Morality and the Supervision of Indian Women Working in Phoenix, 1906–1930," 114.

60. Ibid., 113.

61. Lomawaima, *They Called It Prairie Light*, 81.

62. See Robert A. Trennert, "Corporal Punishment and the Politics of Indian Reform," *History of Education Quarterly* 29, no. 4 (1989): 595 (discussing executive secretary of the American Indian Defense Association John Collier's report on corporal punishment at Phoenix Indian School in 1930, which the author argues was undertaken to force the Bureau of Indian Affairs to restructure and for political gain).

63. Ibid., 598. The Phoenix Indian School building included a jail as early as 1893, three years after opening its doors. While attendance at boarding schools is no longer mandatory, some original punitive policies have continued with little or no modification. At least one "holding cell" in a government-run Indian boarding school was documented to exist as recently as 2003: Cindy Lou Bright Star Gilbert Sohappy, a sixteen-year-old student, died in the "holding cell" at Chemawa Boarding School in Oregon (a federally run boarding school which originally opened in 1880). Earl E. Devaney, Office of Inspector General, *Investigative Report on the Chemawa Indian School Detention Facility* (Washington, D.C.: U.S. Department of the Interior, 2005), 3–6. An official federal report on

the death indicates that Cindy Lou was placed in a cell due to alcohol intoxication. Despite regulations that required her well-being to be monitored every fifteen minutes, Cindy Lou was left alone in the cell for nearly three hours, during which time she died of alcohol poisoning.

64. Lomawaima, *They Called It Prairie Light,* 23.

65. Ibid.

66. Smith, *Conquest.*

67. Jackie Lynne, "Colonialism and the Sexual Exploitation of Canada's First Nations Women," paper presented at the American Psychological Association 106th Annual Convention, San Francisco, Aug. 17, 1998, http://www.prostitutionresearch.com/colonialism%20and%20the%20sexual%20exploitation%20of%20canada%27s%20first%20nations%20women.pdf.

68. Trafficking Victims Protection Act, 22 U.S.C. § 7101(b)(4) (2008).

69. Yellow Horse Brave Heart and DeBruyn, "The American Indian Holocaust," 64–65.

70. Ann Metcalf, "Navajo Women in the City: Lessons from a Quarter-Century of Relocation," *American Indian Quarterly* 6, nos. 1–2 (1982): 83.

71. Ibid., 72.

72. Gary D. Sandefur, Ronald R. Rindfuss, and Barney Cohen, eds., *Changing Numbers, Changing Needs: American Indian Demography and Public Health* (Washington, D.C.: National Research Council, 1996), 109.

73. Joan Ablon, "American Indian Relocation: Problems of Dependency and Management in the City," *Phylon* 26 (Winter 1965): 362.

74. See Theodore D. Graves, "Urban Indian Personality and the 'Culture of Poverty,'" *American Ethnologist* 1 (1974): 66.

75. Metcalf, "Navajo Women in the City," 73.

76. Ibid. (stating that "the BIA provided one-way transportation to the selected city").

77. Ablon, "American Indian Relocation," 363. Many Native people found it difficult to secure employment due to racial prejudice specifically targeted at Indians. For example, a University of Minnesota study of South Minneapolis businesses in 1970 revealed that anti-Indian sentiment was common. Richard P. Gibbons et al., *Indian Americans in Southside Minneapolis: Additional Field Notes from the Urban Slum* (1970) (available at http://files.eric.ed.gov/fulltext/ED067209.pdf). Among some of the interviewees were a flower shop owner ("[Indians] don't belong in the city but back at home on the reservation with their own people"), a real estate agent ("[Indians] are very dishonest and only tell you what you want to hear"), and a gas station owner ("The Indian women, they're pigs").

78. Ablon, *"American Indian Relocation,"* 365.

79. Graves, *"Urban Indian Personality and the 'Culture of Poverty'"* (internal quotations omitted).

80. See, e.g ., Donald H. J. Clairmont, *Deviance among Indians and Eskimos in Aklavik, N.W.T.* (1963) (available at http://files.eric.ed.gov/fulltext/ ED039073.pdf). Clairmont's report, which is typical of social science publications on Native people during that time period, explicitly establishes the ideal social standards as "middle class white values." The report then references "official" whites, who offered critiques of the parenting of Native parents as the cause of social problems such as poverty, "illegitimacy," and alcohol abuse.

81. Albon, *"American Indian Relocation,"* 368.

82. Clairmont, *Deviance among Indians and Eskimos in Aklavik, N.W.T.,* 61.

83. A. M. Ervin, *New Northern Townsmen in Inuvik* (1968) (available at http:// files.eric.ed.gov/fulltext/ED031332.pdf), 11.

84. Ibid.

85. Farley and colleagues explain how this dynamic emerges: "First Nations youth who leave their home communities for urban areas are particularly vulnerable to sexual exploitation in that they are both homeless and in an unfamiliar cultural environment." Melissa Farley, Jacqueline Lynne, and Ann J. Cotton, "Prostitution in Vancouver: Violence and the Colonization of First Nations Women," *Transcultural Psychiatry* 42, no. 2 (2005): 257. See also Nancy Shoemaker, "Urban Indians and Ethnic Choices: American Indian Organizations in Minneapolis, 1920–1950," *Western History Quarterly* 19, no. 4 (1988): 443.

86. Investigate Indian Affairs: Hearings Before the Subcommittee of the Committee of Indian Affairs, 78th Cong. (1944), 675–77 (testimony of Mrs. Amabel K. Bulin, volunteer social worker, Minneapolis Indian Service). Although Mrs. Bulin was Indian, her testimony reflects racial prejudice against black people—particularly the "colored men" she accused of taking advantage of the Indian girls in the "slums" of Minneapolis. Ibid., 675.

87. See generally Robert E. Kuttner and Albert B. Lorincz, "Promiscuity and Prostitution in Urbanized Indian Communities," *Mental Hygiene* 54 (1970): 79 (expressing two doctors' opinions on factors promoting prostitution of Native women in an urban setting).

88. Ibid.

89. Ibid., 84.

90. See Hodge, *"Sexual Trafficking in the United States,"* 148 ("Traffickers deliberately seek out obscure venues to avoid detection. Victims often remain in the shadows because of the fear of arrest; reprisals from traffickers; or the fear that officials are corrupt, unconcerned, or aligned with the traffickers").

91. Ibid., 145. One study of aboriginal women prostitutes in Vancouver found that "the youngest age at recruitment into prostitution was 10 years." Farley, Lynne, and Cotton, "Prostitution in Vancouver," 249.

92. See Yellow Horse Brave Heart and DeBruyn, "The American Indian

Holocaust," 61 (noting that "indigenous people throughout the world can trace social pathologies and internalized oppression to similar historical legacies"). Many of the official strategies used to deal with the "Indian problem" in the United States have a parallel strategy in Canada. For example, the urbanization of Native people in both countries was part of an effort to find employment. See, e.g., Allison M. Williams, "Canadian Urban Aboriginals: A Focus on Aboriginal Women in Toronto," *Canadian Journal of Native Studies* 17, no. 1 (1997): 79–80 (discussing the push factors of the Aboriginal Reserve and the pull factors of the government, both of which caused employment to be a major factor in the movement of indigenous people into cities, where they were subject to assimilation strategies).

93. See Farley, Lynne, and Cotton, "Prostitution in Vancouver," 245 (noting that "in a number of communities across Canada, Aboriginal youth comprise '90% of the visible sex trade'") (quoting Save the Children Canada, *Year One: 1999–2000: Out of the Shadows and Into the Light; A Project to Address the Commercial Sexual Exploitation of Girls and Boys in Canada* [Vancouver: Save the Children Canada, 2000], 7).

94. Dara Culhane, "Their Spirits Live within Us," *American Indian Quarterly* 27, nos. 3–4 (2003): 597 (citing Sue Currie, Ministry of Women's Equality, Province of British Columbia, *Assessing the Violence against Street Involved Women in the Downtown Eastside/Strathcona Community* [2000]).

95. Mike McIntyre, "Hundreds of Kids in Sex Trade," *Winnipeg Free Press,* Feb. 20, 2007, http://www.cyc-net.org/features/viewpoints/c-sex trade.html.

96. Ibid.

97. Ibid.

98. See Alexandra (Sandi) Pierce, *Shattered Hearts* (Minneapolis: Minnesota Indian Women's Resource Center, 2009).

99. Melissa Farley et al., *Garden of Truth: The Prostitution and Trafficking of Native Women in Minnesota* (St. Paul, Minn.: William Mitchell College of Law, 2011), http://www.prostitutionresearch.com/pdfs/Garden_of_Truth_Final_Project_WEB.pdf.

100. Ibid., 3.

101. Ibid.

102. Alex DeMarban, "Sex Trafficking Rings Target Rural Girls New to Anchorage," *Alaska Dispatch News,* Oct. 7, 2010.

103. Ibid.

104. Ibid.

105. Associated Press, "Sex Traffickers Targeting Alaska Native Girls," *News Miner,* Dec. 3, 2010.

106. Hodge, "Sex Trafficking in the United States," 150.

107. Damon Buckley, "Firsthand Account of Man Camp in North Dakota from Local Tribal Cop," *Lakota Country Times*, May 22, 2014, m.lakotacountrytimes.com/news/2014-05-22/Front_Page/Firsthand_Account_Of_Man_Camp_In_North_Dakota_From.html#.VRMsKnjdKOI.

108. Sierra Crane-Murdoch, "On Indian Land, Criminals Can Get Away with Almost Anything," *Atlantic*, Feb. 22, 2013, http://www.theatlantic.com/national/archive/2013/02/on-indian-land-criminals-can-get-away-with-almost-anything/273391; Mary Annette Pember, "Brave Heart Women Fight to Ban Man-Camps, Which Bring Rape and Abuse," *Indian Country Today*, Aug. 28, 2013, http://indiancountrytodaymedianetwork.com/2013/08/28/brave-heart-women-fight-ban-man-camps-which-bring-rape-and-abuse-151070.

109. Sari Horwitz, "Dark Side of the Boom," *Washington Post*, Sept. 28, 2014, http://www.washingtonpost.com/sf/national/2014/09/28/dark-side-of-the-boom.

110. Bureau of Public Affairs, *The Link between Prostitution and Sex Trafficking* (Washington, D.C.: U.S. Department of State, 2004), 1.

111. Andrew Karmen, *Crime Victims: An Introduction to Victimology*, 7th ed. (Belmont, Calif.: Wadsworth Cengage Learning, 2009), 7. See also Angela Bortel et al., *Sex Trafficking Needs Assessment for the State of Minnesota* (Minneapolis: Advocates for Human Rights, 2008), 17 ("With some exceptions, the government response to sex trafficking in Minnesota currently focuses on the arrest, prosecution, and punishment of prostituted women rather than sex traffickers. This misplaced focus leads to harmful criminal and/or immigration consequences for trafficked persons").

112. Elizabeth Grobsmith, "Review of *Inventing the Savage: The Social Construction of Native American Criminality* by Luana Ross," *Great Plains Research* 9 (Apr. 1999): 176. See also Lori De Ravello, Jessica Abeita, and Pam Brown, "Breaking the Cycle/Mending the Hoop: Adverse Childhood Experiences among Incarcerated American Indian/Alaska Native Women in New Mexico," *Health Care for Women International* 29, no. 3 (2008): 301–2.

6. PUNISHING THE VICTIM

1. United States v. Deegan, 605 F.3d 625, 636 (8th Cir. 2010) (Bright, J., dissenting).

2. Ibid., 625.

3. Ibid., 628 (quoting the district court presentencing order). Moreover, the U.S. attorney at the time of the crime described the crime as "violent and vicious" and described Dana's actions as heartless. Paul Walsh,

N.D. "Mom Sentenced in 'Slow-Motion' Death of Newborn Left Alone for Two Weeks," *Minneapolis Star Tribune*, May 13, 2008, http://www .startribune.com/local/18894054.html.

4. *Deegan*, 628.

5. Ibid.

6. See letter from Phillip J. Resnick, director of forensic psychiatry, Case Western Reserve University School of Medicine, to William D. Schmidt, assistant federal public defender, Districts of South Dakota and North Dakota (Apr. 9, 2008) (on file with author) (psychological evaluation documenting Dana's history of trauma and violence).

7. Ibid.

8. Ibid.

9. Ibid.

10. Carol Devens, "'If We Get the Girls, We Get the Race': Missionary Education of Native American Girls," *Journal World History* 3 (Fall 1992): 237.

11. See generally Charles Horejsi et al., "Reactions by Native American Parents to Child Protection Agencies: Cultural and Community Factors," *Child Welfare* 71, no. 4 (1992): 329 (describing the societal and historical influences that influence a Native's way of thinking about outside intervention).

12. This dynamic is explored by Michele Bograd, "Strengthening Domestic Violence Theories: Intersections of Race, Class, Sexual Orientation, and Gender," in *Domestic Violence at the Margins: Readings on Race, Class, Gender, and Culture*, ed. Natalie J. Sokoloff with Christina Pratt (New Brunswick, N.J.: Rutgers University Press, 2005), 31 ("Psychological consequences of battering may be compounded by the 'microaggressions' of racism, heterosexism, and classism in and out of the reference group").

13. Suzanne L. Cross, Angelique G. Day, and Emily C. Proctor, "Working on the Front Lines: The Role of Social Work in Response to the Indian Child Welfare Act of 1978," in *Facing the Future: The Indian Child Welfare Act at 30*, ed. Matthew L. M. Fletcher, Wenona T. Singel, and Kathryn E. Fort (East Lansing: Michigan State University Press, 2009), 3.

14. Claudia R. Long and Mary Ann Curry, "Living in Two Worlds: Native American Women and Prenatal Care," *Health Care for Women International* 19, no. 3 (1998): 211 (noting that all the Native American elders who participated in the study perceived the history of federal policies as having "broke[n] the family circle").

15. Cook-Lynn, "The Big Pipe Case," in *Why I Can't Read Wallace Stegner and Other Essays*, 110.

16. For example, some tribes (largely influenced by state models) will prosecute a woman for child neglect if she fails to leave her abuser or fails to report or seek help for the abuse she and her children suffer.

See, e.g., James G. White, Hallie Bongar White, and Jane Larrington, *Criminal Prosecution of Battered Native Women for Failure to Protect* (2005), 1, http://www.swclap.org/pdfs/FAILURETOPROTECT.pdf. While the intent of such laws may be to protect children, they also present enormous disincentives for a mother to report abuse or ask for help; see ibid., 8–9. A Native woman might "stay" in an abusive marriage—not because she lacks self-esteem or has learned helplessness, but because of a well-justified fear of losing custody of her children.

17. In the Canadian parallel, Kline explains, "While First Nation women are often victims of the child welfare system, they are not passive victims." Marlee Kline, "Complicating the Ideology of Motherhood: Child Welfare Law and First Nation Women," *Queen's Law Journal* 18 (1993): 316.

18. White, White, and Larrington, *Criminal Prosecution of Battered Native Women for Failure to Protect,* 9.

19. Christine A. Fazio and Jennifer L. Comito, "Rethinking the Tough Sentencing of Teenage Neonaticide Offenders in the United States," *Fordham Law Review* 67, no. 6 (1999): 37.

20. Ibid., 40.

21. Ibid., 38.

22. Natalie K. Isser and Lita Linzer Schwartz, "Engendered Homicide," *Journal of Psychiatry and Law* 36, no. 4 (2008): 585.

23. Susan Ayres, "*Kairos* and Safe Havens: The Timing and Calamity of Unwanted Birth," *William and Mary Journal of Women and the Law* 15, no. 2 (2008): 227–89.

24. Jenny Michael, "Case Helped Inspire Safe Haven Law," *Bismarck Tribune,* May 18, 2007, A1, available at LexisNexis. Safe Haven laws, however, present specific complications in the case of Native mothers as a result of the Indian Child Welfare Act. Further study of this issue is needed.

25. Resnick letter, 5; see note 6, this chapter.

26. See, e.g., Carrie A. Martell and Sarah Deer, "Heeding the Voice of Native Women: Toward an Ethic of Decolonization," *North Dakota Law Review* 81, no. 4 (2005): 816.

27. See, e.g., Mishuana R. Goeman and Jennifer Nez Denetdale, "Guest Editors' Introduction, Native Feminism: Legacies, Interventions, and Indigenous Sovereignties," *Wicazo Sa Review* 24, no. 2 (2009): 9–13.

28. *Deegan,* 641 ("Ms. Deegan's state of despair and depression was not merely the result of the physical, verbal, and sexual abuse she suffered. Ms. Deegan lived in extreme poverty and isolation").

29. The pardon attorney makes clemency and pardon recommendations to the White House; the president has the final say on disposition.

30. State of North Dakota v. Laura J. Rafferty, Criminal Judgment and Commitment CR-00–1202 (June 28, 2000).

31. *Deegan,* 662.

7. THE ENIGMA OF FEDERAL REFORM

1. Kimberly Robertson, "Rerighting the Historical Record: Violence against Native Women and the South Dakota Coalition Against Domestic Violence and Sexual Assault," *Wicazo Sa Review* 27, no. 2 (2012): 22 (explaining that the Tribal Law and Order Act "develops out of numerous historical moments, grassroots efforts, and indigenous struggles against settler-colonialism and heteropatriarchy").

2. Jacqueline Agtuca, *Safety for Native Women: VAWA and American Indian Tribes,* ed. Dorma Sahneyah (Lame Deer, Mont.: National Indigenous Women's Resource Center, 2014).

3. 42 U.S.C. § 16901 (2006).

4. Virginia Davis and Kevin Washburn, "Sex Offender Registration in Indian Country," *Ohio State Journal of Criminal Law* 6, no. 13 (2008): 3.

5. Ibid.

6. See, e.g., statement by Kevin Leecy, chairman, Minnesota Indian Affairs Council, July 30, 2005 (on file with author).

7. Matthew L. M. Fletcher, "Toward a Theory of Intertribal and Intratribal Common Law," 43 *Houston Law Review* 43 (2006): 719.

8. Vincent J. Felitti and Robert F. Anda, "The Relationship of Adverse Childhood Experiences to Adult Medical Disease, Psychiatric Disorders and Sexual Behavior: Implications for Healthcare," in *The Impact of Early Life Trauma on Health and Disease: The Hidden Epidemic,* ed. Ruth A. Lanius, Eric Vermetten, and Clare Pain (Cambridge: Cambridge University Press, 2010).

9. Ibid.

10. Indian Law and Order Commission, *A Roadmap for Making Native America Safer* (Los Angeles: Indian Law and Order Commission, 2013), i.

11. Office on Violence Against Women, About the Office, http://www.justice.gov/ovw/about-office.

12. Jacqueline Agtuca, "Beloved Women: Life Givers, Caretakers, Teachers of Future Generations," in Deer et al., *Sharing Our Stories of Survival.*

13. The tribal provisions primarily apply to women who live on Indian reservations or trust land, or, in some other way, fall under the auspices of tribal jurisdiction. Native women living off reservation or in rural areas are not covered by the tribal provisions, although other aspects of VAWA might be applicable.

14. Debora Ortega and Noël Busch-Armendariz, "In the Name of VAWA," *Affilia* 28, no. 3 (2013): 225–28.

15. Deborah Parker, vice chairwoman, Tulalip Tribes, Remarks on the Violence Against Women Act, April 25, 2012, http://youtu.be/yIV7-XASQy8.

16. Grassley, "Senator Grassley Doesn't Think Native Americans Can Hold Fair Trials," http://youtu.be/BRpjxtLrTcE.

17. 159 Cong. Rec. S582 (Feb. 11, 2013) (statement of Sen. Grassley).
18. 159 Cong. Rec. H795 (Feb. 28, 2013) (statement of Rep. Hastings).

8. TOWARD AN INDIGENOUS JURISPRUDENCE OF RAPE

1. Philosopher Ann J. Cahill describes this as "the ethical wrongs of rape." See Ann J. Cahill, *Rethinking Rape* (Ithaca, N.Y.: Cornell University Press, 2001), 167. Legal theory should be distinguished from a behavioral "causal" theory, which seeks to explain *why* rape happens.
2. See, e.g., Julie Horney and Cassia Spohn, "Rape Law Reform and Instrumental Change in Six Urban Jurisdictions," *Law and Society Review* 25, no. 1 (1991): 117 (concluding that "the ability of rape reform legislation to affect case outcomes is limited").
3. Sylvana Tomaselli, introduction to Tomaselli and Porter, *Rape*, 2.
4. The vast majority of sexual assaults are committed by men against women. Lawrence A. Greenfeld, *Sex Offenses and Offenders: An Analysis of Data on Rape and Sexual Assault* (Washington, D.C.: Department of Justice, 1997), 24.
5. Robert Allen Warrior, *Tribal Secrets: Recovering American Indian Intellectual Traditions* (Minneapolis: University of Minnesota Press, 1995), xx.
6. Andrea Smith, "The Sexual Colonization of Native Women," in *Remembering Conquest: Feminist/Womanist Perspectives on Religion, Colonization, and Sexual Violence*, ed. Nantawan Boonprasat-Lewis and Marie M. Fortune (Binghamton, N.Y.: Haworth Press, 1999).
7. David Stannard, *American Holocaust: Conquest of the New World* (New York: Oxford University Press, 1993), 121.
8. Genocidal rape forces women to be "vessels through which the dilution, disappearance, and destruction of their own ethnic group occur." Sherrie L. Russell-Brown, "Rape as an Act of Genocide," *Berkeley Journal of International Law* 21 (2003): 355.
9. See Clara Sue Kidwell, "What Would Pocahontas Think Now? Women and Cultural Persistence," *Callaloo* 17, no. 1 (1994): 149–50.
10. Sarah Winnemucca Hopkins, *Life among the Piutes* (1883; repr., Reno: University of Nevada Press, 1994), 48.
11. See, e.g., Andrea Smith, "Not an Indian Tradition: The Sexual Colonization of Native Peoples," *Hypatia* 18, no. 2 (2003): 70–85.
12. Nadera Shalhoub-Kevorkian, "Towards a Cultural Definition of Rape: Dilemmas in Dealing with Rape Victims in Palestinian Society," *Women's Studies International Forum* 22 (1999): 171.
13. Keith Burgess-Jackson, "Rape and Persuasive Definition," *Canadian Journal of Philosophy* 25, no. 3 (1995): 443. Eric Reitan describes this approach to rape as "territorially defined." Eric Reitan, "Rape as an Essentially Contested Concept," *Hypatia* 16, no. 2 (2001): 51.
14. Burgess-Jackson, *"Rape and Persuasive Definition,"* 444.

15. Ibid., 446.
16. Ibid., 448.
17. See, e.g., Carine M. Mardorossian, "Toward a New Feminist Theory of Rape," *Signs* 27, no. 4 (2002): 747.
18. Laura Hengehold, "Remapping the Event: Institutional Discourses and the Trauma of Rape," *Signs* 26, no. 1 (2000): 211.
19. Mishauna Goeman, "(Re)mapping Indigenous Presence on the Land in Native Women's Literature," *American Quarterly* 60, no. 1 (2008): 295.
20. See, e.g., Valencia-Weber and Zuni, "Domestic Violence and Tribal Protection of Indigenous Women in the United States," 69.
21. See, e.g., Janice Gould, "American Indian Women's Poetry: Strategies of Rage and Hope," *Signs* 20, no. 4 (1995): 797–817.
22. Roberta Makashay Hendrickson, "Victims and Survivors: Native American Women Writers, Violence Against Women, and Child Abuse," *Studies in American Indian Literature* ser. 2, 8, no. 1 (1996): 13–24.
23. See, e.g., Rosalva Aída Hernández Castillo, "Reinventing Tradition: The Women's Law," *Cultural Survival Quarterly* 19, no. 1 (1995): 24.
24. Ibid., 12.
25. Condition of the Indian Tribes: Hearing Before the Special Comm. Appointed under Joint Resolution of March 3, 1865, 39th Cong. 2d sess., 370–371 (1867) (statement of Strike-the-Ree).
26. See generally Russel Lawrence Barsh, "Putting the Tribe in Tribal Court: Possible? Desirable?" *Kansas Journal of Law and Public Policy* 8 (1998): 74–96.
27. See, e.g., Pat Sekaquaptewa, "Evolving the Hopi Common Law," *Kansas Journal of Law and Public Policy* 9 (2000): 761–84.
28. See generally Carrie E. Garrow and Sarah Deer, *Tribal Criminal Law and Procedure* (Lanham, Md.: AltaMira Press, 2004).
29. Maria-Barbara Watson-Franke, "A World in Which Women Move Freely without Fear of Men: An Anthropological Perspective on Rape," *Women's Studies International Forum* 25, no. 6 (2002): 601 (quoting Claire R. Farrer).
30. Dawn Martin-Hill, "She No Speaks and Other Colonial Constructs of the Traditional Woman," in Anderson and Lawrence, *Strong Women Stories*, 107.
31. Raymond D. Fogelson, "Who Were the Ani-Kutani? An Excursion into Cherokee Historical Thought," *Ethnohistory* 31, no. 4 (1984): 255–63.
32. Harlan I. Smith, "Some Ojibwa Myths and Traditions," *Journal of American Folklore* 19 (1906): 215–30.
33. Mona M. Smith, "The Strength of Native Women," *News from Indian Country* 5 (1991): 15.
34. Ibid.

35. Johnny Frank, "Taa'ii' Ti," in *Neerihiinjik: We Traveled from Place to Place* (Fairbanks: Alaska Native Language Center, 1995), 279.

36. This juxtaposition is described in depth by Ross Harrison, "Rape: A Case Study in Political Philosophy," in Tomaselli and Porter, *Rape*, 41–56.

37. See Poupart, "The Familiar Face of Genocide: Internalized Oppression among American Indians" (drawing a line between the historical and contemporary oppression of Native people and the high rate of intra-tribal violence which plagues some tribal communities).

38. Marcie R. Rendon, "Facing Spiritual and Sexual Abuse in the Native Community," *Circle* 18 (July 1997): 9.

9. THE TROUBLE WITH PEACEMAKING

1. Nancy A. Costello, "Walking Together in a Good Way: Indian Peacemaker Courts in Michigan," *University of Detroit Mercy Law Review* 76 (1999): 875.

2. James W. Zion, "The Dynamics of Navajo Peacemaking," *Journal of Contemporary Criminal Justice* 14, no. 1 (1998).

3. Martha Minow, "Between Vengeance and Forgiveness: Feminist Responses to Violent Injustice," *New England Law Review* 32 (1998): 967–81.

4. *Navajo Nation Peacemaking: Living Traditional Justice*, ed. Marianne O. Nielsen and James W. Zion (Tucson: University of Arizona Press, 2005).

5. Ibid.

6. Connie Fife, "Dear Webster," in *Reinventing the Enemy's Language*, ed. Joy Harjo and Gloria Bird (New York: W. W. Norton, 1997), 480.

7. See generally Rupert Ross, *Returning to the Teachings: Exploring Aboriginal Justice* (Toronto: Penguin Canada, 2006), 27–51.

8. Rupert Ross, "Aboriginal Community Healing in Action: The Hollow Water Approach," in McCaslin, *Justice as Healing*, 184–89.

9. Cheryl Regehr and Thomas Gutheil, "Apology, Justice, and Trauma Recovery," *Journal of the American Academy of Psychiatry and the Law* 30, no. 3 (2002): 427 (noting that victims can be "further traumatized by the reopening of wounds and the recounting of events").

10. Berma Bushie, "Community Holistic Circle Healing: A Community Approach," http://www.iirp.org/library/vt/vt_bushie.html (last visited Nov. 2, 2008).

11. Donna Coker, "Restorative Justice, Navajo Peacemaking, and Domestic Violence," *Theoretical Criminology* 10, no. 1 (2006): 67.

12. Dawn Martin-Hill, "She No Speaks and Other Colonial Constructs of the 'Traditional Woman,' " in Anderson and Lawrence, *Strong Women Stories*.

13. Ross, "Aboriginal Community Healing in Action."

14. Ibid.
15. Wanda D. McCaslin, "Introduction: Reweaving the Fabrics of Life," in McCaslin, *Justice as Healing.*
16. Charlene Levis, "Circle Sentencing: The Silence Speaks Loudly" (master's thesis, 1998, University of Northern British Columbia).
17. Emma D. LaRocque, "Violence in Aboriginal Communities," *Public Health Agency of Canada,* http://www.phac-ascpc.gc.ca/ncfv-cnivf/familyviolence/pdfs/vac/pdf.
18. Kathleen Daly, "Setting the Record Straight and a Call For Radical Change: A Reply to Annie Cossins on Restorative Justice and Child Sex Offences," *British Journal of Criminology* 48, no. 4 (2008): 359.
19. Kristin Bumiller, "Fallen Angels: The Representation of Violence against Women in Legal Culture," *International Journal of the Sociology of Law* 18 (1990): 125.
20. John V. Butcher, "Federal Courts and the Native American Sex Offender," *Federal Sentencing Reporter* 13 (2000): 85.
21. Taiaiake Alfred and Jeff Corntassel, "Being Indigenous: Resurgences against Contemporary Colonialism," *Government and Opposition* 40, no. 4 (2005): 597.
22. Anderson, *Chain Her by One Foot,* 119.
23. Allen, *Off the Reservation,* 83.

10. "RIGHTING" TRIBAL RAPE LAW

1. Pub. L. No. 73–383, 48 Stat. 984 (1934) (codified as amended in scattered sections of 25 U.S.C.).
2. Russel Lawrence Barsh and J. Youngblood Henderson, "Tribal Courts, the Model Code, and the Police Idea in American Indian Policy," *Law and Contemporary Problems* 40, no. 1 (1976): 26.
3. For example, at least one tribal government has a "prompt complaint" requirement in its rape statute, which prohibits charging a sex offense if the victim waited more than thirty days to report the crime. No other crime in the tribal code imposes this requirement on victims. Colorado River Indian Tribe Law and Order Code Sec. 320(d), http://www.crit-nsn.gov/crit_contents/ordinances/Law_and_Order_Code.pdf.
4. Cassia Spohn and Julie Horney, *Rape Law Reform: A Grassroots Revolution and Its Impact* (New York: Plenum, 1992), 21.
5. Spiritual leaders who abuse authority are, by definition, not true spiritual leaders. Thus, I have framed the issue as a "so-called" spiritual leader—often, these are people who claim to have spiritual authority and use it to justify or conceal their abusive actions.
6. See Esaúl Sanchez, "Peggy Reeves Sanday Takes a Historic Look at Rape and Accountability," Compass, March 19, 1996, http://www.upenn.edu/

pennnews/features/1996/031996/sanday.html; quoted in Sarah Deer, "Toward an Indigenous Jurisprudence of Rape," *Kansas Journal of Law and Public Policy* 14 (2004): 127. LaRocque, "Violence in Aboriginal Communities."

7. See generally Michelle Alexander, *The New Jim Crow: Mass Incarceration in the Age of Colorblindness* (New York: New Press, 2010).

8. Office of the Inspector General, *Neither Safe nor Secure: An Assessment of Indian Detention Facilities* (Washington, D.C.: U.S. Department of the Interior, 2004), http://www.hsdl.org/?view&did=688492.

9. Valli Kalei Kanuha, "Native Hawaiian Batterer Intervention Program Project Summary" (2007), 2, http://www2.hawaii.edu/~kanuha/ CV%20&%20Publications_files/KAL%20SUMMARY%20REPORT %20JULY%202007-1.pdf.

10. Barbara Creel, "The Right to Counsel for Indians Accused of a Crime: A Tribal and Congressional Imperative," *Michigan Journal of Race and Law* 18, no. 2317 (2013): 321.

11. See, e.g., Eileen Luna, "Protecting Indian Women from Domestic Violence," *National Institute of Justice Journal* 246 (Jan. 2001): 28–30.

12. Ibid.

13. Tribal protection order statutes are not unique in this regard. Most state statutes governing protection orders have similarly defined eligibility requirements, which often do not allow a survivor of sexual assault to obtain a civil protection order.

14. Crime Victims Research and Treatment Center, *Rape in America: A Report to the Nation* 5 (Arlington, Va.: National Victim Center; Charleston, S.C. / Crime Victims Research and Treatment Center, 1992).

15. See, e.g., Amanda Konradi and Tina Burger, "Having the Last Word: An Examination of Rape Survivors' Participation in Sentencing," *Violence Against Women* 6, no. 4 (2000): 351–95.

16. Unfortunately, reports of law enforcement officers raping Native women are not unusual. See, e.g., Jim Holland, "Man Sentenced for Rape of Woman and Her Daughter," *Rapid City Journal,* Jan. 29, 2003 (describing the sentencing of a former tribal police officer convicted of rape).

17. Lyn Schollett, "ICASA Pursues Innovative Legal Remedy for Rape Victims," *ICASA Coalition Commentary* (Winter 2001).

18. See, e.g., MONT. CODE ANN. § 40–15–102 (2001); Md. Cts. Jud. Proc. § 3–1503 (2002).

19. Charging survivors of crime for filing petitions for civil protection orders is contrary to public policy and victim safety, since it would create an undue barrier for indigent victims. Moreover, jurisdictions that charge victims for the filing, issuance, service, or registration of a protection order are prohibited from receiving funding under the Vio-

lence Against Women Act. 42 U.S.C. §§ 3796gg-5(a)(1) and 3796hh(c) (4).

20. This component is similar to most statutory requirements for receiving a domestic violence protection order. Note that the tribal government must define the prohibited contact in order to facilitate the remedy.

21. Similar to domestic violence protection orders, this remedy is independent from any action taken by the tribal prosecutor in regard to a criminal case. Moreover, the burden of proof for obtaining a civil protection order is lower than that required for criminal conviction in most tribal courts.

22. The burden of proof issue in a civil protection order case should not require medical evidence. Indeed, many survivors of sexual assault do not have physical evidence of the assault.

23. 18 U.S.C. § 2265 (2000).

24. Although VAWA requires states to recognize and enforce tribal protection orders, there is still resistance to implementing this requirement in some states. See Sarah Deer and Melissa L. Tatum, "Tribal Efforts to Comply with VAWA's Full Faith and Credit Requirements," *Tulsa Law Review* 39 (2003): 412–13; more awareness and education on the full faith and credit provisions in VAWA are needed to help ensure the safety of all survivors who obtain protection orders.

25. Joe Doe BF v. Diocese of Gallup, 10 Am. Tribal Law 72 (Navajo Nation Supreme Court, 2011).

26. See, e.g., Trokov v. Off. of the Director of Reg., No. GDTC-AA-99-107, 2000 NAMG 0000001 (Mohegan Gaming Disputes Trial Ct. of Appeals [May 8, 2000]) (upholding the authority of the tribal gaming regulators to terminate the employment of a person arrested for sexual assault).

27. Brenda Hill, *Ending Violence Against Native Women from the Roots Up*, 17.

Publication History

Portions of this book were published as "Garden of Truth," *The Federal Law-yer* (April 2012) and as "Demanding Justice," *Indian Country Today* (May 4, 2007).

Portions of chapter 1 were published as "Violence against Native Women: Facts and Figures," in the conference transcript of "Heeding Frickey's Call: Doing Justice in Indian Country," *American Indian Law Review* 37 (2012): 347, 374; as "Domestic Violence in Indian Country," *Indian Country Today*, January 19, 2007; and as "Widening the Gap," *Indian Country Today*, March 23, 2007.

Portions of chapter 2 were published as "Heeding the Voice of Native Women: Toward an Ethic of Decolonization," *North Dakota Law Review* 81 (2005): 807; reprinted with permission.

Portions of chapter 3 were published as "Sovereignty of the Soul: Explor-ing the Intersection of Rape Law Reform and Federal Indian Law," *Suffolk University Law Review* 38 (2005): 455.

Portions of chapter 4 were published as "Federal Indian Law and Violent Crime: Native Women and Children at the Mercy of the State," *Social Justice* 31, no. 4 (2004): 17–30.

Portions of chapter 5 were published as "Relocation Revisited: Sex Traf-ficking of Native Women in the United States," *William Mitchell Law Review* 36 (2010): 621.

Portions of chapter 6 were published as "Protecting Native Mothers and Their Children: A Feminist Lawyering Approach," *William Mitchell Law Review* 40 (2014): 943.

Portions of chapter 8 were published as "Toward an Indigenous Jurisprudence of Rape," *Kansas Journal of Law and Public Policy* 14 (2004): 121.

Portions of chapter 9 were published as "Decolonizing Rape Law: A Native Feminist Synthesis of Safety and Sovereignty," *Wicazo Sa Review* 24, no. 2 (Fall 2009): 149–67.

Portions of chapter 10 were published as "Expanding the Network of Safety: Tribal Protection Orders for Survivors of Sexual Assault," *Tribal Law Journal at the University of New Mexico School of Law* 4 (2003–4), reprinted with permission; as "Violence against Women and Tribal Law," *Indian Country Today*, July 16, 2012; and as "Punishment and Tribal Law," *Indian Country Today*, August 30, 2012.

Index

advocacy for rape survivors, x, 122,
   156, 159–60
Agtuca, Jacqueline, 93
Alaska, xii–xiii, xiv, 26–27, 77,
   120–21
Allen, Paula Gunn, 51, 135–36
Amnesty International, 3, 99
Asetoyer, Charon, 5
assimilation, 16–17, 20, 69–71

Bachman, Ronet, 4, 9
banishment, 145–46
Black Bear, Tillie, xiii
boarding schools, 48, 69–71, 85
Bureau of Indian Affairs, 37, 46–48,
   53–54, 72–73, 139–40

California, 33, 63, 67–68
Canada, xxiii, 76
Cherokee Nation, 66, 119–20
child removal, 84–86
child sexual abuse, xi, 36, 48, 70,
   97–98, 102, 155
Chilocco Indian School, 71
Clairmont, Bonnie, xvi, 138
clans, 19–20, 25–27
Cole, Tom, 104

Columbus, Christopher, 32–33
Confederated Tribes of Coos,
   Lower Umpqua, and Siuslaw, 59
confidentiality, 156, 160
Cook-Lynn, Elizabeth, 22, 86
courts: federal, 56–58; tribal, 25–30
Creel, Barbara, 149
Crow Dog. See Ex Parte Crow Dog
custody. See child removal

Dakota. See U.S.–Dakota war
Davidson, Cristine, 76
Davis, Virginia, 94
Deegan, Dana, 80–91
Deloria, Vine, Jr., 61
divorce, 27–29
Doctrine of Discovery, 51
domestic violence, xvii–xviii,
   28–29, 83–84, 149–50

EchoHawk, Larry, 45
elders, 26, 29, 69, 118
Elk, Lavetta, 55–58
emergency contraception, 161,
   173n15
Erdrich, Louise, 1, 10
Ex Parte Crow Dog, 35–36

Farley, Melissa, 76
Federal Bureau of Investigation, 37, 53
feminisms, 24–25, 88–89
Fife, Connie, 127
Fletcher, Matthew L. M., 97
Forbes, Jack D., xv
Fort Berthold Reservation, 78, 80
Fort Peck Court of Appeals, 30

gangs, 77–78
Gardner, Jerry, 138
Georgia, 66
Goeman, Mishuana, 115
Gover, Kevin, 46–48

Haskell Indian Nations University, xi
Haudenosaunne women, 20
Ho-Chunk culture, 29
Hootch, Lenora, xiii–xiv
Hudon, Eileen, 76

incarceration, 40, 80–81, 83, 101, 134, 143–45
Indian Civil Rights Act, 34, 39–41, 143
Indian Health Service, 53–55, 125, 161
Indian Law and Order Commission, 31
Indian Removal Act, 68

Jones, B. J., 34–35
jurisdiction, tribal, 6–8, 34–42

Lakota culture, 20
LaRocque, Emma, 18, 132, 144
laws: American rape, 23–24; tribal rape, 16–18, 111–12
Littlewolf, LeAnn, 11
Lopez, Guadalupe, 76

Major Crimes Act, 34–37, 82
Manifest Destiny, 51
matrilineal descent, 19, 25–27
Matthews, Nicole, 76
Million, Dian, xv, 14
Minneapolis, 60, 74
Minnesota Indian Women's Resource Center, 76
Minnesota Indian Women's Sexual Assault Coalition, 10–11, 76–77
Miranda, Deborah, 9
Montana, 30, 65
Muscogee. *See* Mvskoke Nation
Mvskoke Nation, 16–18, 30, 112

National Congress of American Indians, 99
Navajo Nation, 42, 123; peacemaking courts, 123–26; tribal court, 27–28, 155
North Dakota, 78

Obama, Barack, 1–2, 46, 55, 102, 104
Oklahoma, 67, 71
Oliphant v. Suquamish, 7–8, 34, 41–42, 102, 104
order for protection. *See* protection orders
Oregon, 59
Osage women, 67

Paiute culture, 50
Parker, Deborah, 102
peacemaking, 123–36
Porter, Robert Odawi, xii, 31–32
Poupart, Lisa, 21
prostitution. *See* sex trafficking
Prostitution Research & Education, 76
protection orders, 149–54, 204n24
Prucha, Francis Paul, 64
public defenders, 148–49

Public Law 280, 34, 37–38
punishment. *See* banishment;
    incarceration

rape laws. *See* laws
relocation, 50, 72–75
restorative justice. *See*
    peacemaking
Richie, Beth, 52
Rosebud Sioux. *See* Sicangu Lakota
    Court of Appeals

Sac and Fox Tribe of the Missis-
    sippi in Iowa, 145–46, 155–56
Sekaquaptewa, Pat, 138
Senate Committee on Indian
    Affairs, 99–100
Sex Offender Registration and
    Notification Act, 94–96
sex trafficking, 60–79
sexual abuse. *See* child sexual
    abuse
Sicangu Lakota Court of Appeals,
    28–29
Sitka Tribal Court, 26–27
slavery, 60–65, 71
Standing Rock Sioux Tribe, 42
Stark, Christine, 76
statistics, ix, 1–15

termination policy, 37–38
Tohe, Laura, 69
Trafficking Victims Protection Act,
    60, 63, 72
Trail of Tears, 50, 68–69
treaties, 56–57
Tribal Law and Order Act, 31, 93,
    100–101, 148
Tribal Law and Policy Institute,
    100, 138
T'tcetsa, 68
Two-Spirit people, 19, 140

U.S.–Dakota War, 33–34, 65

Vicenti, Carey, 58
Violence Against Women Act
    (VAWA), xii, xviii, 93, 101–6, 154

war. *See* U.S.–Dakota War
Warrior, Robert, 112
Washburn, Kevin, 94
White Buffalo Calf Woman Society,
    xiii, 14
Winnebago Supreme Court, 29–30
Winnemucca, Sarah, 112, 117–18

Yup'ik Women's Coalition, xiv

Sarah Deer (Muscogee [Creek] Nation) is a professor at William Mitchell College of Law and a 2014 MacArthur Fellow. She is coauthor of *Introduction to Tribal Legal Studies* and *Tribal Criminal Law and Procedure* and coeditor of *Sharing Our Stories of Survival: Native Women Surviving Violence.*